THE LONG WAVE IN ECONOMIC LIFE

J. J. VAN DUIJN

London
GEORGE ALLEN & UNWIN
Boston   Sydney

George Allen & Unwin (Publishers) Ltd,
40 Museum Street, London WC1A 1LU, UK

George Allen & Unwin (Publishers) Ltd,
Park Lane, Hemel Hempstead, Herts HP2 4TE, UK

Allen & Unwin Inc.,
9 Winchester Terrace, Winchester, Mass 01890, USA

George Allen & Unwin Australia Pty Ltd,
8 Napier Street, North Sydney, NSW 2060, Australia

First published in 1983
Second impression 1985

British Library Cataloguing in Publication Data

Duijn, Jacob van
    The Long Wave in Economic Life
1. Economics
I. Title
330.1   HB171
ISBN 0-04-330330-7
ISBN 0-04-330331-5 Pbk

Library of Congress Cataloging in Publication Data

Duijn, Jacob J. van
    The long wave in economic life
    Translation of: De lange golf in de economie
1. Business cycles.
I. Title
HB3711.D77 1983   338.5'42   82-11497
ISBN 0-04-330330-7
ISBN 0-04-330331-5 (pbk.)

Printed in Great Britain by
Blackmore Press, Shaftesbury, Dorset

ACKNOWLEDGEMENT

Parts of this book have appeared previously as separate papers or as contributions to books, either in English or in Dutch (Van Duijn 1980a, 1980b, 1981a, 1981b, 1981c). The permission by IPC Business Press to re-publish parts of 'Fluctuations in innovations over time', *Futures*, Vol. 13, 264-75, is gratefully acknowledged.

CONTENTS

PREFACE

Of all fluctuations in economic activity, the long wave or the Kondratieff cycle is easily the most puzzling and the least understood. Does it really exist, and if so, is it only a cycle in prices or a cycle in economic activity at large? What causes it? Is it confined to Europe or does it affect the world economy as a whole? These questions, which seemed of little relevance in the prosperous years of post-war growth, have gained in significance since 1973. With the downturn of the long wave, interest in it rose again, just as in the 1930s. Long wave depressions coincide with peaks in long wave research, and the present depression is no exception. Since 1973 numerous publications on the long wave have appeared, and many of them have added to our insight into what causes the recurrent alternations of growth acceleration and retardation.

Research on the long wave has traditionally been a European affair. Socialist economists in Germany and the Netherlands (Parvus, van Gelderen, de Wolff) discovered the long wave; a Russian 'bourgeois' economist (Kondratieff), in the days after the Soviet revolution, gave it its name. It was an Austrian (Schumpeter) who made Americans familiar with the Kondratieff cycle. Europeans again led the long wave renaissance after 1973. It is hardly surprising, therefore, that this book should come out of Europe – of continental Europe, to be precise. In Britain, as in the United States, little research has been done on the long wave, although this is now changing.

My own interest in the long wave dates back to 1976, and my book on the subject, *De lange golf in de economie* (Assen, Van Gorcum) was published in 1979. Quite soon afterwards, however, I felt that the book ought to have been written in English. I therefore decided to prepare a new version which would incorporate all recent theoretical developments in the literature, including my own views, and which would focus on the long wave as an international phenomenon, affecting all industrialized countries.

In writing this book I have benefitted from the fact that the Netherlands is still a main centre of long wave research. In a small country it is easy to arrange workshops and seminars in which researchers are brought together. In my case, meetings with the Free University (Amsterdam) group led by Dr Gerrit van Roon proved particularly helpful.

Quite different but equally important assistance has been given by Nicholas Brealey of George Allen & Unwin, by Jean Sanders who did a marvellous job in editing the manuscript, by Netty Born who did the typesetting, and by Annette van der Reyken, whose typing was fast and accurate and whose mood was always cheerful.

Jaap van Duijn

Delft
February 1982

To Sara Julie

PART I
CYCLES AND TRENDS

I

CYCLICAL FLUCTUATIONS

FOUR CYCLES

Between 1900 and 1980 the gross national product of the United States, at constant prices, increased more than twelvefold. This increase in an 80-year period, amounts to an annual growth rate of 3.2 per cent. Obviously, part of this growth was caused by the increase of population, but even if we eliminate this factor, a considerable growth of real per capita GNP remains: 1.8 per cent. Some countries did better than the United States: Japan's growth rate over the same period was 4.3 per cent. Some others did less well: the United Kingdom showed only a 1.7 per cent growth rate, which in per capita terms becomes 1.3 per cent. The growth of output, however, has not been even (Figure 1.1). The United States growth rate of 3.2 per cent can, for instance, be split into 2.7 (1900-40) and 3.7 per cent (1940-80). In the postwar years growth accelerated, only to slow down again after 1973. The period up to World War II saw years of rapid growth, but also years of decline. In addition to long periods of acceleration and retardation we also see fluctuations of shorter duration: the recessions of 1953/54, 1957/58, 1969/70 and 1973/75 are postwar examples. Other countries have experienced similar interruptions of growth. Cyclical fluctuations are therefore an essential feature of the growth process, and affect virtually all aspects of economic life: production, income, employment, prices, interest rates, to name some of the more important. Sometimes they are hardly noticed, but their impact becomes clear when they take the form of absolute decreases in gross national product.

We have used the term 'cyclical fluctuations'. The word *cycle* has the connotation of regularity, suggesting a self-repeating type of fluctuation of fixed length and amplitude, around some trend. In reality, of course, no cycle in economic life will have such features. The lengths of cycles vary considerably and so does their severity. Yet they are self-repeating, and theoretical models have been built to explain why this is so. In fact, the essence of every cyclical fluctuation model is the explanation of the turning-points: why does an expansion turn into a contraction, and why does the economy get out of a trough

---

A note to this chapter may be found on p. 19.

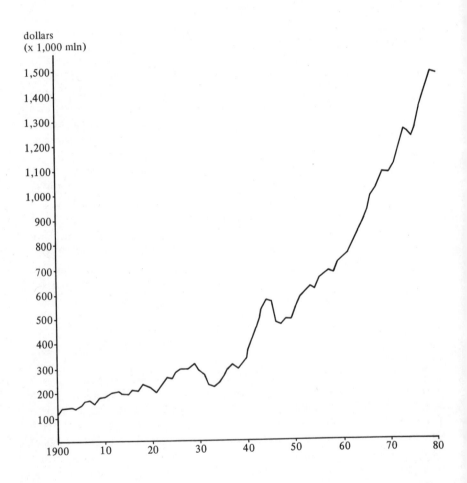

Figure 1.1 *Gross national product of the United States, at 1972 prices, 1900-1980*

again? Nevertheless, the term 'cycle' as in the American 'business cycle' and the English 'trade cycle' may be misleading, and it is interesting to note that not all languages use this expression to refer to economic fluctuations. In continental Europe the term 'conjuncture' is used, derived from the Latin *coniungere*, meaning 'to connect'. The conjuncture is the interplay of movements that together make up the direction in which the economy is going. The conjuncture is usually set against the structure of the economy, i.e. its more durable characteristics (production structure, labour market structure). To indicate the phases of a cycle different terms are used (Figure 1.2). If only an upswing and a downswing phase are distinguished, the following terminology is often used: lower turning point or trough, upswing or expansion, upper turning point or peak, and downswing or contraction. We shall use these terms later in this book. In daily life various other expressions are used to indicate the state of the economy, without these expressions having a precise meaning: boom, slump, hesitation.

The economic literature distinguishes different types of cycles. The *Foundation for the Study of Cycles* in Pittsburgh, USA, has collected hundreds of time series which display cyclical behaviour (see Wilson 1964). The existence of some cycles is firmly acknowledged, in other cases it is doubtful whether the observed fluctuation is self-repeating or just some kind of irregular movement. Usually the doubt arises because no satisfactory theoretical explanation can be found for the alleged cycle. And as it turns out, the longer the cycle, the more

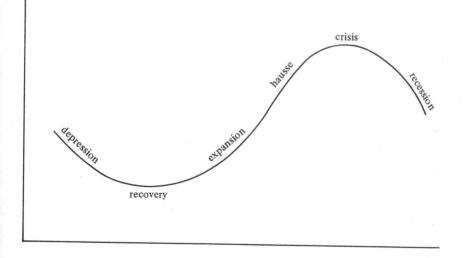

Figure 1.2 *The phases of a cycle*

difficult it becomes to separate specific one-time factors from systematic influences which should explain the self-perpetuating character of a cycle. Therefore, in the following list of four most-frequently listed cycles, the firmness of the cycle is inversely correlated with its length. These are:
(a) the Kitchin or inventory cycle, with a length of 3-5 years;
(b) the Juglar or investment cycle, with a length of 7-11 years;
(c) the Kuznets or building cycle, of 15-25 years duration;
(d) the long wave or Kondratieff cycle, which is said to be of 45 to 60 years.

All these cycles have been named after their discoverers (see Kitchin 1923, Juglar 1862, Kuznets 1930 and Kondratieff 1926. For all cycles except that of Kuznets, Schumpeter was the man to provide the lables. All four cycles exist simultaneously, which raises the question of whether they operate independently of one another, or instead fit together. Schumpeter (1939: 173-74) thought that they were linked. In his view one Kondratieff consisted of six Juglars, and one Juglar consisted of three Kitchins. If we take the average length of the Kondratieff to be 54 years, and if we set the Kuznets cycle (not mentioned by Schumpeter) at 18 years, the Juglar at nine, and the Kitchin at 4½ years, the interconnections become even neater: 1 Kondratieff = 3 Kuznets cycles = 6 Juglars = 12 Kitchins. It is very tempting but also very simplistic to see economic development as the result of four thus interwoven cycles. Yet, simplistic as it may seem, there is some truth to this representation. For indeed, Kuznets peaks have preceded Kondratieff upper turning points and three Kuznets cycles occurred during each of the last two Kondratieffs; also, post-World War II evidence points to an alternation of mild and serious recessions, from which one may conjecture that Juglar influences were felt in alternate Kitchin troughs. For what it's worth, the reader may decide what empirical evidence exists for any of these schemes. Clearly, however, the disentanglement of cycles is no simple matter.

The alternative notion is that the four cycles operate independently. What we then observe is some composite cycle, built up from cyclical fluctuations of different length. The system dynamics long wave model built by Forrester (see Chapter VII) yields such a composite cycle. This view can lead to statements such as: 'the seriousness of the 1929-1932 crisis can be explained as the coincidence of Kitchin, Juglar, Kuznets, and Kondratieff downswings'. With our present knowledge it is impossible to say which of these two views comes closest to reality. A perfect fit is certainly at odds with the non-mechanical way in which economic subjects behave; on the other hand, complete independence seems equally mechanical.

Fluctuations in investment are often seen as the engine of economic cycles. Our list of four cycles reflects this view. The economic fluctuations of different lengths are each associated with a particular type of investment: the Kitchin with inventory investment, the Juglar with investment in machines and equipment, the Kuznets cycle with building investment, and, finally, the Kondratieff with the construction of so-called basic capital goods, such as big plants, railways, canals, land improvement projects, etc. The different lengths are then determined by the differences in durability of the various types of capital goods and by the lags between final demand impulses and the completion of new capital goods.

We do not intend to suggest that all cycles are caused by fluctuations in investment only. Indeed, one of the purposes of this book is to argue that in generating long waves another impulse, i.e. that of basic innovations, is at least as important. Basic innovations in turn lead to increased investment activity. The two sources of instability are thus related. It should also be noted that in the literature variables other than investment have been singled out as causing fluctuations of shorter duration. Thus, there are under-consumption theories (Malthus, Marx, Hobson, Sweezy), a psychological business cycle theory (Pigou), theories of the political business cycle (Kalecki, Nordhaus, Frey), and various monetary business cycle theories (Hawtrey, Friedman). Or what about the sunspot theory of Jevons and Moore?

Yet it is certain that fluctuations in investment play an important role in all four cycles. It is only debatable whether the behaviour of investors in itself is sufficient to generate a cyclical process, or whether there are other basic impulses which affect investment behaviour.

This is only a brief introduction to the phenomenon of cyclical fluctuations. Much more extended and detailed treatments can be found in such texts as Haberler (1937), Hansen (1964), Dauten & Valentine (1978), Moore (1980), plus many others. Very specific on the issue of empirical testing is the excellent Evans (1969). Finally, we should clear up some terminological confusion. First of all: cyclical fluctuations can vary in length, but if the term 'business cycle' is used nowadays, we refer to the shortest of the four cycles (and also the one that can be most easily verified): the inventory cycle. This has not always been the case. In the 19th century and early 20th century literature the business cycle was meant to indicate the 7-11 year investment cycle. In this book we shall use the term Juglar when reference is made to this fixed investment cycle.

Secondly: we speak of the contraction or downswing phase of a cycle without necessarily implying absolute decreases in variables such as industrial production or national income. The upswing and downswing phases of a cycle are determined relative to a trend, i.e. the underlying long-run tendency in economic activity. This trend can be uncovered by eliminating the cycle, for instance through the calculation of moving averages or by applying ordinary least squares to estimate the trend line. What then is considered to be the trend may well be (part of) the cycle of next higher order, or as Schumpeter (1939: 205) put it:

'Every cycle of higher order may be considered as the trend of the cycle of the next lower order.' Even the trend that underlies the long wave is not a log-linear trend (with a constant rate of growth), as many people believe. Rather, it is what has been called the 'life cycle of economic development': an S-shaped curve stretching over a period of more than a century (see Chapter III).

THE INVENTORY CYCLE

The short 3-5 year cycle which we have come to call 'business cycle' is in fact the inventory investment cycle. This is to say, turning points of the business cycle are in the first instance caused by turning points in inventory investment. Klein & Popkin (see Evans 1969: 291) have shown that if 75 per cent of the fluctuations in inventory investment could be controlled, the economy would not have had any postwar recessions. Admittedly Klein & Popkin's study was published in 1961, so that subsequent recessions were not included in their analysis. Even so, it is useful to look in more detail at the mechanisms which keep the inventory cycle in motion.

Firms have various reasons for holding inventories. Firstly, they need them for transaction purposes and will make inventory investments to adjust the actual inventory to its desired level, the latter being a function of sales volume. Secondly, they may desire to hold extra inventories for speculative purposes, for instance if price increases or material shortages are expected. Thirdly, firms may want to hold buffer stocks to meet extra demand. In addition to these forms of desired inventory investment, changes in the inventory level, either positive or negative, may be undesired. Undesired inventory investment is the result of discrepancies between production and demand. If demand stagnates, inventories will rise above their desired levels. Reversely, demand increases will deplete inventories.

Inventory cycles can be easily generated with an inventory-accelerator model, as developed by Metzler (1941). This belongs to the class of multiplier-accelerator models, the simplest version of which will be presented in the next section. The essential feature of the Metzler inventory model is that it focusses on the impact which errors, made in forecasting sales, will have on inventory and overall output. The generation of such an inventory cycle is briefly described below (for the mathematical model itself see, for instance, Lovell 1975: 450-56).

Suppose the actual inventory is below the level desired for transaction purposes. Firms will replenish their inventories: inventory investment is positive. This production creates income which in turn will create additional demand. The result is more inventory investment. However, this chase between extra demand and extra inventory investment (based on anticipated future sales) may easily end in an inventory which exceeds the desired level, for instance, because actual sales fall short of anticipated sales. Firms will then start to liquidate stocks. The demand impulse emanating from desired inventory investment drops to zero. The decrease of overall production also means that income and therefore sales will drop, leaving firms with the need to liquidate stocks even further. This downswing phase of the cycle will end when inventories have become too small. When that point is reached, inventory investment will again start to act as a positive demand impulse.

The cyclical fluctuations described here can be reinforced if stocking for speculative purposes is added to sales-related inventory investment.

The inventory investment cycle has a length of approximately 4? years – at least, this has been its length in postwar Europe. In the USA the length of the short cycle appears to be closer to 40 months. In Table 1.1 an average trough-to-trough length of 38 months is indicated for eight postwar cycles. For the USA, however, it makes a difference whether one takes a growth cycle chronology, as in Table 1.1, rather than a classical NBER business cycle chronology. Growth cycles are fluctuations around a long-run trend. Growth cycle recessions could occur without absolute decreases in output. In the NBER chronology, all business cycle contractions are periods of falling aggregate economic activity. If the NBER dating is taken, the growth cycle recessions of 1951/52, 1962 and 1966/67 disappear and, up to 1975, six postwar cycles remain with an average trough-to-trough length of 59 months.[1]

Thus, the traditional, and still widely referred to, NBER business cycle is longer than its modern counterpart, the growth cycle. From a long-wave point of view we have a clear preference for using the growth cycle concept. During a long-wave expansion business recessions will not always involve absolute drops in output. If, on the other hand, a long-wave downswing has set in and the underlying movement is just slightly upward, or possibly even downward, recessions will more likely be characterized by production decreases.

In this particular case, however, another factor may have affected the difference in length between classical cycles and growth cycles. It should be pointed out that the NBER also distinguishes between wartime and peacetime cycles. The earlier mentioned growth cycle recessions of 1951/52, 1962 and 1966/67 all occurred during what are labelled 'wartime expansions'. In Europe, 1951/52 and 1966/67 were true recessions. Without war-induced demand, U.S. output could possibly have fallen and the cycle would have been more in line with the European pattern. As it was, actual contractions of U.S. economic activity occurred long after the European economies had peaked: 1953 instead of 1951, and 1969 instead of 1966. Only from 1972 onwards did the U.S. and European cycles again become synchronized.

Because war activity did occur, however, differences in average cycle length

Table 1.1. *Postwar growth cycle chronologies for the United States, United Kingdom, West Germany and the Netherlands*

	United States	United Kingdom	West Germany	The Netherlands
P	8-48			
T	11-49			4-49
P	5-51	5-51	1-51	2-51
T	7-52	11-52	2-54	12-52
P	3-53			
T	9.54			
P	2-57	12-55	5-56	8-56
T	5-58	11-58	2-59	8-58
P	2-60			
T	2-61			
P	4-62	3-61	3-61	11-60
T	4-63	2-63	2-63	12-62
P	6-66	2-66	3-66	1-65
T	10-67	3-67	8-67	12-67
P	6-69	11-68	5-70	5-70
T	11-70	2-72	7-72	5-72
P	3-73		8-73	5-74
T	5-75		5-75	8-75

Average length (in months)

expansion	22	30	27	29
contraction	16	26	26	24
P-P	37	53	54	56
T-T	38	58	51	53

Sources: Center for International Business Cycle Research, Rutgers University, New Jersey (US, UK and Germany); Van Duijn (1978) (The Netherlands).

between the U.S. and Europe cannot be explained solely in terms of different behavioral parameters in a Metzler-type inventory accelerator model, but war demand impulses and the speculation motive for inventory holding must be brought into the analysis.

The three European cycles presented in Table 1.1 are remarkably synchronous. The addition of the cycle chronologies of two other large European economies, viz. those of France and Italy, would cause little change to this picture. There are major differences between the European cycle and the U.S. cycle, however, which are large enough to make the old saying 'when the U.S. economy sneezes, Europe catches cold' inaccurate, at least for the postwar years.

If the short cycle is associated with inventory investment, its ups and downs will show up in an inventory investment time series, as is made clear by Table 1.2. The table lists annual changes in business inventories for the United States. Recession years can be recognized as years with little or even negative inventory investment: 1949, 1954, 1958, 1961, 1970, 1975, 1980. Note that the three recessions which were only growth cycle recessions (1951/52, 1962, 1966/67) were indeed minor re-adjustments which occurred without sharp drops in in-

Table 1.2. *Change in U.S. business inventories, 1949-80 (1000 mlns of dollars)*

1948	4.7	1959	5.2	1970	3.8
1949	-3.1	1960	3.8	1971	6.4
1950	6.8	1961	2.2	1972	9.4
1951	10.3	1962	6.5	1973	17.9
1952	3.1	1963	6.0	1974	8.9
1953	.4	1964	5.8	1975	-10.7
1954	-1.5	1965	9.5	1976	10.0
1955	6.0	1966	14.3	1977	21.9
1956	4.7	1967	10.1	1978	22.3
1957	1.3	1968	7.7	1979	17.5
1958	-1.5	1969	9.4	1980	-5.9

Sources: *Economic Report of the President* (1980); *Survey of Current Business* (various issues 1981).

ventory investment. It should be admitted, however, that these annual data are not well-suited for a business cycle analysis. For that purpose quarterly data, or, if available, monthly data should be used. Yet Table 1.2 demonstrates very clearly the strongly fluctuating character of inventory investment as well as its synchrony with the business cycle.

THE FIXED INVESTMENT CYCLE

The greater importance of inventory investment compared to fixed investment as a determinant of business cycle turning-points, is indicated by the timing of the fixed investment category: it is a lagged cycle indicator. Investment in fixed assets, however, includes all kinds of capital goods: machines, equipment, buildings, ships, airplanes. The 7-11 year investment cycle is specifically associated with fluctuations in investment in machines and equipment. The actual existence of the investment or Juglar cycle can therefore only be demonstrated if we manage to eliminate investment in buildings and other capital goods of long durability from our series.

In this book we shall refer frequently to the *multiplier-accelerator model* – also in connection with the long wave. This model, published at the age of 24 by the later Nobel Prize winner Samuelson (1939), offers an elegant explanation for the generation of cyclical fluctuations in overall economic activity, originating from fluctuations in investment. In its simplest version, the model contains only five equations:

(1.1) $\quad C_t \quad = \alpha_0 + \alpha_1 Y_{t-1}$

(1.2) $\quad K_t^* \quad = \kappa Y_{t-1}$

(1.3) $\quad I_t \quad = K_t^* - K_{t-1}$

(1.4) $K_t = K_{t-1} + I_t$

(1.5) $Y_t = C_t + I_t$

Here   C = consumption
       Y = income
       I = net investment
       K = capital stock
       K* = desired capital stock

Furthermore α_0 stands for autonomous consumption, α_1 is the marginal propensity to consume, and κ the capital-output ratio. The subscript t denotes time. Finally, if time is measured in years, the model implies that capital stock K is measured at the end (rather than at the beginning) of the year.

Equations (1.1) and (1.3) are behavioral relations. They describe the behaviour of consumers (whose purchases of consumer goods are determined by last year's income) and producers (who purchase enough plant and equipment to have eliminated the gap between actual and desired capital stock at the end of the year). Equation (1.2) is a technical relation, showing how much capital stock is needed to produce a national income of a certain size.

The model contains two lags. Consumers base their purchases on last year's income; producers derive their estimate of the optimal capital stock from last year's output. These lags are essential for the model. Without lags, no cycles would ever be generated.

The multiplier-accelerator model can be solved. The result is a second-order difference equation:

(1.6) $Y_t = \alpha_0 + (\alpha_1 + \kappa) Y_{t-1} - \kappa Y_{t-2}$

For certain combinations of values of α_1 and κ, equation (1.6) will generate cyclical fluctuations of Y, but not for all combinations. Monotonously diverging or converging time paths of Y are other possible solutions. But with reasonably realistic values oscillations will result. Take, for instance, $\alpha = 0.6$ and $\kappa = 0.8$ (on the choice of reasonable parameter values, see Evans 1969: 364-66). In this case damped cycles will be generated, with a cycle length of 9.35 years. In Table 1.3 we have simulated this cycle by taking initial values $Y_0 = 100$, $K_0 = 75$ and $\alpha_0 = 40$. The damped character of the cycle becomes clear if one compares values of Y during the two cycle peaks shown. In year two Y reaches a value of 107, but during the next peak, reached nine years later, Y is only 102.4. Eventually the cyles will fade and the simple economy of Table 1.3 will converge to an equilibrium at Y = 100.

The most remarkable facet of the multiplier-accelerator model is that seemingly reasonable firm behaviour (all firms do is to adjust their capital stock to its desired level, which is determined by recent actual outcomes) still can generate strong economic fluctuations. This is even more remarkable if we consider the

Table 1.3. *A multiplier-accelerator cycle*

Year	Y	C	I	K
1	105	100	5	80
2	107	103	4	84
3	105.8	104.2	1.6	85.6
4	102.5	103.5	-1.0	84.6
5	98.9	101.5	-2.6	82.0
6	96.4	99.3	-2.9	79.1
7	95.9	97.9	-2.0	77.1
8	97.1	97.5	-0.4	76.7
9	99.2	98.3	1.0	77.7
10	101.2	99.5	1.7	79.4
11	102.4	100.7	1.6	81.0
12	102.3	101.4	0.9	81.9
.	.	.	.	.
∞	100	100	0	80

aggregate character of our model. In reality, disaggregate decision making of firms — each acting on its own, each over-estimating what the market can bear — is another source of instability. In this model government could be the only decision maker; yet one central planner, acting according to equation (1.3), could invoke business cycles.

Obviously, the multiplier-accelerator model as presented here is far too simple. The investment decision is determined by only one variable, Y (or rather: the change in Y). Output, or related variables as sales or sales expectations, is important, of course, but financial variables (retained profits, interest rates) and investment costs surely also play a role in the decision-making process. Such influences may be expressed by inserting an adjustment coefficient β in equation (1.3), which then becomes:

$$(1.3^a) \qquad I_t = \beta (K_t^* - K_{t-1}) \qquad 0 \leqslant \beta \leqslant 1$$

A value of $\beta < 1$ implies that the gap between actual and desired stock will not be eliminated in one year, e.g. for lack of financial means.

Another shortcoming of the model, which should be mentioned for the sake of completeness, is the fact that investment can be positive as well as negative. Of course, net investment can be negative (if depreciations exceed new additions); in the multiplier-accelerator model, however, investment could be strongly negative for a number of years and wipe out the entire capital stock.

Despite these limitations — which in actual econometric models are overcome by applying the model in adjusted form — the multiplier-accelerator mechanism is a crucial element in the explanation of cyclical fluctuations. We have seen that it is used to explain the short inventory cycle (1.2); we shall see later that it is also used to explain long waves (Forester; see Chapter VII *infra*).

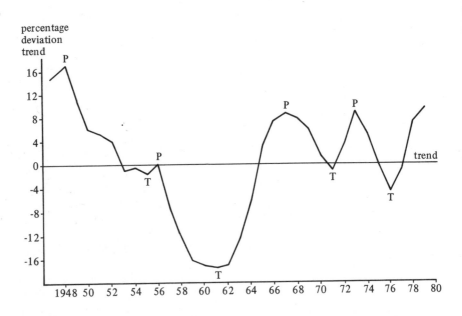

Figure 1.3. *Investment in producers' durable equipment, USA, 1947-1979*

Does the 7-11 year cycle still exist? To answer this question we shall examine
the U.S. time series of investment in producers' durable equipment (excluding
structures). This series quantifies the type of investment activity which generates
this cycle. In order to eliminate the effects of the short inventory cycle we have
taken a three-year moving average, and have furthermore expressed the series as
percentage deviations of a log-linear trend (the postwar trend rate of growth
being 4.2 per cent). The result is shown in Figure 1.3. Four complete cycles
can be recognized – although the 1956 peak is not very pronounced – with an
average length of approximately eight years. It is interesting to see that the
minor cycles have disappeared. For one reason this is the result of smoothing,
through the application of moving averages, for another this is inherent in the
nature of the series: investment in machines and equipment rather than in inventories or structures.

There is no longer much public interest shown in the ups and downs of this
'classical' investment cycle, i.e. Schumpeter's Juglar. All the attention that was
left for cyclical fluctuations during the Keynesian growth era quite under-
standably focussed on the short cycle. Policy makers are oriented towards directly observable, short-term fluctuations; underlying cycles of higher order are not

immediately recognized and therefore do not constitute a base for policy action. Yet, as Table 1.3 shows, the amplitude of the major cycle is quite considerable. There is clearly more than just 'a business cycle'. The major cycle or Juglar is still very much alive.

THE KUZNETS CYCLE

The Kuznets cycle is an 'American' cycle. It was discovered by American economists (Kuznets 1930, 1952; Burns 1934; Long 1940; Abramovitz 1956, 1964); the United States is also the country in which the Kuznets or building cycle is most clearly visible, or perhaps we should say: was visible. This last addition is necessary because in the present period the existence of a Kuznets cycle is no longer commonly accepted. Rostow (1975: 730) argues that it is restricted to the period between 1840 and 1914 and therefore has no general validity: 'I propose, therefore, to set aside the twenty-year Kuznets cycle' (see also Abramovitz 1968). Although it is questionable whether the Kuznets cycle has indeed passed away, it certainly existed in the time period mentioned by Rostow.

It is true that 19th century U.S. data seem to lend more support to the existence of a long cycle (i.e. the Kuznets cycle) than of a long wave (i.e. the Kondratieff cycle). The question at issue is how the events of the last quarter of the 19th century should be interpreted. Was this a period with two Kuznets-depressions (the 1870s and the 1890s) with a Kuznets-upswing in between (the 1880s), or is the term 'Great Depression', used in Europe to characterize the years between 1873 and 1896, also an adequate description of the state of the U.S. economy during that period? Lewis (1978) sees the Kuznets cycle as the dominant pattern. In Chapter IX we shall argue that 19th century U.S. data do not disprove the existence of a long-wave pattern.

The conflict can be easily resolved, however, if it is realized that both cycles can manifest themselves simultaneously. This holds for all four cycles discussed in this chapter. In all likelihood, the U.S. economy of the 19th century was dominated by Kuznets-type fluctuations, but this does not deny the presence of a downward tendency of the Kondratieff.

The Kuznets cycle is associated with construction activity, which includes investment in residential as well as non-residential structures. Most research has been done, however, with respect to the first category. Table 1.4 presents the turning points of the Kuznets cycle for the U.S. economy. These concern aggregate construction. The average length of the cycle is 16 years, with an expansion phase of roughly 11 years and a contraction phase of five years, but deviations around these averages are considerable.

The explanation of the Kuznets cycle relies heavily on the interaction be-

Table 1.4. *Turning points of the Kuznets cycle, USA*

turning points		duration in years			
trough	peak	contraction	expansion	trough-trough	peak-peak
1861	1871		7		
1878	1892	7	14	17	21
1898	1912	6	14	20	20
1918	1927	6	9	20	15
1933	1941	6	8	15	14
1944	1959	3	15	11	18
1960	1972	1	12	16	13
1975		3		15	
average		4.6	11.3	16.3	16.8

Source: adapted from Dauten & Valentine (1978) and brought up-to-date.

tween economic and demographic variables. In the model developed by Easterlin (1968) for the explanation of long swings in residential construction, the following pattern emerges. Taking an economy which operates below full capacity as a starting point, an increase in investment demand induces an increase in overall spending; this leads to an upward pressure on labour-market variables (wages, employment, participation rates, but also immigration); these in turn induce family formation and consequently population-related investment such as residential construction. A schematic rendition of the Easterlin model is given in Figure 1.4. Klotz & Neal (1973) have tested this model for the United States. Using spectral analysis they found statistically significant relations in the 16-year and 24-year bands between the five variables of Figure 1.4.

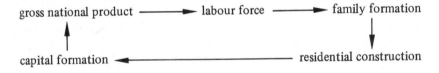

Figure 1.4. *Easterlin's model of the Kuznets cycle*

The strength of the Kuznets fluctuations before World War I has been ascribed to the migration waves from Europe to the New World. 'In the period 1870-1914 at least it does appear that a systematic element was present, and the effect of migration is the most plausible explanation' (Matthews 1959: 110). The Kuznets expansion phases of 1861-71, 1878-92 and 1898-1912 all coincided with considerable emigration from Europe to the United States. Lewis (1978: 183) has even suggested that the U.S. Kuznets cycle was initiated earlier in the 19th century in response to immigration from Europe promoted by European demographic cycles. Whatever the case may be, we find the counterpart of U.S.

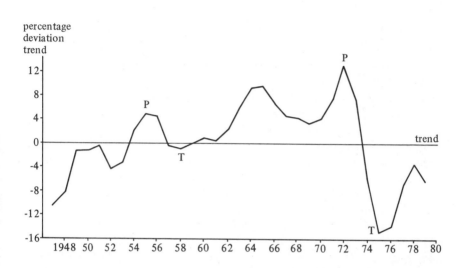

Figure 1.5. *Investment in structures (residential plus non-residential), United States, 1947-1979*

immigration in Great Britain's building cycle which, even until the end of World War II, was the inverse of the U.S. cycle: building peaks in the U.S. roughly coincided with building troughs in Great Britain (Matthews 1959: Chapter 6).

Again, we may ask whether this particular cycle shows up in the actual data. The appropriate time series to consider is investment in structures. We have taken postwar U.S. data on residential plus non-residential investment, smoothed the series again by taking three-year moving averages, and expressed the resulting series as a percentage deviation from a log-linear trend (with an estimated growth rate of 2.8 per cent). The graphical outcome of this exercise is shown in Table 1.5. Kuznets peaks appear in 1955 and 1972, troughs in 1958 and 1975. It is clear, however, that by taking three-year moving averages, we have left some form of Juglar-pattern in the series, the elimination of which would require an eight or nine-year moving average. If such a recalculation is made – the results are not shown here – only two peaks remain, one in 1955 and another which has moved backward to 1969.

It should be noted that Kuznets peaks tend to precede Juglar peaks: 1955 before 1956, and 1972 before 1973. Historically, major downturns in aggregate

economic activity have always been preceded by downturns of the Kuznets
cycle: 1871-73, 1927-29, and, in our time, 1972-73.

THE KONDRATIEFF CYCLE

Of the four cycles discussed in this chapter, the long wave or Kondratieff cycle is
easily the most disputed. This is not remarkable: the longer a cycle, the harder it
is to prove its existence. No-one can deny the Kitchin or inventory cycle for it
can be directly observed, but to recognize cycles of higher order in actual time
series the cycles of lower order have first to be eliminated. This does not create
many problems for the Juglar, for the Kuznets it gets a little harder, but it seems
very difficult to get any grip at all on the Kondratieff cycle.

A second reason why the Kondratieff has not been generally accepted may be
found in the postwar record of the Western economies up to 1973. The apparent
evenness and durability of economic growth made any explanation of growth
from a long-wave perspective seem absurd. As a result, economic textbooks until
recently gave little or no attention to the long wave. Only the Dutch economists
have always shown an interest in the Kondratieff cycle, perhaps because two
Dutchmen, Van Gelderen en De Wolff, did pioneering work in developing the
long wave notion (see Chapter IV). As a result, the three major Dutch textbooks
all give considerable attention to the long wave (Andriessen 1980: 129-30;
Delfgaauw 1973: 169-71; Korteweg & Keesing 1978: 138-39, 155-56).

English-language texts show a different story. For instance, Samuelson (1980:
241) deals with the long wave in a footnote: 'whether these long waves are
simply historical accidents due to chance gold discoveries, inventions, and
political wars, it is still too soon to say.' Lipsey & Steiner (1981: 537) make a
passing remark on a 'longer cycle, associated with major innovations (40 to 50
years).' Most other books do not even mention the long wave, or Kondratieff.
Even Schumpeter, who conceptualized the economic history of the industrial
nations as a sequence of long waves, triggered by variations in the rate of innovations, hardly survived the modern growth era. In the textbooks he has become a
footnote-economist. If textbooks may be taken as the measure, Dauten &
Valentine's (1978: 286) comment should even be considered an understatement:
'This theory of long waves has not been generally accepted by economists.'

The 'agnostic, if not highly sceptical position' with respect to the long wave
which Hansen (1964: 57) professed to, seems to be changing in the post-1973
era. A great many theoretical and empirical studies on the long wave have been
published since the 1973 downturn in Germany, the Netherlands, France,
Britain, but notably also in the United States, the one country whose economy
Dauten & Valentine claim has not been affected by the Kondratieff cycle:
'There is no statistical evidence in production series in the United States of any

long wave fluctuations of 50 or 60 years' (1978:286). In Chapter IX, however, we shall see that there is such evidence. The renewed interest in the long wave has not yet trickled down to the economic textbooks. Considering the lag with which these record reorientations of the economics profession, this is hardly surprising. Yet a first swallow has already arrived. In a recent macroeconomics text, Cherry (1980) emphasizes the role of technological innovation in explaining Kondratieff investment waves.

The present book is about the long wave, about the different theories brought forward to explain it, about the empirical tests made to show its existence, and about economic policy measures which it suggests. There are very few comprehensive treatments of the long wave in existence. We may mention Imbert (1959), a French text, and Weinstock (1964), a German one. Both have been made somewhat out of date, however, by the recent renaissance of the long wave and the new theoretical explanations that came with it. In this book we intend to cover the whole range of modern long wave theories.

We end this chapter as we began it: with some numbers about the United States economy. We have seen that the annual rate of growth of U.S. gross national product between 1900 and 1980 was 3.2 per cent. Let us now divide these 80 years into four subperiods: 1900-29, 1929-48, 1948-73, and 1973-80. The average annual growth rates then become, in order, 3.4 per cent, 2.3 per cent, 3.8 per cent, and 2.4 per cent. In the following chapters we shall show that neither this periodization, nor the alternation of growth acceleration and growth retardation, are coincidental; neither for the U.S. economy nor for any other Western economy.

NOTE

1. The NBER reference dates are:

trough	peak
October 1945	November 1948
October 1949	July 1953
May 1954	August 1957
April 1958	April 1960
February 1961	November 1969
November 1970	November 1973
March 1975	January 1980
July 1980	

The latter three turning-points are tentative and subject to revision.

II

GROWTH AS AN S-SHAPED PHENOMENON

The process of growth can be represented in a number of ways. In macro-economics, in recent decades, the domination of the neoclassical growth model has given rise to the perception of long-term economic development as a process in which the growth of physical output converges to a steady-state rate that is determined by two parameters, both assumed to be stationary: the rate of technological change, and the rate of growth of the labour force.

In the simple neoclassical model, steady-state growth follows from the steady-state assumptions built into the model. The neoclassical economist will then confront the conclusions of his model with actual macroeconomic performance. Can the long-term growth of nations indeed be represented by one steady-state growth rate? Or is this not possible, for instance because the underlying rates of technological change and the rate of growth of the labour force are not steady-state rates?

The competing view of growth, that of Schumpeter, developed long before the neoclassical model gained its prominence, argues that the rate of technologi-cal change is not constant over time. In Schumpeter's view, growth and cycle are fused, growth coming in spurts and appearing as cyclical upswings. In his own words: 'The recurring periods of prosperity of the cyclical movement are the form progress takes in capitalist society' (Schumpter 1927: 295). Progress here is due to the arrival of new innovations, incorporating technological change, and introduced by Schumpeter's entrepreneurs.

Obviously, the long-term economic performance of a nation can always be summarized through a single growth rate. As we have seen in Chapter I, for the U.S. this growth rate has been 3.2 per cent, if GNP is taken as the growth indi-cator, and 1889-1979 as the long term. There have been considerable fluctua-tions, however, around this trend rate. Estimated over the period 1895-1913, the annual growth rate is 4.5 per cent; during the inter-war years 1920-39 it was a mere 2.1 per cent; while an estimate for the postwar period of 1948-73 would give an annual growth rate of 3.7 per cent. Thus, it would appear that the

---

Notes to this chapter may be found on pp. 43-44.

U.S. data give at least some support to the perception of 'growth in spurts', or in other words, of long-term growth as a process of acceleration and deceleration.

One implication of such a wave-like growth pattern is that the accelerations apparently cannot be sustained. Whichever forces carry the economy during those periods of prosperity — as implied above, they may last as long as a quarter-of-a-century — they eventually diminish. Growth rates will abate long before absolute downturns occur, as from 1929 to 1933, or 1973 to 1975. This retardation of growth took place in the 1920-29 period and again in 1966-73 (see Appendix A). It is not restricted to the U.S. experience, but also holds for other industrialized countries, as we shall see in subsequent chapters.

All this points to a concept of growth which in fact is much older than the steady-state growth notion of recent years, one which underlies the Schumpeterian idea of progress, and which has frequently been used in describing the growth of all kinds of phenomena: that of growth as an S-shaped curve.

GROWTH AS AN S-SHAPED CURVE

The French sociologist Gabriel Tarde is usually attributed with having first thought of the S-shaped growth curve. In his *Les lois de l'imitation*, first published in 1890 and translated into English in 1903, he formulated the three phases through which every innovation, whether a new product, idea or belief, has to pass:

A slow advance in the beginning, followed by rapid and uniformly accelerated progress, followed again by progress that continues to slacken until it finally stops: these, then, are the three ages of those real social beings which I call inventions or discoveries ... . This is the law which, if taken as a guide by the statistician and, in general, by the sociologist, would save them from many illusions (Tarde 1903: 127).

It is noteworthy that Tarde saw his law of growth specifically as describing how *new things* spread through imitation: i.e. the adoption by the public of a new idea, a new product, etc. At first, the novelty will be unfamiliar and growth will be slow. But once the initial barriers have been overcome, the innovation will continue to spread rapidly, until it becomes established. Then growth will taper off and might even become negative, if the original innovation is replaced by another.

Tarde's lead was followed by other social scientists.[1] Prescott (1922) seems to have been the first to employ Tarde's law for forecasting purposes, using a Gompertz curve. Prescott's interest was the future demand for automobiles, a favourite topic for many later forecasters. By far the most comprehensive work on growth patterns for individual commodities and industries, however, was that by Kuznets (1930) and Burns (1934). Before we discuss their findings, it is useful to look at other areas in economics in which the concept of S-shaped growth has been successfully applied.

The S-shaped growth curve has undoubtedly found its most widespread application in the field of marketing, where it has become known as the *product life cycle*. This term was coined by Joel Dean (1950), who distinguished three stages in a product's life (introduction, rapid expansion, maturity), and who argued that the length of this cycle is governed by the rate of technical change, the rate of market acceptance, and the ease of competitive entry. The concept was further explored by Patton (1959) and Mickwitz (1959), and in the 1960s, began to appear in the marketing textbooks (Cundiff & Still 1964, and Kotler 1967; see also Levitt 1965, a marketing classic).

Four phases are now usually distinguished (Fig. 2.1), but five-phase models may also be found (Fig. 2.2). If we adhere to the four-phase cycle, the following are the characteristics of the different stages as seen by Levitt (1965).

(1)   *Introduction*. This is when a new product is first brought to market, before there is a proven demand for it, and often before it has been fully proven technically in all respects. Sales are low and sluggish.

(2)   *Growth*. Demand begins to accelerate and the size of the total market expands rapidly. This stage might also be called the 'take-off stage'.

(3)   *Maturity*. Demand levels off and, for the most part, grows only at the replacement and new family-formation rate.

(4)   *Decline*. The product begins to lose consumer appeal and sales drift downwards.

The total length of the life cycle and the length of each stage may vary considerably. Fashions may have a total cycle length of no more than a year. But for a product such as the automobile the maturity phase alone may last thirty years. The later phases of a product are especially difficult to predict. Faced with stagnating demand, an industry might develop follow-up products such that overlapping life cycles result (Fig. 2.3a). Colour television may replace black-and-white; the cut-throat razor may be replaced by the safety razor. Alternatively, new uses may be found for an existing product so that its life cycle is extended (Fig. 2.3b). Nylon may be a case in point here. The repeated cycle (re-cycle) is another variant. After the life cycle has been completed, the product revives and a new cycle is started (Fig. 2.3c). An (European) example of the re-cycle is the bi-cycle, originally used as a means of transportation (and as such replaced by moped and automobile), and now revived as a recreational vehicle. Finally, it could be that a product becomes an integral part of a nation's consumption pattern, not being given new uses nor being replaced by alternatives. Consumer durables such as the refrigerator and the vacuum cleaner are examples

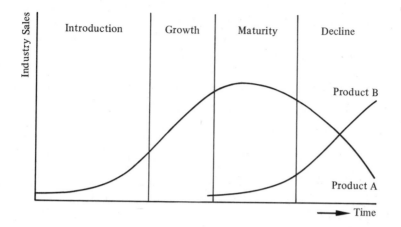

Figure 2.1 *The product life cycle: four-phase model*

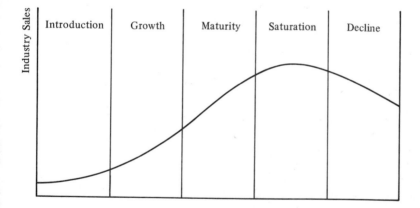

Figure 2.2 *The product life cycle: five-phase model*

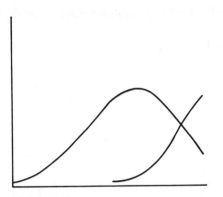

(a) Substitution

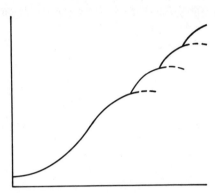

(b) Extensions of the Life Cycle

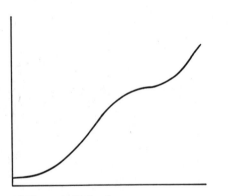

(c) Change in Technology

(d) Extended Maturity Phase

Figure 2.3 *Variations to the Simple Life-Cycle Pattern*

of products with a very long maturity stage (Fig. 2.3d). In marketing, exploiting the product life cycle means using it in designing marketing policy for a certain product in the strategic planning of new products (Levitt 1965), and in the management of sales forecasting (Chambers, Mullick & Smith 1974; Eby & O'Neill 1977).

Another area in which the product life cycle concept has been applied with success is that of international trade. The seminal contribution here is that by Vernon (1966). This article, which set out to resolve the so-called Leontief-paradox, has given rise to a Vernon School, with major contributions by Hirsch (1967), Wells et al (1972) and Claudon (1977). The Leontief-paradox arose when Leontief (1953; 1956) found that the capital-labour ratio in U.S. exports was lower than the capital-labour ratio in U.S. production which had been displaced by competitive imports. This result contradicted the capital-intensity of U.S. exports, which might have been expected on the basis of the Heckscher-Ohlin theorem of comparative advantage. Using the product life cycle concept, Vernon argued that the U.S., as the most likely country to introduce innovations, would produce and export relatively many products in their early life cycle stages. Production in these stages tends to be labour-intensive. Thus, the U.S. export package would also be labour-intensive. As a product matures, production techniques will become more capital-intensive, but by that time, the U.S. will have become a net importer of that particular product.

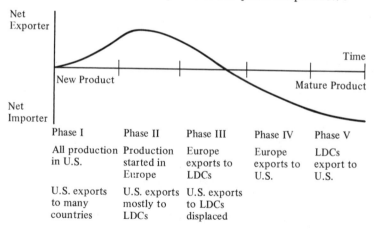

Phase I	Phase II	Phase III	Phase IV	Phase V
All production in U.S.	Production started in Europe	Europe exports to LDCs	Europe exports to U.S.	LDCs export to U.S.
U.S. exports to many countries	U.S. exports mostly to LDCs	U.S. exports to LDCs displaced		

Figure 2.4 *A schematic presentation of the U.S. trade position in the product life cycle*

Source: L.T. Wells (ed): *The Product Life Cycle and International Trade* (Boston, Division of Research, Harvard University Graduate School of Business Administration, 1972), 15. Reproduced by permission.

In the international trade version, the *spatial* implications of the product life cycle are explored. It is recognized that technological information and market information are not freely available at all points in space. Innovation is not only restricted temporally, but also spatially. Assuming that entrepreneurs in the United States are the first to be aware of innovation opportunities, the Vernon School has schematically presented the net trade position of the U.S. in the consecutive stages of an industrial life cycle (Fig. 2.4).

While Vernon et al use national boundaries as spatial demarcation points, one could equally well imagine a life cycle decentralization pattern within a national economy. More specifically, the industrialization of peripheral regions may be interpreted as the decentralization of labour-intensive production processes which started their early life cycle phases in the agglomerated areas (Krumme & Hayter 1975; Van Duijn 1979b).

Finally, there is the application of S-shaped growth in technological forecasting literature, where S-shaped curves correspond to individual technologies, and successions of technologies can be visualized as in Figure 2.5 (Jantsch 1967: 167).

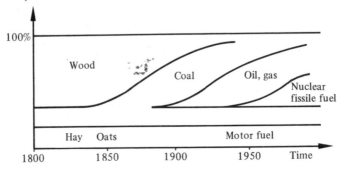

Figure 2.5 *Succession of technologies*

Source: E. Jantsch, *Technological forecasting in perspective*, OECD, 1967.

INDUSTRY GROWTH PATTERNS

Kuznets (1930) has observed that the long-term economic development of a nation is characterized by a succession of leading sectors. An industry which at one time had developed rapidly, would not continue its vigorous growth indefinitely, but would eventually slacken its pace, and finally be overtaken by another industry, whose period of rapid development had started later. Why is it that industries do not continue to expand at a constant rate? Why does the growth of an industry eventually slow down? Kuznets indicates three basic forces: (1) growth of population; (2) changes in demand; (3) technical changes, including improvements in business organization. These three factors are clearly interdependent, but there was no doubt in Kuznets's mind that technical change was the driving force. The slackening of an industry's growth would ultimately have to be explained by technical change-related causes.

A relation between industrial growth and technological change had been noted in 1912 by the German economist, Julius Wolf, who formulated his four 'laws of retardation of progress'. One of these reads:

Every technical improvement, by lowering costs and by perfecting the utilization of raw materials and of power, bars the way to further progress. There is less left to improve, and this narrowing of possibilities results in a slackening or complete cessation of technical development in a number of fields (Wolf 1912: 236-237).

Kuznets tested his hypothesis of growth retardation on 57 production series, the data being drawn from five early industrialized countries: Britain, France, Belgium, Germany and the United States. Using the logistic curve and Gompertz curve (see Appendix B) to fit the data — both curves imply a continually decreasing growth rate — Kuznets concluded that these curves satisfactorily described the long-time movements of growing industries and, with certain modifications, those of declining industries. Yet Kuznets was cautious not to take his conclusions too far. His equations should not be treated as expressions of a 'law of growth', nor should they be used for forecasting purposes (Kuznets 1930: 197-198). The only thing that Kuznets wished to establish was that during the period covered (roughly 1850-1924, with variations due to differences in data availability), industries did indeed exhibit declining growth rates.

Kuznets's work was carried on by Burns (1934), who investigated growth patterns in U.S. industries, covering the 1870-1929 period. His 104 continuous production series included 23 series in agriculture, fisheries and forestry; 22 in mining; 47 in manufacturing & construction; and 12 in transportation & trade. Despite the many manufacturing series, these covered only 22 per cent of manufacturing output. As opposed to this, his coverage of agriculture (65 per cent) and mining (83 per cent) was very high. Yet the latter areas are not necessarily the most interesting when it comes to studying industry growth patterns.

Burns fitted a logarithmic parabola to his 104 series which allowed him to estimate a rate of retardation (see Appendix B) and — for those cases in which growth rates were falling — the year in which output would reach its peak value. Abatement in the rate of growth was found for 92 series; in 44 of these, Burns estimated that the peak level would occur before 1930. These results led him to formulate the following 'rule of uniformity': 'an industry tends to grow at a declining rate, its rise being eventually followed by a decline' (Burns 1934: 173).

This generalization, however, should be interpreted with the same qualifications that Burns added: (1) the rule of retardation may not hold in the late life cycle stages of some industries; (2) in the introduction phase growth may accelerate rather than abate; (3) the rule of retardation does not hold throughout for the secular trends even of established industries, though it does hold for their primary trends — which are movements of longer duration than secular trends; (4) an industry may be invigorated or rejuvenated as a result of a structural change, such that the rule of retardation may only hold for the periods prior to and following the structural change (Ibidem: 172).

With all these qualifications, little or nothing can be predicted about the life path of one particular industry, partly because nothing is known about the length of the various phases. All that remains is a rudimentary S-shaped growth pattern. The only statement that can safely be made is that the high growth rates of a young industry cannot be maintained forever. The simple algebra of growth rates makes a slowdown inevitable. In that respect, it is relevant to note that Burns's industry records cover the period in which the U.S. economy completed its drive to technological maturity, and transited into the stage of high mass-consumption, to use Rostow's terms. It is hardly surprising that the high growth rates enjoyed by various sectors in their late 19th-century development, tapered-off in the 20th century.

Despite Burns's caution, qualifications to a generalization tend to be forgotten: a tentatively stated growth pattern is given absolute validity, and the 'law of growth' is consequently rejected if actual patterns appear to be less uniform than the generalization implies. Perhaps Burns was not sufficiently cautious. The absolute decline of production, which he saw as part of his stylized growth pattern, has occurred only in a few branches. A decline in production is easy to visualize in a closed economy with constant population, but such conditions have not been characteristics of the U.S. economy.

It is not surprising, therefore, that Gold (1964), who added the 1930-1955 period to some of Burns's time-series, found that growth to a peak, followed by a declining trend, was exhibited in only four of the 35 series which he examined. In fact, Gold found 12 different patterns of growth.

One problem with the approaches adopted by Burns and by Gold is that they lump together in one analysis many kinds of industries, from agricultural staples to industrial inputs, from capital goods to consumer goods, and then look for one growth pattern. Even apart from the complications that arise due to the openness of the U.S. economy, different development patterns may be expected over time for a consumer good, such as cigarettes, as opposed to an industrial input, such as steel. Elsewhere (Van Duijn 1980a), we have examined growth patterns for different categories of products, extending Burns's and Gold's work to the present time. This has shown series that in many cases cover a century (1873-1973), and in a few instances, such as pig iron, well over a century. Our findings suggest the existence of an S-shaped growth pattern up to the maturity phase of an industry, with various possible patterns thereafter. What actually happens to a commodity once it has reached its maturity phase, would seem to depend on a number of factors.

International Specialization

Agricultural staples are a case in point here. For the period 1870-1929, i.e. that covered by Burns, virtually all principal U.S. agricultural products showed declining growth rates. Burns therefore rightly concluded that retardation of growth had taken place. The predictive value of these findings for the post-1929 years is zero. For some products the U.S. became or remained a major exporter (soybeans, corn, wheat, cotton, tobacco, rice), specializing in these at the expense of other products. National production figures therefore give no insight into the development of national consumption. Life cycle patterns, including a decline phase, would most likely be found for national per capita consumption; only in a few cases are they to be found for national production.

The Development of Substitutes

Substitutes for existing products or production processes are most likely to be developed in the maturity phase of an industry (see also Chapter X). In the growth phase there is little incentive inside the industry to innovate, while intruders who have no past investment outlays to defend, will be strongly discouraged from entering a market with their substitutes. In the maturity phase, however, as growth rates begin to decline, both insiders and outsiders may attempt to revive a life cycle or to develop substitutes, thereby creating new life cycles. The consumer electronics sector offers many examples of this sequential innovating. On the other hand, a viable substitute for the car has so far not been developed.

Sensitivity to Long Wave Fluctuations

Although we have not yet developed a theoretical framework for a discussion of long waves, it should be clear that they will have some impact on the long-term development of industries. Sectoral output will be boosted during a long wave upswing phase, and will be depressed, with possibly negative growth rates, during a downswing phase. Negative growth rates should not be considered evidence that a life cycle is declining since they are likely to become positive again when the economy embarks on a new long expansion.

The result of the interplay between industry life cycle and long wave fluctuations is hard to foretell. Young industries may grow even through a Kondratieff downturn. Mature industries may be affected in such a way that negative growth rates result. Thus, in a number of sectors, U.S. industry growth rates during the 1873-1895 period, generally accepted as the second Kondratieff downswing, exceeded those of 1895-1913, which was undoubtedly a period of long wave expansion.

Neither Burns nor Gold considered their data material from a long wave perspective.[2] To some extent, this explains why Burns fitted a mathematical function with a decline phase to his data; and also why Gold found such diverse growth patterns: the severity of the 1930s depression and the following war-induced recovery determined his choice of growth pattern (Gold 1964: 68-71).

Both the sensitivity to long wave fluctuations, the development of substitutes and, to some extent, the role of international specialization, can be illustrated with examples taken from the U.S. iron and steel industry.

Table 2.1 presents annual growth rates, measured from Juglar-peak to Juglar-peak for U.S. pig iron shipments.[3] These growth rates show a clear long-cyclical pattern. Reaching 'local' peaks during the 1864-1873, 1895-1903, and 1937-1948 Juglars, growth rates declined for the next two or three Juglars, to rise to a new peak thereafter. Fluctuations of long wave length seem to dominate. Yet peak growth rates show a decline, and if Juglars are combined into Kondratieffs (for which we do not present any justification at this point; see Chapter VIII), a retardation of growth is also revealed, even though the 1948-1973 period covers only the upswing part of a Kondratieff.

Table 2.1 *Pig iron shipments, U.S., 1847-1973*

Juglar	annual growth rate	Juglar	annual growth rate
1847-1856	- 0.2	1913-1920	2.3
1856-1864	3.2	1920-1929	1.7
1864-1873	10.8	1929-1937	-2.0
1873-1882	6.8	1937-1948	3.9
1882-1895	5.7	1948-1956	2.8
1895-1903	8.4	1956-1966	1.9
1903-1913	5.4	1966-1973	1.5

Kondratieff	annual growth rate
1847-1895	5.3
1895-1948	3.3
1948-1973 (upswing)	2.1

Sources: US Dept of Commerce 1975: Series M 217; US Dept of Commerce 1979, for updating.

Raw steel production shows similar waves of decreasing and increasing growth rates, with a clear retardation of secular growth. The double digit growth rates up to 1903 are typical for an industry in its early stages (Table 2.2).

Table 2.2 *Raw steel production, U.S., 1864-1973*

Juglar	annual growth rate	Juglar	annual growth rate
1864-1873	41.2	1920-1929	3.3
1873-1882	31.0	1929-1937	-1.1
1882-1895	10.1	1937-1948	4.2
1895-1903	11.2	1948-1956	3.3
1903-1913	7.9	1956-1966	1.5
1913-1920	4.4	1966-1973	1.7

Kondratieff	annual growth rate
1873-1895 (downswing)	16.8
1895-1948	5.0
1948-1973 (upswing)	2.1

Sources: US Dept of Commerce 1975: Series P 265; US Dept of Commerce 1979, for updatings.

The post-1948 slowdown in U.S. steel production has not been accompanied by a similar slowdown in steel consumption. In 1950, imports of steel mill products constituted only one per cent of total U.S. supply; in 1977 this had increased to 18 per cent. During that period, U.S. exports of steel mill products showed little growth.

The steel industry is interesting because data availability permits us to trace the substitution of steel-making technologies over time. The introduction of the Bessemer process in 1866 signified the start of the modern steel industry. All steel produced prior to that date had been crucible steel (introduced in 1811). In the 1870s the open hearth process was developed as a third technology, becoming paramount early in the 20th century. A fourth technology is that of electric steel making. Finally, in 1952, oxygen steel making was started in Austria, and is now the dominant technology (Fig. 2.6). As raw steel is not a final commodity but rather an input into various production processes, the substitution of new technologies for old is not determined by maturity or saturation phenomena, but occurs during periods of demand expansion. Thus the Bessemer and Siemens-Martin processes were introduced as the demand for steel increased during the 1845-1873 Kondratieff upswing, electric steel making arrived during the 1895-1913 expansion, and oxygen steel making was introduced in the post-1948 upswing.

Figure 2.6 shows the output shares of the different technologies; in absolute terms, crucible steel, Bessemer steel and open hearth steel have increased to peak levels and decreased thereafter. Crucible steel making virtually disappeared during the Second World War; the Bessemer process reached its production peak in 1906; while open hearth steel making peaked in 1955. Bessemer steel making has now also practically disappeared, while open hearth steel making is declining steadily.

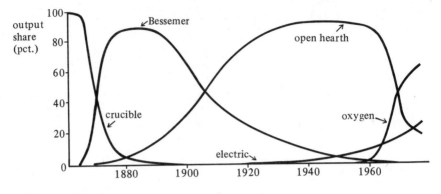

Figure 2.6 *U.S. Steelmaking Technologies, 1860-1977*

Absolute declines therefore occur if new innovations are developed, even in the context of a growing economy; the visibility of decline obviously depends on the industry delineation used. At the 2-digit SIC-level most industries will appear to be growing at all times. Yet within such industries substitution processes will be going on, such as have been illustrated with the steel-making example. Regardless of the level of aggregation selected, however, whether it is the individual product, or the commonly used 2-digit SIC-level, or total industrial production, a constant rate of growth over the entire known life of the unit measured will not be the outcome. We may not be able to foretell what happens past the maturity stage, but retardation of growth following the introduction of a product, production process, or innovation in general, is inevitable. Industrial growth will again be examined in Chapters IX and X: in Chapter IX to look at aggregate industrial production as it has changed over time in the core industrial countries; in Chapter X to trace what by then we shall call innovation life cycles.

ASYMPTOTIC GROWTH CURVES

Growth retardation can be represented by a number of mathematical growth curves. Kuznets (1930) used the logistic curve and the Gompertz curve to estimate growth retardation of industrial output in the early industrial nations; Burns (1934) and Frickey (1942) used the logarithmic parabola on U.S. data.

The equation for the *logistic curve* is:

$$(2.1) \quad y_t = \frac{k}{1 + ae^{-bt}} \qquad (k, a, b > 0),$$

where y_t = output at time t
        k = asymptote

e = base of the natural logarithm
t = time index.

The constant a determines the position of the curve with respect to the time axis (to increase a means to shift the curve to the right); the constant b determines the slope of the curve.

A special property of the logistic curve is its symmetry with respect to its inflexion point, between y = 0 (at t = -∞) and y = k (at t = +∞). To determine its point of inflexion the second derivative d^2y/dt^2 is set equal to zero. Then t = (ln a)/b and y = k/2. In words: at the point of inflexion the output level is exactly half the saturation level. In life-cycle models the point of inflexion is sometimes used to mark the transition from growth phase to maturity phase. In those instances where the parameters of the logistic curve can be estimated, this transition can thus be uniquely determined.

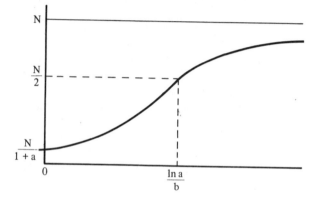

Figure 2.7 *The logistic curve*

The most attractive property of the logistic curve, however, is that it exhibits growth at a continually decreasing rate. The instantaneous rate of growth equals

(2.2) $$\frac{dy}{dt} \cdot \frac{1}{y} = \frac{ab}{e^{bt} + a}$$

and is indeed continually decreasing.

The logistic curve can be derived from simple behavioral assumptions, one of which is to view S-shaped growth as the growth of knowledge. The basic assumption then is

(2.3) $$\frac{dI}{dt} = bI_t,$$

where I_t = accumulated information, or state of knowledge, at time t. Equation

(2.3) assumes that the information gain is proportional to the amount of information existing at time t. Integration between t = 0 and t = T would yield an exponential increase of information.

(2.4) $I = I_0 (e^{bT} - 1)$

(I_0 = amount of information at time t = 0). However, accumulated information is bound to an upper limit k, and a correction factor (k - I) /k is introduced, such that (2.3) becomes

(2.3a) $\dfrac{dI}{dt} = bI_t \dfrac{k - I_t}{k}$

Integration now yields the logistic growth curve:

(2.4a) $I = \dfrac{k}{1 + (\dfrac{k}{I_0} - 1)e^{-bt}}$

A similar derivation, but with a different interpretation of the variables, is obtained by assuming that the rate of adoption by the public of a new product is proportional to the number of people already familiar with the product. By replacing I in (2.3) with a variable which measures numbers of buyers, an equation is obtained which gives the rate of increase of number of buyers of the new product. Since the number of potential buyers is limited (to k), a correction factor can be applied to prevent the number of buyers from growing exponentially, yielding the logistic curve again.

The equation for the *Gompertz curve* is

(2.5) $y_t = ka^{b^t}$ $(k > 0, 0 < a, b < 1)$

where y_t and k are defined as above. The shape of this curve differs from the

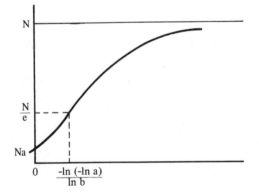

Figure 2.8 *The Gompertz curve*

logistic curve. Which equation will yield the best fit will depend on the phenomenon studied. Gompertz curves, for example, are used to describe income growth. In other instances, however, the logistic curve might be more appropriate.

The Gompertz curve is non-symmetrical with respect to its point of inflexion. This inflexion point is reached for $b = -\frac{1}{\ln a}$; y then equals $k/e = .36788k$. Like the logistic curve, however, the Gompertz has a continually decreasing growth rate, as

(2.6) $\quad \frac{dy}{dt} \cdot \frac{1}{y} = \ln a \cdot \ln b \cdot b^t$

Both the logistic curve and the Gompertz curve, in addition to being asymptotic growth curves, are *S-shaped*; i.e. they have a point of inflexion, which means that the absolute growth increments rise to the inflexion point, and fall beyond it.

The third curve to be mentioned here, the *modified exponential*, is characterized by a constant percentage decrease in the absolute amount of growth. Its equation is

(2.7) $\quad y_t = k + ab^t \quad (k > 0, a < 0, 0 < b < 1)$

with y_t and k again being defined as output at time t and the asymptote respectively. The parameter b represents the ratio between successive growth increments. As these increments decline, the relative rate of growth of the modified exponential must continually decrease. This gives us:

(2.8) $\quad \frac{dy}{dt} \cdot \frac{1}{y} = \ln b \cdot \frac{ab^t}{k + ab^t}$

The fourth growth curve, the *logarithmic parabola*, is strictly speaking not an asymptotic growth curve, and is included here only because Burns and Frickey used it for their estimation of growth retardation of U.S. industrial output. The logarithmic parabola reaches a maximum, after which a decline sets in. It exhibits a constant rate of retardation or of acceleration, as the case may be. Its equation is of the form

(2.9) $\quad \log y = a + bt + ct^2$

If the origin (t = 0) is taken at the centre of the time interval, then a equals the logarithm of the centre observation, b is the log of the growth *ratio*, y, at the centre of the period (e.g. 1.05), while 2c is the log of the average retardation ratio (e.g. 0.998, if the annual rate of retardation is 0.2 per cent). That the average retardation ratio can indeed be obtained in this way, may be seen by writing the logarithmic parabola as follows:

(2.9a) $\quad \log y = a + (\log b')t + (\frac{\log c'}{2})t^2$

Differentiating $\log y$ with respect to t, we get:

(2.10a) $\dfrac{d(\log y)}{dt} = \log y = \log b' + (\log c')t$

and

(2.11a) $y = b'c'^t$

The retardation ratio is now equal to $\dfrac{b'c'^{t+1}}{b'c'^t} = c'$, and as $\dfrac{\log c'}{2} = c$, $2c$ is indeed equal to the log of the retardation ratio.[4]

The logarithmic parabola does have a maximum value. By setting $\dfrac{d(\log y)}{dt} = 0$, one finds $t = -b/2c$ as the period in which this maximum is reached. The maximum value of $\log y$, $\log y^m$, is found as

(2.12) $\log y^m = a - \dfrac{b^2}{4c}$

Finally, a simple expression for the relative rate of growth of the logarithmic parabola can be obtained by setting b and c in (2.9) equal to $\log b''$ and $\log c''$ respectively. Then

(2.13) $\dfrac{dy}{dt} \cdot \dfrac{1}{y} = 2t(\ln c'') + \ln b''$

If there is retardation of growth, then in the original equation $b > 0$ and $c < 0$. This implies that $\ln b'' > 0$ and $\ln c'' < 0$, as should be the case.

APPENDIX A

Measuring the Rate of Economic Growth[5]

The rate of economic growth over a certain time period may be measured in several ways, all of which yield different rates for one identical output time series. The choice of method thus determines the resulting growth rate. In applying a particular method, one should at least be aware of its biases.

A very simple method is to calculate the growth rate as the arithmetic average of year-to-year growth rates:

$$(A.1) \quad \frac{\sum_{t=1}^{n} \frac{y_t}{y_{t-1}}}{n-1} - 1 \ \times \ 100$$

This method takes the development of actual output from year to year into account, but can produce peculiar results if strong fluctuations in output should occur. A series such as 100, 110, 99, 108.9, 98.01 would yield a zero average growth rate with this method. Yet, a continuation of alternating 10 per cent increases and decreases would imply a falling trend. For instance, after 20 years output would have fallen to 90.44, but the 20-year span would still be characterized by a zero growth rate.

Another method, which uses all output data in a series, involves fitting a growth curve

$$(A.2) \quad y_t = y_0 (1 + g)^t$$

to the data observed. The growth rate of course equals 100g. This method is given fairly wide application, as is the fitting of

$$(A.2a) \quad y_t = y_0 e^{\gamma t} ,$$

with e being the base of the Napierian logarithm and γ being the instantaneous rate of growth.

When applied to the same set of data, the estimated value of γ, $\hat{\gamma}$, will be lower than $\hat{g}$, the estimated value of g, because the instantaneous growth rate in (A.2) equals

$$(A.3) \quad \frac{dy}{dt} \cdot \frac{1}{y} = \ln (1 + g)$$

and $\ln (1 + g) > g$.

An exponential curve cannot be fitted directly to a set of data, and logarithms of the observed data are therefore first taken. However, using ordinary least squares then implies that the product (rather than the sum) of the actual values is made equal to the product (rather than the sum) of the estimated values. This, according to Pesek (1961: 301), is a meaningless procedure from the standpoint of economics. His 'improved' estimation method (see below) equalizes the sums of actual and estimated output and minimizes the sum of the squared deviations between actual and estimated output.

A third method by which to measure the growth rate over a certain period is to apply the compound interest-rate formula to the initial and terminal years of the time series, i.e. to calculate r from

$$(A.4) \qquad y_T = y_I (1+r)^{T-I}$$

where T and I denote terminal year and initial year respectively. This is probably the most widely-used method, even though it has some serious drawbacks. Its advantage is that it is extremely easy to compute an annual growth rate with this method, as

$$(A.5) \qquad r = \sqrt[T-I]{\frac{y_T}{y_I}} - 1$$

and many pocket calculators nowadays contain x/y-buttons that make growth rate calculation a matter of mere seconds. Its main disadvantages are:

(1) the sensitivity of the outcomes to the actual selection of initial and terminal years;

(2) the disregard of all information other than that contained in initial and terminal years.

The first problem poses itself when the actual time path fluctuates as a result of business cycles. Consider, for instance, the following series:

year	output	year	output
1	100	6	110
2	96	7	114
3	99	8	118
4	105	9	124
5	110	10	123

Measuring annual growth with I = 1 and T = 8 gives 2.4 as the growth rate; measuring it with I = 2 and T = 9, also a 7-year span, gives a 3.7 growth rate. One way by which to reduce the arbitrariness of point selection is to choose only comparable business-cycle years as initial and terminal years. A further reduction is obtained if only peak-to-peak measurements are made. Business cycle peaks are limited by productive capacity ceilings. Troughs, on the other hand, although comparable in terms of cycle phase, can vary in their rate of under-utilization of productive capacity, which makes them less desirable points. In our particular example, years 1 and 9 are assumed to be business cycle peaks. Connecting those points gives a 2.7 annual growth rate. Connecting the troughs – years 2 and 10 in the example – would yield a 3.1 rate, as recession in year 10 is clearly less serious than in year 2.

The compound interest-rate method does not take into account all data in the series, and a growth rate computed by this method cannot be called an *average* growth rate. It is an annual growth rate, calculated to measure the change in output from one business-cycle peak to another, for example.

To overcome the two disadvantages of the compound interest-rate method and to do away with the anomaly of working with products of outputs rather than sums, as implied by regular exponential growth curve fitting, Pesek (Ibidem: 305-306) has devised a method which suffers none of these drawbacks. With Pesek's growth rate, g_p, equalling (b - 1) x 100, his method determines the rate of economic growth using the following formula:

$$(A.6) \quad \frac{b^n + 1}{b + 1} = \frac{\sum_{t=1}^{n} y_t b^{t-1}}{\sum_{t=1}^{n} y_t}$$

The disadvantage of this method in actual applications is clear: it requires a substantial computational effort.

Finally, in illustration, the various methods of measuring the rate of economic growth are applied to postwar industrial production in the United States. The data are reproduced in Table A.1. Under the first method, computation of the

Table A.1 *U.S. index of industrial production, 1947-1979 (1967 = 100)*

year	index	year	index	year	index
1947	39.4	1958	57.9	1969	111.1
1948	41.4	1959	64.8	1970	107.8
1949	38.8	1960	66.2	1971	109.6
1950	44.9	1961	66.7	1972	119.7
1951	48.7	1962	72.2	1973	129.8
1952	50.6	1963	76.5	1974	129.3
1953	54.8	1964	81.7	1975	117.8
1954	51.9	1965	89.8	1976	130.5
1955	58.5	1966	97.8	1977	138.2
1956	61.1	1967	100.0	1978	146.1
1957	61.9	1968	106.3	1979	152.2

Source: *Economic Report of the President* (January 1980).

arithmetic average of 32 year-to-year growth rates yields an average growth rate of 4.475.

Fitting $\log y_t = \log y_0 + (\log b)t$ to the 33 industrial output data with 1947 being $t = 1$, produces the following estimates:

$$\hat{y}_0 = 37.949$$
$$\hat{b} = 1.04390 \qquad R^2 = .982$$

The growth rate therefore equals 4.390. Examination of the residuals, however, reveals a dominance of negative residuals up to 1964, then positive residuals through 1974, and negative residuals again for the remaining years. This suggests a slowdown of growth in the latter part of the 1960s and in the 1970s. The representation of the U.S. postwar industrial growth by one growth rate might therefore not be entirely adequate. To verify this, two data segments are considered, 1948-1966 and 1966-1979,[6] and the exponential growth curve is fitted to each of the segments. The results are:

	1948-1966	1966-1979
$\hat{y}_0$	39.159	94.658
$\hat{b}$	1.04458	1.03222
R^2	.953	.916

and we do indeed find a lower growth rate for the second sub-period.

Estimating the instantaneous rate of growth from $y_t = y_0 e^{\gamma t}$ for the 1947-1979 series yields:

$$\hat{y}_0 = 37.914$$
$$\hat{\gamma} = 0.0430$$
$$R^2 = .982.$$

This estimate is identical to that of the instantaneous rate of growth in the exponential function above, since $\ln \hat{b} = \ln (1.0439) = 0.0430$.

Calculating the rate of growth of industrial production with the compound interest-rate formula, with $I = 1947$ and $T = 1979$, gives a rate of 4.314. Care should be taken, however, in the choice of initial and terminal years. Assuming that 1979 will prove to be a business cycle peak, it is known that 1947 was not so. To measure annual growth from peak year to peak year, the 1948-1979 period should be considered. As it happens, the growth rate over this period is also 4.314.

The slowdown of growth noticed in the latter part of the postwar period, might also be revealed by dividing the period into business cycles, and by measuring growth rates from peak to peak. The result is:

1948-1956   5.081
1956-1966   4.817
1966-1973   4.127
1973-1979   2.689[7]

showing that peak-to-peak growth rates have gradually declined.

To sum up: dependent on the method chosen, U.S. industrial output in the 1947-1979 period grew at an annual rate of 4.5, 4.4 or 4.3 per cent.

APPENDIX B

Estimating the Parameters of Asymptotic Growth Curves

Logistic curve, Gompertz curve and modified exponential, all have three parameters: an asymptote and two other parameters. Straightforward regression analysis cannot be applied. It has to be done indirectly, or an entirely different method has to be used.

To fit a *logistic curve* to a set of data, Pearl's three-point method is often used. The three-point method determines the parameters of the logistic curve

$$(B.1) \quad y_t = \frac{k}{1 + ae^{-bt}} \qquad [8]$$

through the selection of three, equidistant observations of y_t, say y_0, y_1 and y_2, with the observations being n periods apart. It can be shown that

$$(B.2) \quad k = \frac{2y_0 y_1 y_2 - y_1^2 (y_0 + y_2)}{y_0 y_2 - y_1^2}$$

Once k has been determined, a and b can be obtained:

$$(B.3) \quad a = \frac{k - y_0}{y_0}$$

$$(B.4) \quad b = -\frac{1}{n} \ln \frac{y_0 (k - y_1)}{y_1 (k - y_0)}$$

A drawback of this method is that the choice of the three equidistant points is entirely arbitrary. Each set of points will yield its own set of parameter values. It might even be that a particular selection produces unacceptable outcomes, such as negative values for k and/or b.[9]

In estimating the parameters of the logistic through linear regression a transformation

$$(B.5) \quad z_t = \frac{1}{y_t}$$

is first applied. From the equidistance of the y_t - values it follows that

$$(B.6) \quad z_{t+1} = e^{-b} z_t + \frac{(1 - e^{-b})}{k} \ .$$

Once b and k have been estimated, an estimate for a can be found.

In applications of the logistic curve it is sometimes useful to assume that y_t contains a fixed part, $\bar{y}$, which does not increase, or at any rate not as a logistic function. When estimating the parameters of the logistic through linear regression, $\bar{y}$ can be chosen as that $\bar{y}$ which produces the best fit.

Estimates of the *Gompertz curve* and of the *modified exponential curve* can be obtained by the method of partial totals. To apply this method, (equidistant) data are divided into three segments of equal time length, and summed for each segment: Σ_1, Σ_2, and Σ_3.[10] Recalling the Gompertz curve

(B.7) $\quad y_t = ka^{b^t}$,

we first write it in logarithmic form:

(B.8) $\quad \ln y_t = \ln k + (\ln a)b^t$

Then:

(B.9) $\quad \ln k = \dfrac{1}{n} \ \dfrac{(\Sigma_1 \ln y)(\Sigma_3 \ln y) - (\Sigma_2 \ln y)^2}{\Sigma_1 \ln y + \Sigma_3 \ln y - 2\Sigma_2 \ln y}$,

where n is the number of time periods in each third of the data. Also:

(B.10) $\quad b^n = \dfrac{\Sigma_3 \ln y - \Sigma_2 \ln y}{\Sigma_2 \ln y - \Sigma_1 \ln y}$

(B.11) $\quad \ln a = (\Sigma_2 \ln y - \Sigma_1 \ln y) \ \dfrac{b - 1}{(b^n - 1)^2}$

The calculation of b^n can be used as a quick check on whether a series does indeed have an asymptote. If $b^n > 1$, and therefore $b > 1$, this is not the case and the series cannot be adequately represented by an asymptotic Gompertz curve.[11]

The parameters of the modified exponential can be obtained in similar fashion. Its applicability in economics is limited, however, and we shall not give the formulae here. The interested reader is referred to Croxton, Cowden & Klein (1967: 262 ff.), who also derive the expressions for the Gompertz curve given above.

NOTES

1. Ogburn (1922); Chapin (1928).
2. Kuznets did do so, but he showed 'a hesitancy to accept this notion of the secondary secular movements as periodic cycles, our main ground for it being an absence of factors that would explain the periodicity' (Kuznets 1930: 264).
3. On the measurement of growth rates, see Appendix A.
4. Instead of estimating the parameters of (2.9a), one could obtain estimates of log b' and log c' by letting y be the dependent variable.
5. See also Pesek (1961).
6. On the choice of initial and terminal years, see Note 7.
7. 1966 is not officially recorded as a business cycle peak year in the U.S., although 1965

or 1966 was so recorded in European countries. The U.S. economy experienced a minor slowdown in 1967, but due to the escalation of the Vietnam War, the real recession was postponed until 1970. The other benchmark years chosen here are true industrial production peak years.

8.   Sometimes the logistic is specified, and fitted, with common logarithms:

$$y_t = \frac{k}{1 + 10^{c + dt}}$$

9.   One restriction that has to be imposed on the asymptote k is $k > y_2$.
Now if $y_0 = y_1 - \eta$

$$y_2 = y_1 + \epsilon ,$$

where $\eta, \epsilon > 0$, then the middle observation y_1 has to be chosen such that

$$\eta \leqslant y_1 \leqslant \frac{\eta \epsilon}{\epsilon - \eta} \quad \text{in order to obtain a value of } k > y_2.$$

10.   The rationale of this method is that, as both curves are determined by three parameters, three equations are needed to obtain estimates of these three parameters.
11.   It could be the case that the series in question again has a fixed part, such as discussed for the logistic curve.

III

SECULAR TRENDS

ROSTOW'S STAGES OF ECONOMIC GROWTH

In the previous chapter economic growth has been shown as an S-shaped phenomenon . The S-shaped curve may be an adequate visualization of the growth of products, or industries, or even national industrial output during a certain length of time, but would it also be suitable to describe the secular growth of an economy? Do economies follow a certain growth pattern in their transition from agricultural to industrial and post-industrial societies? And if so, how is the long wave intertwined with this growth pattern?

By far the best-known theory of long-term economic growth is Rostow's stages theory (Rostow 1971a). First published in 1960 as a 'non-communist manifesto', Rostow's theory distinguishes five stages: (1) traditional society; (2) preconditions for take-off; (3) take-off; (4) the drive to technological maturity; (5) the age of high mass-consumption. Later, he added a sixth stage: the search for quality (Rostow 1971b).

In the empirical validation of this theory, Rostow has laid most emphasis on stages 3, 4 and 5. Traditional society, in his view, is the pre-Newtonian world: the world of medieval Europe, or the dynasties in China. The second stage points at the kind of transformation Western Europe went through during the late 17th and early 18th centuries, as the insights of modern science began to have their impact on production in agriculture and industry. Rostow elaborated this stage in a separate work in 1975. But by far the most important stage is the third one, the take-off into sustained growth, 'the great watershed in the life of modern societies' (Rostow 1971a: 7). During take-off new industries expand rapidly, the rate of effective investment will rise, the basic structure of the economy and the social and political structures of the society are transformed in such a way that a steady rate of growth can thereafter be regularly sustained.

During take-off the economy is focussed on a relatively narrow complex of industry and technology. During its drive to technological maturity, new leading sectors emerge (historically, textiles was followed by railroads, steel, electricity, and the chemical industry). Maturity sets in when an economy demonstrates its

A note to this chapter may be found on p. 56.

capability of absorbing the most advanced fruits of (then) modern technology. Then follows the age of high mass-consumption. The leading sectors shift towards durable consumers' goods and services. Beyond consumption lies the search for quality.

Immediately after its publication the stages-of-growth theory became the subject of much discussion – and criticism. A debate was staged between Rostow and his critics in Konstanz, through a conference organized by the International Economic Association (1961; the papers and proceedings of this conference were published in Rostow 1963). The criticisms concentrated mainly on two aspects: the quick rise in the rate of investment which Rostow assumed to characterize take-off, and the sequence of leading sectors. The critics (Phyllis Deane and Kuznets among them) argued that in the British case the increase in the rate of investment had been gradual rather than sudden. Deane, for one, could not detect a clear sequence of leading sectors. Kuznets questioned whether Rostow's two most crucial stages, the take-off and the drive to technological maturity, could be identified on the basis of the available statistical data.

It is somewhat unfortunate, considering the common origins of their work, that the stages-of-growth debate set Kuznets against Rostow. In his lengthy comment on the stages-of-growth discussion (Preface and Appendix B of Rostow 1971a), Rostow argued that Kuznets's early work on *Secular Movements in Production and Prices* (1930), had provided the inspiration in his work on the process of economic growth.

Kuznets (1930) is indeed full of 'Rostowian' insights: the sectoral rather than the macro-economic approach to economic development, the linking of new technologies to new leading sectors, the slackening of growth once these technologies have been fully absorbed, the overtaking by new industries, the incorporation of new technologies. But the generation of aggregate statistical data, on an international basis, set Kuznets on a different course – although his work in the late 1960s and early 1970s shows that he returned to his own sources again – while Rostow further developed and elaborated his sectoral approach. In Rostow's view this was at the heart of their controversy: should growth be analyzed in terms of broad aggregates only, or should these aggregates be linked to movements in the sectors and sub-sectors within which new technologies are efficiently absorbed into an economy? (Rostow 1971a: ix). Rostow's answer has been clear from the start. It would seem that recent economic developments and the sudden rise in popularity of the 'meso' level as the appropriate level of aggregation for the study of current economic problems, have vindicated his judgement.

A direct consequence of Rostow's linking of stages of growth with the sequence of leading sector complexes is the denial of any relation between his stages and an aggregate measure such as GNP. In his own words:

I would hold that the most fundamental approach [to growth] is to identify the extent to which particular technologies have been absorbed efficiently into the economy, and the sequence in which they are absorbed. This means we must look at the sectors and sub-sectors, not merely the aggregates. Technology is not absorbed in GNP. Movements in GNP reflect the process of absorption, as well as other variables (Ibidem: 180).

Thus, cotton textiles and pig iron were the leading sectors of Britain's take-off, railroads and steel and the early phase of electricity the leading sectors of its drive to technological maturity, while the age of high mass-consumption was entered with the arrival of automobiles. Because of Britain's initial lead, its leading sectors are widely spaced. The latecomers of the 19th century (e.g. Sweden, Italy, Japan, and Russia) were able to draw from a cumulative pool of technology created by countries whose take-off had taken place earlier. The latecomers of the 20th century could draw from an even larger pool. Yet in most cases the imperatives of modernization and of the income elasticity of demand still decree a sequence of absorption which bears a family relation to those of the historical past: cotton usually precedes steel and heavy engineering; motor vehicles and durable consumer goods in general, electronics and modern chemicals come still later (Rostow 1978: 378-89).

A particular stage of growth therefore corresponds with a particular degree of absorption of technology, and not necessarily with a particular level of per capita GNP. During take-off, some countries may already be relatively rich (Australia); others may still be poor in their drive towards technological maturity (India). But while stage of growth and level of per capita income may not be rigorously related, theory and empirical observation both suggest a relation between *stage* of growth and *rate* of per capita GNP growth.

Such a theoretical relationship has been suggested by Kristensen (1974), who argues that the growth of per capita GNP depends on the rate of absorption of the stock of existing and unfolding knowledge. Absorption of knowledge requires capital and skilled manpower. Countries which have both the capital for investment and a reasonably high standard of education can attain fairly rapid economic growth. As a general rule these will be the medium income countries. Higher income countries will generally have slower growth, mainly because they already apply modern knowledge to a large extent. Low income countries, on the other hand, usually lack both capital and trained manpower. Consequently, their rate of growth will also be low.

'Existing knowledge' is Kristensen's key variable. If the level of existing knowledge were constant, production per capita would gradually approach a ceiling determined by this level. But if new knowledge is produced, this ceiling will move upwards. Also, the transfer of knowledge to economically less developed countries will allow them to catch up with those that are more advanced.

For the latter this means a dampening effect on growth. 'Thus', Kristensen concludes, 'if there is something that can be called the typical growth curve for GNP
per capita, it is not an exponential curve but rather an S-shaped curve that may
or may not approach an upper limit' (Ibidem: 29).

More recently, Rostow has backed down from his earlier rejection of GNP as
an aid to secular growth analysis. In Rostow & Fordyce (1978) he endorses
Kristensen's assessment of the role of the diffusion of technologies, adding,
however, that cross-sectional analyses, such as Kristensen's, hide important
aspects of the story of growth that do show up when growth is looked at from
an historical perspective. Yet Rostow appears willing to let his drive-to-technol-
ogical-maturity phase correspond with Kristensen's middle-income range, and
the later part of his stage of high mass-consumption with Kristensen's high-
income range. In Rostow's terminology then, once take-off or modern growth
has begun, growth will accelerate during the drive to technological maturity,
and decelerate in those countries far into the stage of high mass consumption.

The long-term path of growth of per capita GNP will therefore be S-shaped.[1]
Every student of economic growth knows, however, that the quarter-century
from 1948 to 1973 showed a remarkable acceleration of growth, for the early
entrants as well as the latecomers. Why were 1948-1973 growth rates higher
than ever before during the past two centuries? Rostow mentions four explanatory factors.

1. The postwar commitment of governments to maintain full employment,
    backed by a wide range of instruments for affecting the level of effective
    demand.
2. The backlog of technologies, ready for absorption by Western Europe and
    Japan; the added impetus of demand for capital goods in countries which
    had suffered physical war damage.
3. The efforts of the developing regions of Latin America, Africa, the Middle
    East and Asia to increase investment rates and absorb the backlog of un-
    applied technologies.
4. An environment of relatively falling energy prices and, from 1951 to 1972,
    relatively falling or low prices of foodstuffs and raw materials.

The long-term per capita growth patterns of the four industrial core countries
(Great Britain, United States, France and Germany) are illustrated below, plus
those of two later entrants (Sweden and Italy), by showing percentage deviations
of an estimated log-linear trend (Figures 3.1 through 3.6). As the estimated
trend rates of growth — and therefore also the residuals — are rather sensitive to
the length of the time series over which they are estimated, we have taken
Rostow's take-off decades for each of these countries in order to determine the
initial year of the respective time series. The take-off stage marks the beginning
of modern growth; the S-shaped curve should start to unfold itself during that
particular stage.

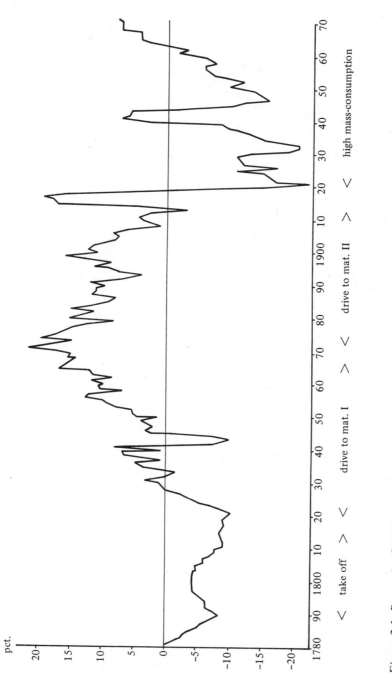

Figure 3.1 *Per capita GNP Great Britain, per cent deviations log-linear trend*

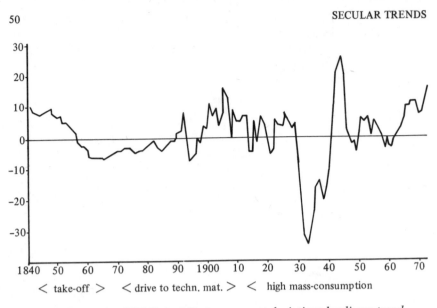

Figure 3.2 *Per capita GNP United States, per cent deviations log-linear trend*

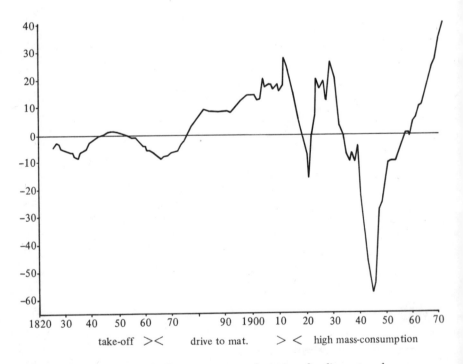

Figure 3.3 *Per capita GNP France, per cent deviations log-linear trend*

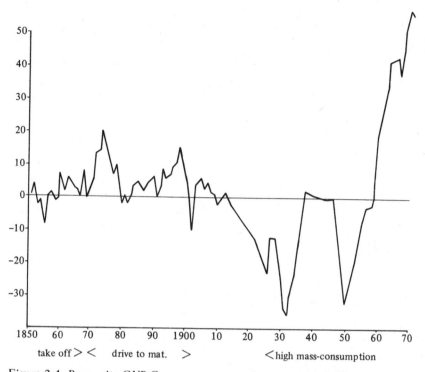

Figure 3.4 *Per capita GNP Germany, per cent deviations log-linear trend*

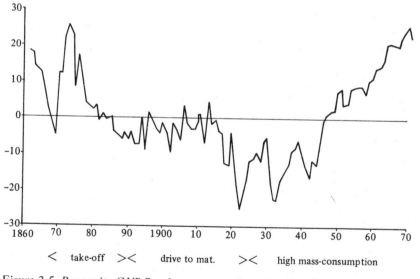

Figure 3.5 *Per capita GNP Sweden, per cent deviations log-linear trend*

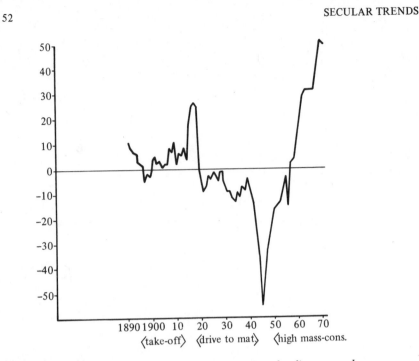

Figure 3.6 *Per capita GNP Italy, per cent deviations log-linear trend*

The stylized pattern of percentage deviations from the log-linear trend should look as follows: negative residuals during take-off, becoming smaller and turning positive during the drive to technological maturity; residuals will become negative again in the age of high mass-consumption, but the unique set of postwar circumstances will yield positive residuals again, at least for the 1960s, and possibly also for the 1950s. This is shown in Graph 1.

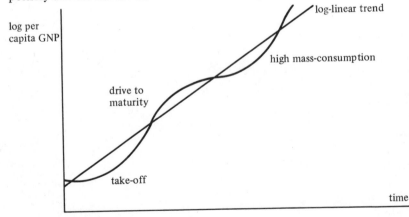

Graph 1 *Long-term per capita growth*

The basic contours of such a growth pattern can be found in the graphs of all countries, with the exception of Sweden. During the take-off phase a trough can be recorded, marking the point after which growth starts to accelerate. This acceleration occurs sometime during Rostow's take-off stage, not necessarily at its beginning (see Table 3.2). The first major peak of the residuals series is situated at the end of the drive to technological maturity of Great Britain, United States and France, but much earlier in the cases of Germany, Sweden and Italy. The next trough is reached either in 1932-33, or in 1944-45, after which the postwar boom starts to move the residuals series up again.

Sweden's residual pattern is different. It is the kind that would result from fitting a log-linear trend to a series which exhibits a gradually increasing growth rate: first the residuals are positive, then negative, and finally positive again. Note also that Sweden's estimated per capita growth rate is higher than anywhere else: 2.4 versus 1.6-1.7 for the United States, France, Germany and Italy, and 1.3 for Great Britain (Table 3.1).

With the amendment for the unique set of postwar growth conditions added, the S-shaped secular growth hypothesis seems to hold up well when confronted with actual per capita growth data. The question is, however, whether the postwar experience is just a one-time divergence from an otherwise dominant pattern, or whether growth deceleration followed by growth acceleration is likely to be a recurrent phenomenon. Postwar growth was boosted by a rather unique combination of factors, but is it not likely that the available pool of innovations would have accelerated growth even without relatively cheap energy and raw materials? Would not a next round of growth witness the entrance of new latecomers, who would be able to absorb the available backlog of unapplied technologies and would have a stimulating effect on the older industrialized nations?

The question at issue is that of secular growth, intertwined with the international rhythm of the long wave. It would appear that both phenomena exert their influence on a country's growth record. If only the S-shaped secular growth pattern is looked for, one needs an amendment to explain the 1948-1973 boom; if long-wave patterns only are sought, downturns may be hidden if they coincide with a country's drive to technological maturity. It is for this latter reason that the long wave shows up much more clearly in world industrial production data than in the industrial production records of individual countries, as we shall see in Chapter IX.

In short, insight into both phenomena is necessary for an adequate understanding of the process of long-term economic growth. The S-shaped growth pattern is needed, according to the interpretation given by Kristensen and Rostow. The long-wave pattern is also necessary, but its theoretical explanation has yet to be provided. For that reason we shall abstain here from interpreting Figures 3.1 through 3.6 from a long-wave perspective. We wish only to emphasize that S-shaped secular growth is very much a national phenomenon, with

Table 3.1 *Estimating log-linear trends of per capita GNP, six countries*

	Time series	Estimated growth rate	R^2
Great Britain	1781-1971	1.268	.980
United States	1841-1973	1.752	.980
France	1826-1971	1.713	.943
Germany	1851-1971	1.584	.920
Sweden	1862-1971	2.434	.978
Italy	1891-1971	1.660	.773

Data source: Rostow & Fordyce (1978)

Table 3.2 *Residual patterns and stages of growth, six countries*

	Take-off	T	Drive to maturity	P	High mass-consumption	T
Great Britain	1783-1830	1821	1830-1870 1870-1913	1871	1920-	1932
United States	1843-1870	1864	1870-1910	1906	1910-	1933
France	1830-1870	1866	1870-1913	1912	1920-	1944
Germany	1840-1870	1855	1870-1913	1898	1925-	1932
Sweden	1868-1890	(1895)	1890-1925	(1913)	1925-	1933
Italy	1895-1913	1897	1920-1940	1917	1950-	1945

T = trough; P = peak

the 'time length' of the S being determined by the available, international, pool of technologies; the long wave, on the other hand, is predominantly an international phenomenon, related to the clustered appearance of new technologies, or better, new basic innovations. But even this comment anticipates matters that have yet to be discussed.

ECONOMIC GROWTH IN THE VERY LONG RUN

Above we have argued that S-shaped growth as interpreted by Kristensen and Rostow is applicable to national economies. In their models, limits to growth are determined by the level of existing knowledge. There is, however, an S-shaped growth curve which spans an even longer period than the 200 years that have passed since the Industrial Revolution, and which applies to the world as a whole. The upper limits to this global growth process are not technological, but physical and social.

The physical limits to growth were widely discussed during the early 1970s (Club of Rome 1972; Forrester 1973), at the end of the postwar growth era; later in the 1970s, the social limits to growth also became topic of discussion (Hirsch 1977). It would seem that nowadays more emphasis is put on the social than on the physical constraints to further economic growth (see, e.g. Kahn 1979, and the OECD Interfutures report 1979). What are these social limits to growth? In short, 'growth will taper off because of slackening demand, changed values, and changed attitudes' (Kahn 1979: 71). Rostow's 'search for quality' will apparently imply lower growth rates.

It is interesting to note that both Kahn and Interfutures view the current period as one of transition (see Figure 3.7). Would the same assessment have been made if high growth had continued after 1973? Most likely not! The designation of our times as a period of transition towards slower growth reminds one of the secular stagnation thesis, which enjoyed brief popularity during the late 1930s, and with which the name of Alvin Hansen is associated (Hansen 1938, 1941). Then, too, growth had abruptly stopped, to be followed by a decade of stagnation with no clear indications of permanent recovery. Then, too, this period of stagnation was seen as one of transition when placed in a longer time perspective. To cite Hansen (1941: 349): 'We are passing, so to speak, over a divide which separates the great era of growth and expansion of the nineteenth century from an era which no man, unwilling to embark on pure conjecture, can as yet characterize with clarity or precision.'

Admittedly, Hansen saw the cause of secular stagnation neither in physical limits to growth, nor in social limits. The only alternative to stagnation, in his view, was a more rapid advance of technology: 'The problem of our generation

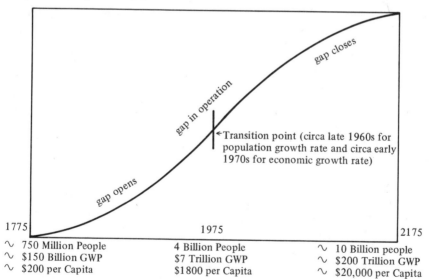

A positive and realistic
image of humanity's earth trek

1775   1975   2175

∿ 750 Million People	4 Billion People	∿ 10 Billion people
∿ $150 Billion GWP	$7 Trillion GWP	∿ $200 Trillion GWP
∿ $200 per Capita	$1800 per Capita	∿ $20,000 per Capita

Note: Plot is logarithmic; GWP = Gross World Product; and sums are fixed 1978 dollars.

Figure 3.7 *Kahn's Great Transition*

Source: Kahn (1979: 66).

is, above all, the problem of inadequate private investment outlets. What we need is not a slowing down in the progress of science and technology, but rather an acceleration of that rate' (Ibidem: 362). Thus, Hansen's analysis is more in the line with that of Kristensen and Rostow. A country which has reached the age of high mass consumption will reach a point of saturation unless it raises its ceiling through the application of new knowledge that is used to meet hitherto unsatisfied needs and wants.

Even so, despite the differing emphases on what actually constitutes the major limit to growth, discussions of secular points of transition are more likely to arise during periods of depression than during years of rapid expansion. This is not to say that the notion of S-shaped growth for the world economy as a whole, as depicted by Kahn, deserves no attention. Certain social limits, because of changing values and changing attitudes, may make themselves felt in the near future. Yet how these changing values and attitudes will be translated into demands for goods and services, and how this demand will be valued in GNP-terms, we do not know. Should the public come to place a high value on certain services, on cultural and recreational activities which do not require large quantities of physical products, then GNP – as the sum of value added – might shoot up. Yet the nature of growth would then be entirely different from that of the recent past. GNP, apart from its other deficiencies, is a time-bound concept, reflecting the values of a particular age. Comparisons between an industrial and a possible post-industrial age, spanning centuries, have little meaning.

It is not inadequate to label this a 'period of transition', but then in the sense that the advanced countries are in the process of moving from one generation of leading sectors to another. Whether the early 1970s also represented a point of inflexion on a curve which measures logarithms of gross world product in 1978 dollars over a 400-year time span, is a question of little operational value.

NOTE

1. This does not mean that logistic and Gompertz curves will necessarily provide a good fit to actual data, as these two functions assume continually decreasing growth rates.

PART II

LONG WAVE THEORIES

IV

THE DISCOVERY OF THE LONG WAVE

FIRST SKETCHES OF A LONG WAVE

In a paper published in the British *Railway Register* for 1847, and entitled 'Physical Economy – a preliminary inquiry into the physical laws governing the periods of famines and panics', Dr Hyde Clarke suggested the existence of a 54-year period which started with the crisis of 1793 and ended with that of 1847. Clarke saw this long period as consisting of five 10-11 year periods (or Juglars, as later authors were to call them), the intervals being the crises of 1804, 1815, 1826 and 1837.

As far as we know, this is the first reference to a possible long wave in economic activity. From the quotations given in Jevons (1844: 202-204), it seems that Clarke's conjectures were based only on a comparison of the famines of 1793 and 1847, both very severe ones. There is no attempt at explanation. Clarke felt, however, that the 10-11 year intervals could not be incidental but that there must be some physical cause, which should be sought with the aid of a science to be called 'physical economy'.

Jevons himself, of course, was also interested in the periodicity of economic crises. His sunspot theory may actually have been the type of physical cause that Clarke was looking for. Remarkably enough, Jevons also did a great deal of work on long-term fluctuations in the price level, which played a key role in the writings of long wave pioneers. Yet Jevons was never able to explain the long alternating periods of rising and falling prices. In 1865 he had to conclude: 'No single cause that I know of can be sufficient to account for so singular an event' (reprinted in Jevons 1884: 127).

Fluctuations in the general price level, as observable in the late 18th and in the 19th century, have been the direct incentive for the search for long fluctuations in economic activity at large. This was due primarily to the fact that price series were the most readily available type of economic time series. For Britain there was Sauerbeck's well-known price-index, starting in 1818; there were also numerous price series for individual commodities, for wages, interest rates, etc. Physical volume series were much harder to come by. In the post-World War II

Notes to this chapter may be found on p. 72.

years the excellent work of economic historians has provided modern researchers with industrial production series with which they can trace all the ups and downs in the industrial history of Western countries, but in the early years of this century such series were not available.

A second reason for investigating price fluctuations was that the long period of overall economic expansion which followed the 1847 crisis and lasted until 1873, coincided with a period of rising prices of equal length. The subsequent Great Depression (1873-96) was a period of steadily falling prices, and events of this period have particularly impressed contemporary economists. Werner Sombart (quoted in Van Gelderen 1913: 458) wrote: 'The so-called natural state of modern economic life is the depression'! This long depression ended in 1896 and a new period of expansion set in, again associated with a rise in the price level. It was then that economists began to wonder whether these alternations of long expansions and contractions were inherent in capitalist economies and, if so, what could cause them.

The first to do this was Parvus, i.e. the Russian Marxist, Alexander Israel Helphand (1867-1924), a prominent member of the German and, for a while, the Russian socialist movement of the late 19th and early 20th century. A socialist-theoretician, Parvus influenced Trotsky's thinking. In fact, Trotsky borrowed from him the idea of long-term capitalist development as a wave-like movement (Trotsky 1923).

In 1901 Parvus published a pamphlet which gave the bare outline of his long wave. There are times, he said, 'when the development in all areas of the capitalist economy – the state of technology, the money market, trade, the colonies – has come to the point that an eminent expansion of the world market must take place, lifting the whole of world production onto a new, more comprehensive basis' (Parvus 1901: 26). According to Parvus, this is when the *Sturm- und Drang* period of capital begins, during which regular business cycles will occur. The cycle upswings will be stronger, however, while the crises will be of shorter duration, and so it will continue until the development potential has worked itself out. Then the sharpest of crises will break out and will develop into an *economic depression*. This will be characterized by a slowdown of economic development; business cycle expansions will become weaker, and crises more prolonged, while production will have difficulty in recovering. This will continue until the potential for a new Sturm- und Drang period has developed (Ibidem).[1]

Parvus was clearly thinking of a continual motion, not necessarily regular in its periodicity, but one in which periods of long expansion and contraction would alternate. A Sturm- und Drang period will eventually be followed by a depression, but in turn, this depression will be followed by a new phase of expansion.

Parvus's work can in no way be called a long wave theory, i.e. he does not explain the turning points (the quintessential test for any theory of economic fluctuations), other than in the vaguest of terms. At best it might be said that he indicated the factors which, in his opinion, had ushered in the new Sturm-und Drang period which started in 1896. Parvus categorized these factors under three headings: (1) the opening-up of new markets; (2) the increase in gold pro-duction; (3) the development of electricity (Ibidem: 28-31). There is almost no empirical support for his thesis, and he surprisingly and erroneously lets the 1850-73 expansion phase start in the 1860s and end in the late 1870s. Yet, here is a truly original thinker who, mainly because of his failure to elaborate his ideas, has never received much credit for this originality.[2]

TWO DUTCHMEN

It is sometimes argued in the Netherlands, somewhat chauvinistically, that the long wave was discovered in that country. The honour should go to two Dutch Marxists, Van Gelderen (writing under the pseudonym J. Fedder) and De Wolff.

The Dutch are right in contesting Schumpeter's association of the long wave with Kondratieff. Van Gelderen's work on the long wave was published in 1913, almost ten years before Kondratieff started writing about his long cycles. De Wolff, like Kondratieff, published in the 1920s. Both authors worked indepen-dently of one another. Kondratieff later became familiar with a German article by De Wolff (1924), but De Wolff never mentioned Kondratieff, even though his main work (De Wolff 1929) was published three years after Kondratieff's article in the *Archiv für Sozialwissenschaft und Sozialpolitik* in 1926.

The Dutch are only partly right, of course. While Van Gelderen was unques-tionably the first economist to study the relation between long price cycles and fluctuations in industrial development, both in its statistical and its theoretical aspects, he was second in the line of Marxist long wave economists which started with Parvus. Van Gelderen has acknowledged this fact (1913:455). As far as the Marxists are concerned, the long wave ought to be called the Parvus cycle.

After studying price series for a number of Western countries, Van Gelderen noted an alternation of long periods of rising and falling prices. He linked these with fluctuations in general economic activity: the period 1850-73 had seen a strong upward surge of the European and United States economies; this was followed by a period of slow economic growth, which ended in the early 1890s. The year 1896 marked the beginning of a new 'springtide', as Van Gelderen called the long-wave upswing phase.

Van Gelderen sought statistical support for his thesis in various series: not merely price series, but also production, financial, international trade and trans-port. At that time, many of the latter series were still very short. If they sup-ported the existence of a wave-like motion, they were far too short to prove the existence of a long *cycle*. Van Gelderen avoided that term altogether, restricting himself to an historical-statistical analysis and looking for economic factors that could explain the observed alternation of springtide and ebbtide. Van Gelderen noted that for a long-wave expansion to occur a powerful increase of production has to take place, whether spontaneous or gradual. This can happen in two ways: (1) through the opening of new territory; (2) through the establishment of new industrial activities, which are able to meet some hitherto unsatisfied need (automobiles, electricity). Demand impulses will be propagated through the economy, through consumption-multiplier and inter-industry input-output effects. Growth will take off, but the acceleration of production carries the seeds of its own destruction. First of all, final-goods markets will be flooded and over-production will occur. Secondly, raw material shortages will develop and drive up production costs. The market, however, cannot carry increases in product prices, actual demand will decrease, profits will fall, and the tide will turn.

The explanation of the lower turning point has proved to be a most difficult task for most long wave economists, and Van Gelderen was no exception. He recognized the conditions under which a long-wave expansion would occur, but failed to explain how and when these conditions will be brought about. In his only reference to the length of the long wave he argues that the explanation of its periodicity lies in 'the quantitatively and qualitatively uncontrolled course of the capitalist production process' (Ibidem: 453).

The 1913-paper was Van Gelderen's only contribution to the long-wave discussion. Although he certainly deserves recognition as a true long-wave pioneer, he was by no means the only economist to notice the wave-like behaviour of prices. In the year of publication of his paper, three French books were published in which reference was made to (price-) movements of long duration: Aftalion (1913: 6), Lenoir (1913: 149) and Von Tugan-Baranowsky (1913: 19). At about the same time, i.e. in 1912 and 1914, Lescure published two articles on long-term fluctuations of prices (re-edited in Lescure 1933). All these authors, however, offered no clear explanation of long waves. Lenoir remarked merely that: 'without doubt, these changes signify a relative shift of the supply and demand curves.' Whether or not they had a valid explanation, however, it is clear that by 1913 long waves had come to the notice of the economists.

In the Netherlands, Van Gelderen's work was to be continued by De Wolff, an active member of the Dutch Marxist-socialist movement and one-time friend of the other. De Wolff made two contributions: a paper in German (De Wolff 1924) and a book in Dutch, *Het economisch getij* (The Economic Tide; 1929), the title of which is a tribute to Van Gelderen's springtide.

De Wolff's long wave is an echo-wave, caused by the reproduction of obsolescent capital goods, seen by Marx as the main cause of business cycles. The length of the business cycle is determined by the life of machines which, in

Marx's days, averaged 10 years; the length of the long wave is determined by capital goods of long duration, such as plants, bridges, wharfs, railway material, etc. By taking average depreciation rates of various categories of durable capital goods, De Wolff calculated an average rate of 2.615 per cent, corresponding to an average life of 38 years. And, lo and behold, long wave peaks at 1873 and 1913 give a length of 40 years, and long wave troughs at 1894 and 1930 a length of 36 years; i.e. an average of exactly 38 years. 'Therefore the long wave is determined by the life of the long-living fixed capital' (De Wolff 1929: 419).

De Wolff assumed a fixed relationship between the short business cycle and the long wave: each long wave phase (upswing and downswing) comprised 2½ business cycles. But the business cycle was getting shorter, as the life of 'labour machines' would get shorter over time. This conforms with the Marxist notion that the frequency of crises in the capitalist system would increase until its final collapse would follow. De Wolff's calculations allow us to predict the year that this collapse should take place: 1994 (Broersma 1978: 18).

In an echo-wave model, cycles are endogenous once they have been set in motion by an exogenous impulse, which De Wolff took to be the application of innovations of the Industrial Revolution. This had set the capitalist mode of production in motion, it also set the long wave in motion. During each phase of prosperity, the stock of durable capital goods would be renewed, to last for the remainder of the cycle.

There is more to De Wolff's analysis. As a true follower of Marx he had to find a place in his theory for such Marxist concepts as the rate of surplus value and the organic composition of capital. We shall not go into this part of his work. Although voluminous, it adds little to his explanation of the long wave and, if anything, confuses it. De Wolff's long wave is in fact nothing other than a reproduction cycle.

KONDRATIEFF

Nikolai Dmitriyevich Kondratyev, or Kondratieff, as his name is usually written in economics literature, was a Russian agricultural economist. Born in 1892, he became Vice Minister of Food in the provisional government of Alexander Kerensky (May-November 1917), worked with the Agricultural Academy in Moscow, and in 1920 founded the Conjuncture Institute, which he directed until his removal in 1928.[3]

Kondratieff developed his long-wave hypothesis in the late 1910s and early 1920s, thus providing support for Schumpeter's view that an individual's creativity peaks before his thirtieth year and that the remainder of his lifetime is spent on working-out his ideas! Kondratieff's first sketch of a long wave appeared in 1922, in an article entitled 'The world economy and its condition during and after the war.' In this article, which was published only in Russian, he was still very cautious about the existence of a long wave: 'we consider the long cycles in the capitalist economy only as probable.' The, mainly negative, reactions of his fellow economists induced Kondratieff to elaborate his ideas further. In 1923, 1924, and 1925 new papers appeared (see Appendix C, which lists all his publications), the last of which contained the results of Kondratieff's statistical investigations. A German version was published in 1926; later on, an abridged English translation appeared, under the title 'The long waves in economic life' (Kondratieff 1935), and it is through this German-English article that Kondratieff's work became known in the Western world.

'The long waves in economic life' does not provide any theoretical explanation of the long cycle. In fact, Kondratieff ends it by stating: 'in the preceding sketch we had no intention of laying the foundations for an appropriate theory of long waves.' This lack of theoretical support was a source of vehement criticism. Nothing daunted, Kondratieff continued his work on the long wave. A new paper, read in 1926 before the Economic Institute in Moscow, made 'a first attempt to give a tentative explanation of the long cycles', but failed to satisfy his critics. In 1928 Kondratieff re-stated his theory in a paper, which was translated into German (Kondratieff 1928), and which proved to be his last. Soon after publication, Kondratieff was removed from his position as head of the Conjuncture Institute. A few months later, the official Soviet Russian Encyclopedia referred to his long wave theory in a single sentence: 'This theory is wrong and reactionary.' In the Autumn of 1930, Kondratieff was arrested as the alleged head of an illegal 'Working Peasants Party' (TKP), and deported to Siberia without trial.

Most of what we know of Kondratieff's life and career as an economist comes from one source, George Garvy (1943). Garvy, himself was a native of Russia, was able to read Kondratieff's Russian articles and the criticisms of Kondratieff's Soviet colleagues. Kondratieff's name, however, appears in quite a different source, namely, Solzhenitsyn's Gulag Archipelago, in which the author discusses the trial of 200,000 'members' of the Working Peasants Party, which was to have taken place in 1931 but which was called off by Stalin. Only some of the big fish, including Kondratieff, were hauled in. Solzhenitsyn does not mention deportation, but states that Kondratieff was sentenced to solitary confinement, became mentally ill and died. When, we do not know.

It is debatable whether there is a relationship between the harsh criticism of Kondratieff's long wave theory and his arrest for alleged counter-revolutionary activities. According to Solzhenitsyn, Kondratieff was merely an 'agricultural economist', and no reference is made to the long wave. Yet it is clear that the violent criticisms were at least partly due to the prediction implied by his theory. The downswing of the long wave which, according to Kondratieff, had started around 1914-20, would eventually be followed by a new upswing, implying that the final disintegration of the capitalist system for which the Soviet leaders were waiting, would not occur. Kondratieff's views therefore ran counter to the official Marxist view. Indeed, one line of attack used by his opponents was to reject his theory because a similar reasoning had been used by 'bourgeois' economists. This is somewhat ironic when it is realized that the long wave theory has Marxist roots, not only because such authors as Parvus, Van Gelderen and De Wolff were all Marxists, but because the inspiration for their long waves came from Marx's own business cycle. The cyclic nature of the dynamic capitalist economy, blown up in the long wave theory to a movement of some 50 years' length, thus conflicts with the Marxist expectation of total disintegration of the capitalist system.

This dilemma is very apparent in the writings of a modern Marxist long-wave author, Ernest Mandel (1980). Mandel is convinced of the existence of a long wave, but in his analysis each interruption of the secular decline in the rate of profit, i.e. each upturn of the long wave, is explained with the aid of exogenous factors. Only in this way can Marxist theory, in which the tendency of the average rate of profit to decline plays a central role, be reconciled with the long wave.

A true Marxist can never explain the long wave with the aid of purely endogenous mechanisms. This is where Kondratieff erred: his analysis clearly implied that a new upswing, caused by the dynamics of the capitalist system, was inevitable.

Kondratieff based his long wave theory first and foremost on the observation of 19th century price series (including interest rates and wages). In addition, he used a few value series (foreign trade, bank deposits) plus a number of (fairly short) volume series, the latter being in the minority. The price series were essential. Without them no long wave theory could ever have been proposed, whether by Kondratieff, or by any other of the long wave pioneers who had to rely on 19th century data. In that respect, the work of all early long wave authors followed a set order:

(1)   a long wave pattern is observed in time series;
(2)   with respect to the second half of the 19th century, a relation is suspected between price movements and economic development at large;
(3)   on the basis of these findings the long wave is described as a phenomenon inherent in the capitalist mode of production; additional characteristics of upswing and downswing phases are laid down in the form of propositions;
(4)   attempts are made to explain the long wave as an endogenous cyclical process.

By 1926 Kondratieff had advanced to step three. Although it was difficult to demonstrate the presence of long waves in volume series with any great conviction (in some series no such waves were evident), he found that the historical material on the development of economic and social life provided sufficient confirmation of the long-wave hypothesis. This led him to formulate the following empirical characteristics.

1. During the rise of the long waves, years of prosperity are more numerous, whereas during the downswing years of depression predominate.
2. During the downswing, agriculture usually suffers an especially pronounced and long depression.
3. During the downswing, many important inventions in the techniques of production and communication are made; however, these are usually applied on a large scale only at the beginning of the next long upswing.
4. At the beginning of a long upswing, gold production usually increases, and the world market is enlarged by the assimilation of new countries, especially the former colonies.
5. It is during the period of the rise of the long wave that the most disastrous and extensive wars and revolutions mostly occur (Kondratieff 1935: 111).

Each of these propositions played an important role in later long-wave literature, but some of them have now been pushed into the background. The winning of gold is no longer a factor in the present world economy. The postwar upswing phase has been completed without wars acting as outlets in the expansion of economic forces. For the present situation, the third of Kondratieff's characteristics is of major importance. Kondratieff did not consider technological change as a datum, but rather as an endogenous economic process: 'Changes in the technique of production presume (1) that the relevant scientific-technical discoveries and inventions have been made, and (2) that it is *economically possible* to use them' (Ibidem: 112). While post-World War II macroeconomics literature shows technological development almost exclusively as an exogenous factor, Kondratieff demonstrated as long ago as 1926 why technological change is endogenous, and why the distinction between invention and innovation is of such importance. 'Scientific-technical inventions in themselves, however, are insufficient to bring about a real change in the technique of production. They can remain ineffective so long as economic conditions favourable to their application are absent' (Ibidem: 112). When we observe today how policy makers repeatedly emphasize the importance of innovation and industrial renewal, but also that many of them do not realize that innovations can only flourish under appropriate economic conditions, then this may be seen as evidence of Kondratieff's sharp insights.

It is sad that Kondratieff, in his later long wave theory, made so little use of his view of the role of technological innovation. The theory which he had to construct in order to satisfy his Soviet critics rested on another mechanism: fluctuations in so-called basic capital goods. 'The material basis of the long cycles is the wear and tear, the replacement and the increase of the fund of basic capital goods, the production of which requires tremendous investment and is a long process.' Basic capital goods included 'big plants, important railways, canals, large land improvement projects, etc.... As a matter of fact, the training of skilled labour belongs in this category' (Garvy 1943: 208).

Kondratieff's explanation of the long wave resembles that of De Wolff. The length of the long wave is linked to durability, production period and investment amount of the particular type of capital good. But why are these capital goods built in clusters, rather than continuously? To answer this question, Kondratieff borrowed from Von Tugan Baranowsky's (1901: 239) theory of free loanable funds. At the beginning of an expansion phase a large supply of loanable capital is available at low interest rates. In addition, the propensity to save will be high and the price level low. As investment in basic capital goods increases, available funds will become gradually depleted and interest rates will go up, causing the investment flow to dwindle. A downturn will follow: prices and interest rates start to fall, the overall level of economic activity will slow down. During the downswing phase the propensity to save will again increase, especially of those whose real income rises due to the sinking price level. The growing supply of savings, low interest rates, and falling prices, will eventually create the conditions for a new upswing phase.

While stressing the cyclical character of the long wave throughout his writings, in his last paper Kondratieff nevertheless admitted that a downswing was not necessarily followed by a new upswing: 'Freilich trägt dieser Anstieg keine absolute Notwendigkeit in sich' (Kondratieff 1928: 38). The 'organic change' of the economic system could deform the dynamic character of the economy. Kondratieff was thus not absolutely sure about the lower turning point, and was not alone in that respect: the explanation of this lower turning point has been a defect of many later long wave theories. And quite apart from the theoretical aspects of long-wave model building: can anyone who lives in the middle of a long wave depression, really feel confident that the economy will pull itself up again?

In falling back on monetary over-investment theory to explain the cyclical nature of long waves, Kondratieff served his own cause very poorly. The irony of it all is that the ingredients needed for an endogenous long wave theory were all at hand. He recognized the importance of technological innovation and had a keen insight into the timing of major innovations with respect to long wave upswing and downswing; he also knew that long wave expansions correspond with increased production of basic capital goods. Yet he failed to link the two: he failed to see that innovations create new industrial sectors and that these require their own infrastructure. Instead, he borrowed from Marx the notion of echo-replacement cycles, used the free loanable funds theory, magnified both to long wave proportions, and came up with an artificial construct that convinced no-one. As a result, even a mild commentator such as Garvy had to conclude: 'Thus Kondratieff's entire theoretical construction emerges, after consideration, as extremely unrealistic' (Garvy 1943: 219).

Ultimately, therefore, the overall judgement of Kondratieff's work is a negative one. His statistical endeavours have been criticized, his theory rejected, while the policy implications of his work eventually ruined his career. What remained is rather meagre: until the 1970s to most economists the Kondratieff cycle was no more than a price cycle without any theoretical explanation.

A BRIEF SURVEY OF PREWAR LITERATURE

By 1935, when Kondratieff's first major article appeared in English, considerable literature already existed on the long wave. This is hardly surprising: was not the Great Depression the clearest possible confirmation of the existence of a long wave?

In this book we shall deal only very briefly with this prewar literature, and shall place our greatest emphasis on modern, post-1973, theories. Only Schumpeter's work, which still forms the foundation of many modern studies, will be discussed in Chapter VI. To some extent, Clark's work, written during the war, may be seen as a bridge between old and new. His perception of 'capital hungry' and 'capital sated' periods produced remarkably accurate forecasts for the postwar years (see Chapter VII *infra*). Other authors provide many arguments that bear on today's problems but very often focus on factors that are no longer considered essential.

If we were to classify the different explanations of the long wave, most prewar contributions could be listed under one of the following categories:

(a)   those stressing *monetary* factors;
(b)   those stressing *wars* as a causal factor;
(c)   those which see the upswing phase as caused by bunches of *innovations*;
(d)   those which explain long waves as accelerations and retardations in the growth of *fixed capital*;
(e)   those which look at long waves as *reinvestment* cycles; and
(f)   those which stress disequilibria on markets of *foodstuffs and raw materials*.

A set of explanatory factors can frequently be attributed either an exogenous or an endogenous character. Those authors who stress the exogenous nature of explanatory variables come up with historical descriptions of individual upswing and downswing movements. What one author considers an exogenous and therefore unexplained phenomenon, however, is seen by another as endogenous, and differences of opinion frequently centre on this point. Monetary theories see changes in the money supply as the cause of accelerations and retardations in real magnitudes. On the one hand, these can be caused by events which are strictly exogenous, e.g. gold discoveries; on the other hand, they may result from endogenous control of money supply as a tool of monetary policy. In the application of monetary policy, inappropriate reactions might well lead the economy into a depression.

It is quite understandable that the exogenous-monetary explanation formerly had many supporters (Table 4.1). The gold discoveries in Australia and California coincided with the beginning of the long upswing of 1850-73; those in South Africa and Alaska with the expansionary movement which started around 1895. In addition, the exogenous-monetary theory can restrict itself in the first instance to an explanation of price movements.

As the importance of the gold supply lessened, advocates of monetary theories switched their attention to the role of monetary policy in creating long waves. The Great Depression of the 1930s has been explained in terms of a strong contraction of the money supply during a prolonged period (Cleveland & Brittain 1975; Friedman & Schwartz 1963).

The role which has been attributed to war in the explanation of long waves, is twofold. On the one hand, wars are seen as the cause of Kondratieffs (Von Ciriacy-Wantrup 1936). In this line of thought, wars give rise to economic expansion as a result of increased government expenditure, the opening-up of new markets, and innovations inspired by military activities. Similarly, the end of a war is followed by a long depression. Readjustment to a peace economy ushers in a period of chronic difficulty. The exogenous war theory could thus be the explanation of long fluctuations in economic activity. On the other hand, wars can be seen as the culmination of the upswing phase of the long wave, i.e. an endogenous phenomenon, a notion which is held by various authors (Table 4.1). Home markets, becoming saturated during the upswing phase, create economic and political tensions which unload in war activity.

Assessment of the role of wars is hampered considerably by the different ways in which they have affected countries on either side of the Atlantic. In the 20th century, the United States has participated in four wars that were waged elsewhere and which led to boom periods in the United States economy. After World War I, a strong pent-up demand was expressed in the United States for commodities that had not been readily available during the war. In Europe, however, those countries which had suffered from war activities faced difficulty in getting back on track. In Europe the upswing phase ended with World War I, while in the United States it was prolonged by the same war. World War II, on the other hand, clearly does not fit the theory.

In conclusion, we should comment briefly on Sirol's (1942) explanation of the long wave as being due to supply rigidities in agricultural production. During the upswing phase, demand for agricultural products will exceed supply, but adjustments in productive capacity will occur only with long lags. Supply increases will tend to overshoot demand, causing a fall in prices and a long-wave downswing. Capital adjustments during the downswing phase will again be lagged. It is thus the specific nature of agricultural production which, in Sirol's view, determines the long wave. Just as a cobweb cycle is caused by short-term supply rigidities, so a long cycle is caused by long-term supply rigidities.

Table 4.1 *A survey of the prewar long-wave literature*

Key variable	Authors
money supply/gold supply	Kitchin (1930) Woytinksi-Lorenz (1931) Cassel (1932) Simiand (1932) Dupriez (1935) Warren & Pearson (1935)
wars	Wagemann (1931) Hansen (1932) Von Ciriacy-Wantrup (1936) Bernstein (1940)
innovations/new industries	Van Gelderen (1913) Lescure (1933) Schumpeter (1939)
basic capital/reinvestment	Kondratieff (1926) (1928) De Wolff (1929) Clark (1944)
foodstuffs & raw materials	Sirol (1942)

Sirol's agricultural hypothesis is also dated. The role of agriculture in postwar industrial societies is far too restricted for slowness of supply responses in this sector to be the cause of a long wave in overall economic activity. If the agricultural sector is extended to a whole primary sector, however, including (other) raw materials and energy sources, our assessment of Sirol's theory may need to be changed. As we shall see in the next chapter, Rostow has made this primary sector, and its price formation in relation to the industrial sector, the central element of a very modern long-wave theory.

Finally, readers may find an extensive treatment of prewar long-wave theories in Imbert (1959; very detailed, but available only in French) and Broersma (1978; but only in Dutch).

APPENDIX C

Kondratieff's writings

(1)   The world economy and its conditions during and after the war (1922), 242ff. Published only in Russian. Contains a first sketch of the long wave theory, together with a tentative dating of the cycles.

(2)   'Some controversial questions concerning the world economy and the crisis', Sotsialiticheskoe Khoziaistvo (1923), No. 4-5, 50-87. This paper, again published only in Russian, is a lengthy reply to the criticism met by his first paper, and contains several of the principal ideas developed in later publications.

(3)   'On the notion of economic statics, dynamics and fluctuations', Sotsialisti- cheskoe Khoziaistvo (1924), No. 2, 349-82. This article deals with the place of the study of cyclical processes in economics. Part of this study has been published in English, as

(3a) 'The static and the dynamic view of economics', Quarterly Journal of Economics, 39 (1925), 575-83.

(4)   The major economic cycles, Voprosy Conjunktury, 1 (1925), 28-79. In this paper the main results of Kondratieff's statistical investigations with respect to the long wave are reported. The German version of this paper made Kondratieff's work known outside the Soviet Union:

(4a) 'Die langen Wellen der Konjunktur', Archiv für Sozialwissenschaft und Sozialpolitik, 56 (1926), 573-609. An abridged version of this was later translated into English:

(4b) 'The long waves in economic life', Review of Economic Statistics, 17 (1935), 105-15.

(5)   'The problems of forecasting', Voprosy Conjunktury, 2 (1926), 1-42. An abridged version of this paper appeared in German, as:

(5a) 'Das Problem der Prognose, in Sonderheit der sozialwirtschaftlichen', Annalen der Betriebswirtschaft, 1 (1927), 41-64 and 221-52.

(6)   'Major economic cycles' (1928; together with D.I. Oparin). This is the pub- lished version of a paper read in February 1926 before the Economic Insti- tute in Moscow, and includes 'a first attempt to give a tentative explana- tion of the long cycles'.

(7)   'On the dynamics of industrial and agricultural prices', Voprosy Con- junktury, 4 (1928), 5-85. This paper re-states the theory proposed in (5). Also, long waves in prices of industrial and agricultural prices are seen in relation to long waves in overall economic activity. An abridged German translation (by A. von Schelting) appeared as:

(7a) 'Die Preisdynamik der industriellen und landwirtschaftlichen Waren (Zum Problem der relativen Dynamik und Konjunktur)', *Archiv für Sozialwissenschaft und Sozialpolitik*, 60 (1928), 1-85.

NOTES

1. Parvus (1901: 27) quotes from an article that he wrote for the *Sächsische Arbeiterzeitung* in the spring of 1896 in which he foresaw that the then ongoing recovery would be the beginning of a new long expansion phase: 'the economic depression has ended – a new Sturm- und Drang period of capitalist industry begins. This should not be interpreted to mean that from now on no setbacks will be encountered and only prosperity will rule. We are dealing here with the pace of development which always follows the law of capitalist waves.'
2. In a later pamphlet, Parvus (1908) again brought up the issue of the long waves, but without adding any new ideas. The central feature to him seems to have been the expansion of world markets, which implied that the socialist movement could no longer deal with capitalism on a national scale. See also his biographers, Scharlau & Zeman (1964).
3. See Kondratieff's note on the research activities of the Conjuncture Institute in the *Quarterly Journal of Economics*, 39 (1925), 320-24.

V

THE KONDRATIEFF AS A PRICE CYCLE

FLUCTUATIONS IN PRICES

Is there a long wave in economic activity or only a long wave in prices? In the previous chapter we have seen that most theorizing on the existence of a long cyclical type of fluctuation in aggregate economic activity originated in the observation of long-run fluctuations in price levels of industrializing countries after the Industrial Revolution. Figure 5.1 shows these fluctuations for the United States, England and France, as compiled by Kondratieff in his famous 1926 article. We see a rising price level from about 1790 onwards, reaching a peak around 1815. Then there is a downward trend from 1815 until 1849, followed by a moderate rise until 1873 (American price history differed during the Civil War). Then follows a steady decline to a trough in 1896. From then until 1913 the price level moves up again, with sharp increases after the outbreak of World War I.

Figure 5.1 has the appearance of a long wave only for those who look for it, i.e. those who have sufficient additional knowledge and time-series available to make them suspect the existence of a long wave. The unconditioned observer might well summarize the 19th century movement of commodity prices as one which exhibited a downward trend from the end of the Napoleonic Wars until the end of the century, with only a temporary interruption during the 1850s and 1860s. And who knows what prices would have done if World War I had not driven them up?

Visual inspection is only one way by which to analyse economic time-series. A look at the data themselves will yield additional insight. For that reason, the data as they appeared in Kondratieff's 1926 article are given in Table 5.1. In order to eliminate the 7-11 years business cycle, Kondratieff took nine-year moving averages from the original indices; the turning points, however, were derived from the unsmoothed data.[1]

Notes to this chapter may be found on p. 92.

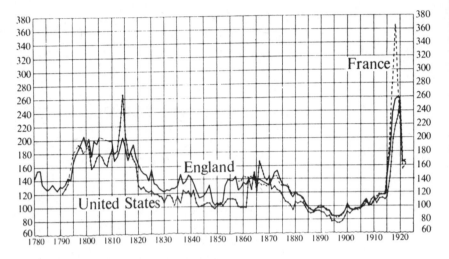

Source: Kondratieff (1935: 106; English translation of Kondratieff 1926).

Figure 5.1. *Kondratieff's index numbers of commodity prices (1901-10=100)*

* The *French* data are taken from the *Annuaire Statistique* [Statistique Générale de la France], 1922, p. 341; the index number has been recalculated on a gold basis through use of dollar-franc exchange rates.
For *England*, there is for 1782-1865 the index of Jevons; for 1779-1850, a new index number, computed by Silberling and published in the *Review of Economic Statistics*, V (1923); for the period after 1846, we have Sauerbeck's index, which at present is carried on by the *Statist*. Since Silberling's index is based upon more complete data of the prices of individual commodities than that of Jevons, we have used the former for the period 1780-1846. From 1846 on we use Sauerbeck's index number. Both indices have been tied together on the basis of their relation during 1846-50, for which period they are both available; after this procedure, we have shifted the series to a new base, 1901-10. For the period 1801-20 and since 1914, in which periods England was on a paper standard, the index numbers have been recalculated on a gold basis.
For the *United States*, we use the following series, which have been tied together: for 1791-1801, H V Roelse (*Quarterly Publications of the American Statistical Association*, December, 1917); 1801-25 A H Hansen (*ibid*, December, 1915); 1825-39, C H Juergens (*ibid*, June, 1911); 1840-90, Falkner (Report from the Committee on Finance of the United States Senate on *Wholesale Prices, Wages, and Transportation*, 52d Congress, 2d session, Report No 1394, Part 1 [Washington: Government Printing Office, March 3, 1893]); since 1890, the BLS index. All index numbers are on the base 1901-10. For the Greenback period (1862-78), they have been recalculated on a gold basis. All data [except Silberling's index] are taken from the *Annuaire Statistique*, 1922 [which utilizes the sources above cited].

Table 5.1 *Kondratieff's index numbers of commodity prices (1901-10=100)*

Year	England	France	USA	Year	England	France	USA
1780	142	–	–	1832	124	–	117
1781	154	–	–	1833	127	–	114
1782	155	–	–	1834	127	–	103
1783	135	–	–	1835	131	–	116
1784	130	–	–	1836	147	–	106
1785	126	–	–	1837	134	–	124
1786	129	–	–	1838	137	–	120
1787	134	–	–	1839	146	–	123
1788	129	–	–	1840	142	–	115
1789	125	–	–	1841	135	–	124
1790	131	–	–	1842	124	–	106
1791	130	–	121	1843	113	–	100
1792	134	–	128	1844	114	–	101
1793	143	–	136	1845	116	–	102
1794	141	–	–	1846	122	–	105
1795	166	–	179	1847	130	–	105
1796	179	–	–	1848	107	–	100
1797	185	–	193	1849	101	–	97
1798	196	–	190	1850	105	–	101
1799	205	–	181	1851	102	–	105
1800	191	–	–	1852	107	–	101
1801	202	–	192	1853	130	–	107
1802	176	–	158	1854	139	–	111
1803	199	–	162	1855	138	–	111
1804	195	–	174	1856	138	–	111
1805	204	–	179	1857	143	–	110
1806	–	–	175	1858	124	137	100
1807	–	–	165	1859	128	137	99
1808	–	–	162	1860	135	144	99
1809	199	–	174	1861	132	142	99
1810	199	–	186	1862	138	142	140
1811	169	–	180	1863	141	143	125
1812	175	–	183	1864	143	141	149
1813	187	–	214	1865	138	132	122
1814	203	–	265	1866	139	134	166
1815	190	–	208	1867	137	131	156
1816	170	–	178	1868	135	132	141
1817	184	–	180	1869	134	130	138
1818	191	–	172	1870	131	133	143
1819	175	–	164	1871	137	138	125
1820	163	–	132	1872	149	144	129
1821	154	–	127	1873	152	144	124
1822	150	–	130	1874	139	132	122
1823	148	–	124	1875	131	129	115
1824	139	–	122	1876	130	130	107
1825	155	–	124	1877	128	131	106
1826	135	–	119	1878	119	120	102
1827	133	–	119	1879	113	117	95
1828	127	–	116	1880	120	120	106
1829	124	–	116	1881	116	117	104
1830	122	–	107	1882	115	114	106
1831	125	–	117	1883	112	110	105

Year	England	France	USA	Year	England	France	USA
1884	104	101	98	1904	96	94	96
1885	98	99	92	1905	98	98	96
1886	94	95	90	1906	105	104	100
1887	93	92	91	1907	109	109	105
1888	96	96	93	1908	100	101	101
1889	98	100	93	1909	101	101	109
1890	98	100	91	1910	107	108	113
1891	98	98	90	1911	109	113	104
1892	93	95	84	1912	116	118	111
1893	93	94	86	1913	116	116	112
1894	86	87	77	1914	116	118	110
1895	85	85	78	1915	144	149	113
1896	83	82	75	1916	182	192	142
1897	85	83	75	1917	234	273	198
1898	87	86	78	1918	256	364	217
1899	93	93	84	1919	259	288	231
1900	102	99	91	1920	258	214	253
1901	96	95	89	1921	167	154	165
1902	94	94	94	1922	163	161	167
1903	94	96	96				

Source: Kondratieff (1926: 600-1; data source as in Figure 5.1).

	England	France	United States
trough	1789		
peak	1814		1814
trough	1849		1849
peak	1873	1873	1866
trough	1896	1896	1896
peak	1920	1920	1920

If we now apply nine-year moving averages centered on Kondratieff's turning points, the following average annual percentage price changes emerge. These may be seen as approximations of the degree of price fluctuations from long-wave trough to peak, and vice versa:

	England	France	United States
1789-1814	+ 1.4 %		
1814-1849	- 1.4 %		- 1.8 %
1849-1873	+ 0.8 %		+ 1.9 % (1849-1866)
1873-1896	- 1.8 %	- 1.8 %	- 1.9 % (1866-1896)
1896-1918	+ 3.7 %	+ 4.0 %	+ 3.6 %

These figures show that the price increases of the 1849-73 upturn in England were indeed modest, if compared with those of 1789-1814 and 1896-1918. The combined effect of two periods of falling prices (1814-49 and 1873-96) with one of moderately rising prices in between was a price level in 1896 which was less than half that of 1814, and less than 70 per cent of that of 1789. Even at the outbreak of World War I, prices in England were still clearly below the 1789 level. In summary, the 19th century was a century of falling prices. Even when periods of prolonged price increases did occur, the speed of these increases nowhere approximated those to which we have grown accustomed in the present century.

The French and U.S. patterns do not differ significantly from that of England. Only the Civil War caused the U.S. price rise in the 1860s to be more pronounced than elsewhere, which brings us to an important cause of price fluctuations: war. The American Civil War was not alone in causing prices to rise and to fall again after war activity had ended. The same applies, with significantly larger fluctuations, to the Napoleonic War and World War I. Or, if we go beyond the limits of Kondratieff's graph, for wars before the Industrial Revolution and after 1920. This is beautifully illustrated by Figure 5.2, a record of three centuries of inflation and deflation in Britain, drawn up by *The Economist* in 1978.

Wars cause prices to rise sharply because of inflationary policies, or because of actual shortages, due to blockades, etc. Once war activity ceases, prices often move back to their prewar levels, albeit sometimes with a considerable lag. Only the post-1945 years form an exception to that pattern.

Does not the occurrence of wars make the appearance of long waves largely illusory, as Dauten & Valentine (1978: 287) maintain? If the Napoleonic Wars were responsible for most of the price increases between 1789 and 1814, if the Crimean War lifted prices in the 1850s, and if World War I more than doubled prices between 1913 and 1920, what remains of the long wave? We shall never know with any degree of certainty, of course, what the price curve in a war-free world might have been, but it does seem certain that price peaks would have been much less pronounced. Nevertheless, fluctuations have not all been caused by war. The fall in prices between 1873 and 1896 was not war-related, neither can the gradual rise of the price level from 1896 to 1913 be attributed to war activity, and it was the 1873-1913 period which gave rise to much of the early work on long waves.

Other causes of price fluctuations must therefore be sought. Kondratieff was never very specific about possible causes, merely arguing that 'the long waves in prices are an integral part of the general long-term fluctuations in the dynamics of the economy' (Kondratieff 1935: 35). He insisted that he had proven this by finding fluctuations of similar duration not only in prices, but also in wages, interest rates, foreign trade, bank deposits, and a number of physical production series. Variations in gold production were emphatically excluded by Kondratieff as a cause of price fluctuations (although he admitted that gold production could have some influence on the price level).

Kondratieff wanted to show a relation between fluctuations in the price level and fluctuations in aggregate economic activity, the outcome of his analysis being that both prices and volumes showed a synchronous movement, *going up*

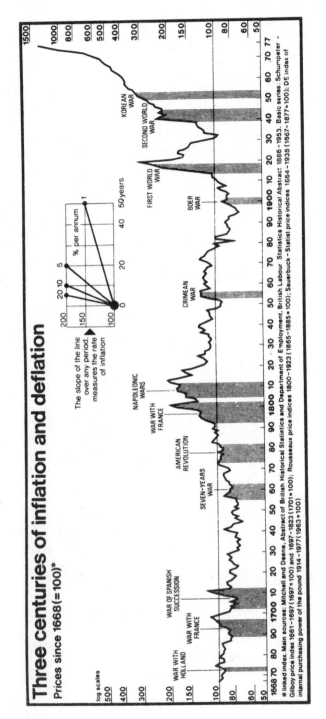

Source: *The Economist* (June 1978)

Figure 5.2. *British prices, 1668-1977.*

and down together. This led him to the long-wave chronology shown in Table 5.2.

Table 5.2. *The dating of the long wave according to Kondratieff*

	1st long wave	2nd long wave	3rd long wave
uspwing	around 1790-1810/17	1844/51-1870/75	1890/96-1914/20
downswing	1810/17-1844/51	1870/75-1890/96	1914/20-

Source: Kondratieff (1926: 590).

His dating of long-wave turning points allows for a margin of error — he considered it impossible precisely to establish troughs and peaks — but in essence his turning points correspond with those of the commodity price series given earlier.

It has often been said that Kondratieff would have encountered serious dating problems had he seen price developments since the 1930s. After reaching a trough in 1932/33, world commodity prices have risen almost without interruption: while the world was still in depression, as after 1933; when the world enjoyed prosperity and rapid growth, as between 1948 and 1973; but also after it had entered a new period of depression, as after 1973. The relation between changes in the price level and changes in production volume has been broken in the 20th century, perhaps because price changes are now the result of conditions that were not operative in the 130 years covered by Kondratieff. Even for the 19th century, however, the synchronous movement of prices and volumes cannot be established as firmly as was suggested by Kondratieff.

Commodity prices can fluctuate for a number of reasons. Firstly, shifts in the demand and supply curves will change (equilibrium) prices and quantities. Simultaneous increases in price and quantity will occur if the demand curve shifts to the right; simultaneous decreases if it shifts to the left. A long wave expansion in aggregate demand could thus result in rising prices and quantities, at least if the aggregate supply curve, affected by productivity changes among other things, does not shift far enough to the right to offset the price increase. If a long-wave downswing is interpreted as a slowdown of growth as historically has been the case, rather than as a prolonged absolute decline of output, then a gradually rightward-shifting demand curve combined with a strongly rightward-shifting supply curve could result in falling prices and small increases in production volume.

A second reason why commodity prices may fluctuate lies in changes in the money supply. When paper currency is convertible into gold, the supply of gold becomes a determinant of the price level. Thus, it has been argued that price rises from 1849 to 1873 should be linked to the gold discoveries in Australia and California; and that the long hausse which started in 1896 was related to the discoveries in South Africa and Alaska. But money is also created by banks and governments. If, for instance, governments finance (part of) their deficits through money creation, prices may rise as a result.

A third reason for price fluctuations stems from the behaviour of money incomes vis-à-vis productivity. If money wages rise faster than productivity, e.g. due to the presence of strong labour unions, this will create an upward pressure on prices. If, on the other hand, money wages are stabilized while productivity growth is positive, falling prices may result. A fourth reason for changes in the level of commodity prices may be the cost-of-living clauses included in wage contracts. Theoretically, such clauses may cause prices to rise and to fall. In a period of falling commodity prices, the price index and therefore money wages could also fall. But if prices have started to rise for whatever reason, cost-of-living clauses could cause that rise to become never ending. A fifth reason, which changes prices only in the upward direction, is the price-setting behaviour of oligopolistic industries. If a ratchet effect operates, commodity prices will rise if input prices go up or if demand increases, but input prices will decrease and slackening demand will not be translated into lower commodity prices.

Considering the variety of these reasons, and the fact that their importance as determinants of commodity prices has changed over time, one should be very critical of any attempt to date long waves solely on the basis of absolute rises and falls of aggregate price levels. That is, if the long wave is seen as an economic cycle, i.e. as an endogenous fluctuation in output growth, in the same way that the Kitchin, Juglar and Kuznets cycles are seen as economic cycles. Even if one is willing to interpret the long wave primarily as a price cycle, however, it is necessary to delve below the surface of the aggregate commodity price level and to separate the various influences that historically have affected prices.

Early 20th century long-wave authors emphasized the role of changes in the demand and supply of commodities and in the money supply. From our point of view, this seems to have been quite reasonable. As for the third reason – money income changes not being in line with productivity changes – Lewis (1980) has shown that, from the 1850s onwards, the pattern has been for money wages to rise whenever unemployment diminished, and to remain more or less constant when unemployment increased. This pattern held for the United Kingdom, France and Germany, but not for the USA. During the long-wave downswing this meant that productivity rose faster than money wages, thus exerting a deflationary influence; during the ensuing upswing, from 1899 onwards, money wages outgrew productivity, thus exerting an inflationary influence. In the second half of the 19th century, therefore, money wages behaved in such a way as to reinforce inflationary tendencies during a long-wave upswing, and deflationary tendencies during a long-wave downswing. In the middle of the 1930s, however, this pattern changed in such a way that wage costs went up despite depression.

Cost-of-living clauses are recent phenomena. Lewis (1980), in comparing two periods of rising prices, 1899-1913 and 1950-79, which did not have a major war for their background, argues that the tying of wages to the cost of living is a dominating element in the present inflationary period, and one which was nonexistent during 1899-1913. Since 1973, wages have continued to rise, mainly because of the linkage with the cost of living, despite an economic slowdown that is comparable to, if not worse than, Kondratieff's 2nd and 3rd long-wave downturns.

Inflationary pressure arising from the price-setting behaviour of concentrated industries, is another factor that is relevant only to the 20th century. We shall not discuss the issue of whether commodity prices in concentrated industries can actually be shown to be downwardly rigid; the point is that for most of the 19th century, production was not sufficiently concentrated (at the turn of the century agricultural output still accounted for almost 60 per cent of total world production) to allow concentration to have a significant influence on the price level.

This leaves us with the first two factors: demand and supply, and the money stock. The expansion of economic activity during Kondratieff's long-wave upswings has been associated with the application of important discoveries and inventions, giving rise to the establishment of new industrial sectors – cotton textiles and pig iron during the first long wave, railroads during the second, anorganic chemicals, electricity and motor vehicles during the third. The reasoning, then, is that increased demand for industrial products and the impact of this demand on input factors, including raw materials, would have caused commodity prices to go up. In the later life-cycle stages of these products the combined effect of slackening demand and cost-reducing innovations on the input side, should cause prices to fall. In this interpretation a separate influence may come from the supply side. During expansion the productive capacity of input factors (raw materials, capital goods) may fall short. As new capacity is added with a lag, an abundance of supply could result at the same time that the growth of final demand is slowing down, and thus reinforce the deflationary tendency.

This all sounds plausible. Unfortunately, however, it does not fit very well with the actual record of the 19th century. To start with, industrial production in Britain did not slow down after 1815. The two leading sectors, cotton textiles and pig iron, continued to lead until the 1860s. In fact, British industrial production grew faster after 1815, despite the falling price level. Secondly, the big railway boom in Britain came before the 1850s, i.e. during the 1st Kondratieff downswing. Railroads continued to be a leading sector until the 1870s, but again, their main expansion came at a time when prices were falling. In other words, the strengths of the three leading sectors in industrial history, the first in the country to industrialize, stretched-out over what is said to be the first long-wave downturn. Not until after 1873 did a slowdown of growth occur together with a fall of the price level. After 1896, too, growth rates and prices moved together.

It would seem, then, that the early long-wave theories were patterned on the experience of the second half of the 19th century and of the years 1900-14, with little regard for the pre-1850 record. Only during the 60-odd years between 1850 and 1913 did output and prices move together.

The interplay of price movements and changes in demand and supply during the last two hundred years may be explained in yet another way, as has been done by Rostow, the only modern long-wave theorist to interpret the long wave as a price cycle. Rostow has not examined just one price level, but has made the crucial distinction between industrial prices and those of basic commodities (foodstuffs and raw materials), enabling a much better explanation of long price cycles. The outcome of his analysis, however, is a theory of Kondratieff-type fluctuations in prices, not one of long waves in production growth.

What about the role of the money supply? Rostow (1980, Chapter 5) has investigated in great detail the relation between money and prices in the pre-1914 world. He has analyzed the role of the monetary system, at both the national and the international levels, and also the impact on the world economy of the gold discoveries in California and Australia around 1850, and those in South Africa and other places around 1890. His main conclusions are summarized as follows:

(1)   The analysis of national monetary systems and the workings of the international system conducted over short periods of time reveal, as a matter of fact rather than hypothesis, their considerable flexibility, and justify the broad judgement that non-monetary factors were paramount in determining price movements.

(2)   Increased gold mining was, indeed, an inherently inflationary activity in the world economy during the phases during which it occurred; but a useful explanation of its impact on prices must be couched in real rather than merely monetary terms (Ibidem: 220).

Monetary policy, to the extent that it existed in the 19th century, was essentially passive and responsive to changes in the real sphere. The gold discoveries certainly added to inflation but, considering other changes that took place in the 1850s and 1890s, did not cause all the price increases that actually occurred.

The outcome of the foregoing discussion is mainly negative. Several factors are at work in determining the price level. Wars undoubtedly have been a major factor; gold discoveries have played a role, although apparently a minor one. Fluctuations in economic expansion are likely to have affected prices, but the match between changes in prices and changes in output growth is far from perfect. In the course of the 20th century, institutional and market changes have further weakened this relationship between output growth and prices. All this makes the notion of a Kondratieff price cycle rather unlikely. Yet, as part of the long-wave renaissance, such a cycle has recently been proposed. It is to that model of the Kondratieff cycle that we now turn our attention.

ROSTOW'S MODEL OF THE KONDRATIEFF CYCLE

'For four decades, W.W. Rostow has argued that trend periods, or Kondratieff cycles, as he has interpreted them, were caused primarily by periodic under-shooting and overshooting of the dynamic optimum levels of capacity and output for food and raw materials in the world economy.' Thus begins Rostow's explanation of the Kondratieff price cycle (Rostow & Kennedy 1979; also Rostow 1980, Chapter 2). Optimum levels are 'those levels which would have been attained in a continuous dynamic equilibrium where capacity was smoothly adjusted to rates of increase in population and income, the income elasticity of demand, the rate and changing structure of industrial growth, and the pace and character of technological change' (Rostow & Kennedy 1979: 2).

Deviations of actual from optimum capacity are caused by three distinctive characteristics of major investments in foodstuffs and raw materials:

(1)   a recognition lag – the lag between the emergence of a profit possibility and the investment decisions designed to exploit it;

(2)   a gestation lag – the lag caused in part by large prior infrastructure outlays before production can begin;

(3)   an exploitation lag – the lag between the completion of the investment and its maximum efficient exploitation, often involving large domestic or international migration.

In agriculture and raw material production, these lags are longer than in manu-facturing. In the former, productive capacity increases discontinuously in large, discrete steps and these increases involve long time lags. Protracted upward shifts in the relative prices of basic commodities act as the catalyst which sets in motion the expansion of productive capacity. However, this expansion over-shoots the dynamic optimum level. The subsequent period of decline in relative prices of basic commodities leads to an investment decline. Demand for basic commodities continues to grow in response to population growth and the trend expansion of industry, and the neglect of investment ultimately causes a reversal of the relative price movements when surplus capacity has been worked off. A new round of expansion of produtive capacity follows.

This cyclical process, which can be traced back for almost two centuries, is reflected in the general price level as well as in patterns of investment. More precisely, it is reflected in the price ratio of basic commodities and industrial commodities. Growth models, in Rostow's view, must allow for the possibility of gross discontinuities in the expansion of capacity to produce basic commo-dities. They have to be two-sector models, focussing on industrial production and the production of basic commodities. In addition to capital and labour as factors of production, they must include 'land', i.e. natural resources, subject to diminishing returns unless new technologies or new resources are found. Devia-tions of actual from optimum sectoral capacity have to be reflected in relative

prices; the price ratio between basic commodities and industrial goods determines the direction of investment; investment in the basic commodity sector,
however, is subject to lumpiness and multiple lags.

Rostow's formal Kondratieff model contains 16 equations, which are presented below (Rostow 1980: 67-69).

Static Conditions

I. *Production Relations*

Define the following variables:

B = basic goods
I = industrial goods
X_B = gross output of B
X_I = gross output of I
Y_B = net output of B
Y_I = net output of I
L_B = labour devoted to production of B
L_I = labour devoted to production of I
K_B = capital devoted to production of B
K_I = capital devoted to production of I
N = land

The production functions are

$$X_B = f_B(e^{vt}L_B, K_B, N) \tag{1}$$

and

$$X_I = f_I(e^{vt}L_I, K_I) \tag{2}$$

The input-output relations are

$$Y_B = X_B - a_{BI}X_I, \tag{3}$$

where a_{BI} is a constant input-output parameter, and

$$Y_I = X_I. \tag{4}$$

There is thus no intermediate input of I goods into B goods production.

2. *Factor Availability*

$$N = \bar{N} \tag{5}$$
$$L_I + L_B = \bar{L} \tag{6}$$
$$K_I + K_B = \bar{K} \tag{7}$$

In the short run, all factors are fixed in supply.

3. *Income Formation and Disposal*

Define the following variables:

Y nominal GNP
w nominal wage
r nominal rental of capital
n nominal rental of resource areas
C_B consumption of B
C_I consumption of I
S savings (= investment, composed totally of I goods)
P_B price of B
P_I price of I.

The prices of output goods are competitively determined through the total cost relations:

$$P_B = g_B(e^{-vt}w, r, n),\qquad(8)$$

and

$$P_I = g_I(e^{-vt}w, r) + a_{BI}P_B\qquad(9)$$

(g_B and g_I are the unit cost functions associated with f_B and f_I);

$$Y = P_I Y_I + P_B Y_B = wL + rK + nN.\qquad(10)$$

Nominal GNP equals the value of net output, which in turn equals total factor payments:

$$P_I S = \sigma Y.\qquad(11)$$

Nominal saving is a constant fraction of nominal GNP:

$$C_B = C_B((I - \sigma)Y, P_B, P_I)\qquad(12)$$

and

$$C_I = C_I((I - \sigma)Y, P_B, P_I).\qquad(13)$$

C_B and C_I are demand functions derived from utility maximization; they satisfy $P_I C_I + P_B C_B = (I - \sigma)Y$.

Equations (1) – (13) determine all the variables in the static solution of the economy. Relative but not absolute prices are determined in this non-monetary model.

The dynamic behaviour of the economy depends on the time paths of availability of factor supplies, that is, the time paths of $\bar{L}$, $\bar{K}$, and $\bar{N}$. Assume

$$\bar{L}_t = e^{\lambda}\bar{L}_{t-1}\qquad(14)$$

i.e. labour grows exponentially at rate λ (the subscript t denotes time). In neo-classical simulations

$$\bar{K}_t = S + (I - \delta)\bar{K}_{t-1}.\qquad(15)$$

Here δ is the depreciation rate. This is the traditional capital-accumulation relation. In most simulations, however, certain social overhead investments are deducted from the available directly-productive capital stock; these only become productive, and are then added to the stock, after a certain gestation lag. In a balanced growth case, land availability would grow as follows:

$$\bar{N}_t = e^{\mu}\bar{N}_{t-1}. \tag{16}$$

In the basic simulations, land becomes available in discrete lumps, although averaged across the very long run it follows equation (16).

In order to generate simulations, parameter values have to be chosen. These values are:

$$\lambda = .01$$
$$\upsilon = .02$$
$$\mu = (\lambda + \upsilon) = .03$$
$$\sigma = .15$$
$$\delta = .10$$

The CES production functions have an elasticity of substitution of .25. Consumer-demand functions are derived from a CES utility function, here with an elasticity of substitution of .70. The distribution parameters are chosen in such a way that, in balanced growth, the share of B in consumption expenditure is .30, and the share of I is .70. (Similarly, distribution shares are determined for production factors under conditions of balanced growth.)

In Figure 5.3 the solid line (K) shows the growth of real GNP, over a 40-year time span, in Rostow's basic run. (All runs are done over a 40-year time-span.)

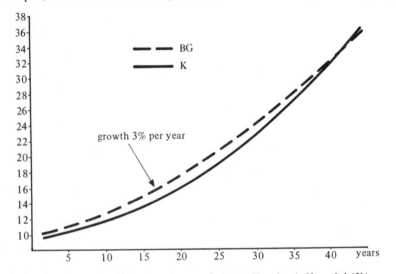

Figure 5.3. *Real GNP growth in Rostow's basic Kondratieff model (K), as compared with a balanced growth model (BG)*

This can be compared with the balanced-growth path (BG), which would follow if land were to become available at a constant growth rate μ (= 3% per annum). Growth rates of real GNP and land availability in the Kondratieff-model can be averaged per decade:

Years	GNP Growth per annum	N-factor Growth per annum
1-11	1.8%	0.0%
11-21	3.1%	2.8%
21-31	4.1%	5.6%
31-41	3.3%	3.7%

After a slow start during the Kondratieff upswing phase, due to the fixed availability of land (or resources in general), followed by slow growth in availability, GNP moves towards the balanced-growth path during the downswing phase, as more and more resources become available and are exploited. The fourth decade ends with a convergence of the balanced-growth and Kondratieff paths.

Scarcity of land and its subsequent abundance during the downswing phase are reflected in the price ratio of basic commodities and industrial goods (Figure 5.4). Since land/resources are used only in the production of basic commodities, the scarcity of this factor during the upswing phase drives up the BP/PI-ratio. A

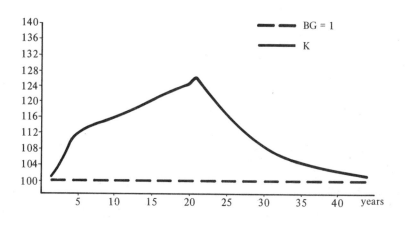

Figure 5.4. *The PB/PI-ratio in Rostow's basic Kondratieff model (K)*

peak is reached in year 21, after which the price ratio converges to its balanced-growth equilibrium level. This Kondratieff-model represents Rostow's basic model. The lumpiness with which additions to the factor land are introduced and the lags involved in this introduction, generates a cycle which, because of the way additional N-capacity is made available, lasts some forty years. Historically, other factors than rigidities in the supply of land have co-determined the shape of Kondratieff-cycles, and have been introduced by Rostow in a number of variants to the basic model. One variant, called the Schumpeter model, uses varying rates of technological progress as a way to capture fluctuations of innovations over time. Another, called the war model, assumes that 25 per cent of resource availability is destroyed at the beginning of the cycle. A third attempts to handle the stagflation phenomenon. Finally, a fourth variant introduces limits to growth by assuming a fixed amount of land.

The main variants, Schumpeter and War, produce a price cycle which in essence differs little from that of the basic run. War destruction results in a much higher and earlier price peak. In both the Schumpeter and War variants, as well as in the basic model, the GNP growth rate is highest during the downswing phase of the cycle. This is quite important: during the upswing phase of the price cycle, aggregate economic growth is lower than during the downswing phase. Rostow's Kondratieff theory thus yields a relation between price changes and output changes which is the opposite to what Kondratieff intended to show. In Rostow's simulations, output troughs occur around year 20, when the price ratio peaks; the uppermost deviation from the balanced growth path of output seems to be located near year 40, when the price ratio reaches its lowest point. Kondratieff used his empirical data to demonstrate that precisely the opposite occurred: prices and output would reach peak and bottom at about the same time.

At this point it is useful to introduce Rostow's own Kondratieff chronology. Rostow (1980) distinguishes the following cycles:

	Upswing	Downswing
1st Kondratieff	1790-1815	1815-1848
2nd Kondratieff	1848-1873	1873-1896
3rd Kondratieff	1896-1920	1920-1933
4th Kondratieff	1933-1951	1951-1972
5th Kondratieff	1972-	

Up to 1920 all his turning points are peaks and troughs in the general price level, and are essentially the same as those indicated by Kondratieff. It is interesting to see that 1933 is considered here by Rostow to have been the trough year marking the end of the Third Kondratieff cycle, whereas in his previous (1978) work he had seen 1920-36 as a trend period. Since 1933, protracted falls in the price level have not occurred. The last two turning points, 1951 and 1972, are therefore to be seen as benchmarks, signalling reversals in the price ratio of basic commodities and industrial goods: after 1951 the terms of trade reversed in favour of industrial goods, a process which ended with the price revolution of the early 1970s. If we accept Rostow's dating of the Kondratieff price cycle (which, up to 1920, is also Kondratieff's own cycle), what is the matching output growth record? Does it accord with Rostow's theory, or with Kondratieff's interpretation of the long wave?

For the 1st Kondratieff we have to rely on British data. Both per capita GNP data and industrial production estimates show higher growth rates for the 1815-48 downturn than for the 1790-1815 upturn. The per capita GNP growth rates are 1.6 (1815-48) and 0.6 (1790-1815) respectively; industrial production grew at 2.4 per cent from 1790 to 1815, to be followed by a 3.5 per cent rate between 1815 and 1848. There is little doubt about the nature of the ratio between agricultural and industrial prices in Britain during the 1st Kondratieff. That ratio reached a peak in 1812, and fell thereafter.[2] In terms of these two outcomes — aggregate growth and price changes — the 1st Kondratieff can thus be said to fit Rostow's Kondratieff-War model. We leave aside here the problem of how to deal with the major innovations of the 1790-1848 interval, how to explain their timing and how to assess their effects on the British economy. It would seem that, in a simulation model, simple variations in the rate of technological progress are unable to grasp the unfolding of new innovation life cycles and their impact on an economy. It is sufficient to establish that the macroeconomic outcomes of Rostow's model are in accordance with British data.

For the second and following Kondratieff price cycles we can make use of estimates of world production compiled by Kuczynski (1980). These data contain series of industrial production, agricultural production, mining and total production, allowing us to separate Rostow's basic good production (agricultural plus mining) from his industrial production. Table 5.3 gives average annual growth rates for the various trend periods, with 1850 (the initial year of the Kuczynski series) instead of 1848 taken as the starting date of the 2nd Kondratieff.

If land, and the resources harvested and mined from land, are the bottleneck factors in a growing economy during a Kondratieff upswing, then the 'basic goods' column of Table 5.3 is a perfect illustration of the alternation of land scarcity and land abundance during Kondratieff trend periods. The growth rates of the basic sector rise and fall in the way predicted by Rostow. The numbers given in this column thus offer strong support for the plausibility of Rostow's Kondratieff model. No such alternation of growth rates emerges from the 'industrial goods' column. Yet if land is a bottleneck in the production of basic commodities, then the latter, which form an input into I goods production, should act as a bottleneck in the production of industrial goods during the up-

Table 5.3. *Annual growth rates of basic, industrial, and total world production during Rostow's trend periods*

	Basic goods	Industrial goods	Total world production
2nd Kondratieff			
1850-1873	1.9	4.3	2.5
1873-1896	2.4	3.2	2.7
3rd Kondratieff			
1896-1920	1.5	2.9	2.0
1920-1933	2.3	1.1	1.8
4th Kondratieff			
1933-1951	1.0	4.9	2.8
1951-1972	2.6	5.2	4.2

Data source: Kuczynski (1980).

swing phase. The sharp increase of B goods during downswing should allow for a vast expansion of the industrial sector during the second part of the Kondratieff cycle. The industrial goods sector, and consequently total production, should follow the same alternating growth pattern as that of the basic goods sector.

This pattern does not occur, however. The downswing growth rates of industrial production are lower than the upswing rates during the 2nd and 3rd Kondratieff cycles – as part of a steadily declining growth rate sequence – while the 1951-72 growth rate exceeds that of 1933-51 by only three-tenths of a percentage point. The change in weights of basic goods and industrial goods over the course of time produces a mixed pattern for total production growth.

One reason why this sequel to Rostow's theory does not fit the historical data is that the basic goods sector can only to a certain extent be considered to be an input of the industrial sector. Few if any agricultural products enter the production function of industry. Examination of the sequence of leading sectors which have emerged since the Industrial Revolution, shows that most of them were not fed by agricultural input but by mining input. In the 19th century, however, the mining sector was small compared to agriculture. Agriculture, on the other hand, was the dominant sector in the world economy (not until 1940 did world industrial production exceed world agricultural output for the first time). It is not surprising, therefore, that the general price level was greatly affected by the interplay of demand for, and the supply of, agricultural products, much more than by developments in industry.

But does industrial production as such show a pattern of long-wave fluctuations over time? Clearly not, if time periods are delineated on the basis of turning points in the price level. A consequence of the foregoing argument, however, is that price peaks and troughs should not necessarily be seen as long-wave benchmarks. The growth over time of industrial production itself should be examined before any decision is taken on appropriate long-wave periods. This will be done in Chapter IX *infra*. At the present moment it is only necessary to discuss some of the main reasons why the rhythm of industrial production came to differ markedly from that of agricultural and raw material production following the 1920-peak in prices.

Wars have had a great deal to do with the various cyclical patterns that have emerged. During World War I new agricultural capacity was added outside Europe, and contributed to the fall in prices after the war. Not until 1936 or thereabouts was this capacity absorbed to the extent that new shortages began to develop and prices to rise. World War II caused prices to rise even further. After 1945, increases in productivity rather than in acreage reversed the movement of prices into a downward one.

The two world wars had quite different effects on industrial production. The first interrupted the growth of the new leading sector complexes which had been established in the first decade of the 20th century (automobiles, chemicals, electricity). This growth was resumed after 1920. World War II stopped the development of some innovations introduced in the 1930s, and speeded-up the introduction of others. When war activity ended and resources were shifted away from their war-time uses, these innovations turned into new growth sectors.

Two different long cycles thus appear to exist: one, a Kondratieff price cycle, whose course is determined by discontinuities in the expansion of productive capacity in agriculture and raw material production; the other, a long wave in industrial production, which results from fluctuations in innovations over time and the way in which these innovations give rise to the establishment of growth sectors.

Historically, the price level has been determined much more by agricultural and raw material prices than by industrial prices. It is reasonable, therefore, to see the long price cycle first and foremost as a reflection of changes in the demand and supply of agricultural products and raw materials. This simple fact has been better understood by Rostow than by many other observers.[3] Only after 1940 did the increasing weight of industry in total world production in the primary and secondary sectors, together with other factors, put an end to the downward trend in the price level during periods of basic sector surplus. Between 1951 and 1970, when the world export price level of food and raw materials fell by 12 per cent, the overall export commodity price level went up by four per cent, primarily because of the increased weight of manufactured goods whose price level rose by almost 18 per cent during the same period.

Within the basic sector, energy sources and raw materials have gained in importance as compared to agricultural products. Productivity increases have become more important than those in acreage. The nature of Rostow's Kondratieff cycle is therefore changing. If there is to be a new Kondratieff downswing, my guess is that a sharp downward break in relative prices of basic commodities awaits the breakthrough to some new, cheap, hopefully infinite and non-polluting, source of energy .... Until a major breakthrough occurs in the cost and supply of energy, a convergence of powerful forces at work in the world economy is likely to keep the prices of basic commodities oscillating in a high range (Rostow 1978: 37).

NOTES

1. The following dates are as they appeared in Kondratieff (1926: 589). Note that the actual turning points in the original series in a few instances differ by one year.
2. Kondratieff's (1928) data indicate that the PB/PI-ratio rose again between 1825 and 1835, as industrial prices, brought down by cost-reducing technological change, fell even faster than agricultural prices.
3. The Frenchman Sirol (1942), not mentioned by Rostow, proposed essentially the same explanation of the Kondratieff price cycle, although he only considered agriculture rather than all products of the land.

VI

INNOVATION THEORIES

INNOVATION

Economists have long seen technological change as an autonomous process. The discovery of the 'residual', the unexplained part of growth, by Abramowitz in 1956 and Solow in 1957 — although Tinbergen in fact had made the same discovery 15 years earlier — gave rise to an impressive body of literature in which attempts were made to divide the residual into different parts. Much of this, however, left unanswered the why and how of technological change. It was assumed, but not explained. This lack of interest in the process of technological change was characteristic of mainstream economics, but did not apply to all its practitioners. Heterodox authors such as Schumpeter, Kuznets, Schmookler, Rosenberg and Heertje, have always worked from a different perspective.

Times have now changed. In the second half of the 1970s 'innovation' became a household word, mainly because it was apparently lacking. Stories in magazines like *Business Week* with titles such as 'The breakdown of US innovation' (16 February 1976), and 'Vanishing innovation' (3 July 1978) typified the awareness that developed in the post-1973 years: technological change, especially that embodied in new products, could no longer be taken for granted. More in general, resistance arose against the failure of neoclassical theory to deal with the phenomenon of innovation: 'The [neoclassical] theory conceals either in aggregation or in the abstract generality of multi-sector models, all the drama of the events — the rise and fall of products, technologies and industries, and the accompanying transformation of the spatial and occupational distribution of the population' (Nordhaus & Tobin 1972; see also Rosenberg 1975, Schmookler 1965, Nelson & Winter 1974, Hirsch 1969 and Nordhaus 1973).

Wherever technological change is considered a datum, the economic analysis will deal most often with the consequences of that change. Economists are not the only ones to follow this 'technology push' approach. Historians are also inclined to discuss innovations in order to explain their impact on economic life; in quite a different field, that of technology assessment, similar impact analyses are made on an *ex ante* basis. The role of the innovator is conveniently left out of the picture, however, rather as though technological change is an autonomous force, unstoppable and uncontrollable.

It was Schumpeter who gave us the distinction between 'invention' and 'innovation'. As an economist, he did not find the act of inventing particularly important: 'As long as they are not carried into practice, inventions are economically irrelevant' (Schumpeter 1961: 88). It is now agreed that Schumpeter overstated his case. Much inventive activity is determined by economic considerations, as we shall demonstrate. Yet most people would also agree that economic progress is only possible if inventions are put into practice. This can be done in a variety of ways. In Schumpeter's words:

> We include the introduction of new commodities which may even serve as the standard case. Technological change in the production of commodities already in use, the opening up of new markets or of new sources of supply, Taylorization of work, improved handling of material, the setting up of new business organizations such as department stores – in short, any 'doing things differently' in the realm of economic life – all these are instances of what we shall refer to by the term Innovation (Schumpeter 1939: 84).

Other authors have given equally broad interpretations of 'innovation'. Nelson & Winter (1974: 894) speak of innovation as the 'change of existing decision rules'; Nyström (1979: 1) goes even further: 'discontinuous changes – that is sudden radical alterations in the company's activities – have been designated here as innovations.' Kuznets (1972: 431) defines innovation as the 'application of a new way of attaining a useful end.' More specific definitions are 'the technical industrial and commercial steps which lead to the marketing of new manufactured products and to the commercial use of new technical processes and equipment' (Central Advisory Council for Science and Technology 1968: 1), and 'the development and successful introduction of new or improved products, services, production and distribution processes' (*Nota inzake de Selectieve Groei* 1976: 209-10). While these latter definitions are more restrictive and as such easier to use, a problem is that they do not consider the scope of innovation. Therefore, marginal product improvements are not distinguished from radical changes. With these definitions it could also be argued that many innovations are being made at the present time, despite the strong and commonly held view that lack of innovation is at the root of our economic problems.

The difference in impact of innovations has led Mensch (1975, 1979) to distinguish between basic, improvement, and pseudo-innovations. This distinction is also apparent in lists of 'important' innovations, of which that of Jewkes, Sawers & Stillerman (1969) is the most widely used. In this book we shall use the term 'basic innovations', without suggesting that any simple criteria for classification exist. Quantitative measures are conceivable (production volume attributable to an innovation; rate of substitution if the innovation replaces an older product or production process; the chain of innovations stemming from one basic innovation); however, the disparity of innovations makes it inevitable that in each particular case different arguments will be used to demonstrate the fundamental nature of an innovation. The best judges of the character of an innovation are the experts in the field. For example, in a study prepared for the U.S. National Science Foundation, an international panel of experts ranked a large number of innovations, introduced into the marketplace between 1953 and 1973. As Table 6.1 shows, only very few of these innovations were classified as radical breakthroughs.

Table 6.1. *'Radicalness' classification of 1242 innovations, 1953-1973*

Category	Frequency
1. Basic innovations	7
2. Radical innovations	29
3. Very important improvement innovations	62
4. Important improvement innovations	145
5. Minor improvements	239
6. Minor product or process differentiation	760
	1242

Source: Mensch (1979: 31).

We have referred above to Schumpeter's separation of invention and innovation. Rather than cutting off the act of invention from the realm of economic considerations, it might be better to see the two as steps in the process of technological change. Six phases could be distinguished:
(a)   fundamental science,
(b)   scientific discoveries,
(c)   invention,
(d)   development,
(e)   innovation,
(f)   diffusion of innovation.
This classification is more detailed than that which is frequently used, which combines our six phases into three pairs: scientific research-invention-innovation. In an economic analysis, i.e. an analysis which deals with the allocation of scarce resources, however, we feel that six steps should be distinguished. A distinction between (a) and (b) should then be made, as we assume that *fundamental science* is not oriented to societal demands. Rather, 'the sequence in which modern science developed is related to ease of observation and tools for experiment and measurement' (Rostow 1975: 139; see also Rosenberg 1974). It is true, however, that the direction in which science moves puts restrictions on the nature of the innovations that can be developed. Thus Shockley et al. had to use Einstein's quantum theory in order to develop the transistor, while maser and

laser are direct results of the application of Einstein's notion of 'stimulated emission', introduced in his quantum theory.

For phase (b) *scientific discoveries*, we assume that the orientation to societal needs is present. The allocation of financial means to particular fields of research involves a choice. The U.S. space programme of the past 25 years is perhaps the most spectacular example of the mobilization of intellectual knowledge and financial means, aimed at fulfilling a need that was felt at that time. Perhaps less spectacular, but an even clearer example of the changing orientation of research, is the field of medical research. Schmookler (1972: 83) speaks of 'the inevitability of the succession of foci of research – an inevitability which follows man's mortality.'

Phases (a) and (b) precede *invention*, the phase in which a new and promising technological opportunity is recognized and worked out in its most essential, rudimentary form. Of all phases in our sequence of six, this seems to be the easiest to measure – or perhaps the least difficult to measure – for inventions can be patented. But that is about all that can be said for it, for the use of patent activity to measure invention has many caveats: (1) not all inventions can be patented; (2) for some inventions patents will not be applied for; (3) criteria for issuing patents differ from country to country; (4) not all inventions will become innovations; (5) sometimes a patent is issued after the moment of innovation; (6) patents are often applied for in more countries simultaneously, hampering international comparisons of patent data. Despite these shortcomings, patent statistics are frequently used as a measure of inventive output. Later, in Chapter X, we shall take as the time of invention the year in which the technological knowledge necessary for innovation became available, which is not necessarily identical to the issuing date of a pertaining patent. At any rate, invention will most often be an economic act (hence: 'necessity is the mother of invention'); Schumpeter's emphasis on innovation as the only truly economic activity should be interpreted in the context of his theory of economic development, in which development was set equal to innovation.

Development (phase d) is nothing more nor less than the D of R & D: 'Development begins where research ends' (Hamberg 1966: 11). Measured in relative size, the transformation of an invention into a product or production process accounts for roughly two-thirds of total R & D expenditure (Rosenberg 1975: 471). It is abundantly clear that economic considerations guide the nature and size of the development process. Three conditions have to be met, before an invention can become an innovation: (i) the technological knowledge must be available; (ii) there must be demand for the new product or process; (iii) the financial means must be available. The moment of *innovation* is that of the first commercial application of the new product or process. The product is brought onto the market, and the timing of this moment is important. Innovations can be rushed; they can also be postponed. When the introduction will be made will depend on how the producer judges demand for the product and on the costs of production – can the innovation compete with existing products or processes? It also depends on the profit prospects of the existing line of products, on the state of the competition, and on many other factors which may hamper or stimulate innovation. Since the introduction of an innovation usually involves great risks, the number of innovation-hampering factors usually outweighs the number of innovation-stimulating factors (see Chapter VIII). This makes it important to explain the moment of innovation and also the fluctuations of innovations over time, especially in a long-wave context.

The importance of the moment of innovation, however, should not be overstated. The ultimate success of an innovation will depend on its *diffusion*. If new sectors of industry are created, it may rightfully be said that the innovation was important, and it may be labelled as 'basic', but this can only be done in retrospect. This observation, of course, somewhat diminishes the importance of the moment of innovation. Television, for instance, would still have become a basic innovation if it had been introduced commercially in 1946, rather than in 1936 when the BBC made its first broadcast. Its successful diffusion, i.e. the acceleration in sales after World War II, ten years after the moment of introduction, together with its huge overall economic impact, made it a basic innovation.

New basic innovations may have been introduced in the post-1973 depression years, but it may take another decade before we know about their diffusion and how radical they proved to be. No-one has any doubts about the overwhelming importance of the electronic computer, but when Jewkes, Sawers & Stillerman wrote the first edition of their *Sources of Invention* in 1958, they felt 'that the electronic digital computer seemed to have so uncertain a commercial future that we decided to exclude it from our case histories then' (Jewkes, Sawers & Stillerman 1969: 11). Nevertheless, we shall continue to attach particular significance to the moment of first commercial application, because 'innovation is an arduous and risky process, and the reluctance of companies to take what they perceive to be unnecessary risks is understandable' (Daniel V. DeSimone, Head of the U.S. Bureau of Standards' Office of Inventions and Innovations, cited in Blair 1972: 238). In Chapter X we shall see what can be said about the timing of innovations when this insight, in addition to what economists such as Schumpeter have taught us, is taken into account.

SCHUMPETER'S THEORY OF ECONOMIC DEVELOPMENT

Joseph Alois Schumpter (1883-1950) has been disrespectfully called 'a footnote economist'. Although considered by some to have been one of the greatest economists ever (a sure Nobel Prize winner, had that prize been given to economists in his time), many postwar students of economics have never been exposed to his work. The textbooks mention his name only in passing, when technological change and business cycles are discussed. When his writings are dealt with more explicitly, it is not his earlier work on economic development, but his later book on *Capitalism, Socialism and Democracy*, first published in 1943, which draws attention. Yet it was Schumpeter who said that an individual is most creative before his 30th birthday; everything done in later life is but an elaboration of ideas developed earlier. What we should first look at, therefore, is Schumpeter's theory of economic development, published in 1912, but formulated between 1908 and 1911 — indeed, well before his 30th birthday (English edition published in 1934; we have used the paperback edition published in 1961).

Schumpeter saw economic agents as continually striving for equilibrium. This ideal state, however, would never be attained since economic life was subject to changes, small changes, but also 'revolutionary' ones. Schumpeter understood economic development as change which was not forced upon the economy from outside, but rather arose from within: 'It is spontaneous and discontinuous change in the channels of the flow, disturbance of equilibrium, which forever alters and displaces the equilibrium state previously existing. Our theory of development is nothing but a treatment of this phenomenon and the processes incidental to it' (Schumpeter 1961: 64).

What are these spontaneous and discontinuous changes? They are essentially what Schumpeter called his *neue Kombinationen*, the new combinations of materials and productive forces. Economic development was the carrying out of new combinations, or innovations, which could take different forms. Schumpeter distinguished five cases: (1) the introduction of a new good; (2) the introduction of a new method of production; (3) the opening of a new market; (4) the conquest of a new source of supply of raw materials or semi-manufactured goods; (5) the carrying out of the new organization of an industry. Schumpeter's definition of innovation therefore covered new products as well as new production processes and organizational changes, just as any modern interpretation of the concept. 'The carrying out of new combinations we call "enterprises", the individuals whose function it is to carry them out we call "entrepreneurs"' (Ibidem: 74). The entrepreneur is not the one who provides the financial means of the enterprise; he is not the risk bearer. Risk falls on the owner of the means of production, 'hence never on the entrepreneur *as such*' (Ibidem: 75). We would see innovation as risk-taking behaviour, but in Schumpeter's view the carrying out of new combinations and financial risk taking are strictly separated. Nor should the manager be confused with the entrepreneur: 'everyone is an entrepreneur only when he actually "carries out the new combinations", and loses that character as soon as he has built up his business, when he settles down to running it as other people run their businesses' (Ibidem: 78). For that reason, 'being an entrepreneur is not a profession and as a rule not a lasting condition' (Ibidem: 78).

Having arrived at this point, we return to Schumpeter's earlier reference to 'spontaneous and discontinuous changes'. Why are innovations discontinuous, 'why is it that economic development in our sense does not proceed evenly as a tree grows, but as it were jerkily: why does it display those characteristic ups and downs?' (Ibidem: 223). 'The answer cannot be short and precise enough: exclusively *because the new combinations are not, as one would expect according to general principles of probability, evenly distributed through time* – in such a way that equal intervals of time could be chosen, in each of which the carrying out of new combinations would fall – *but appear, if at all, discontinuously in groups or swarms'* (Ibidem: 223). This is the essential link between technological change (read: innovation) and cyclical fluctuations: cycles arise because innovations appear in bunches.

But why is it that entrepreneurial activity is clustered? *'Exclusively because the appearance of one or a few entrepreneurs facilitates the appearance of others, and these the appearance of more, in ever-increasing numbers'* (Ibidem: 228). This is a crucial point which has been seen as the weakest link in Schumpeter's theory, and therefore requires further explanation. Schumpeter gave the following arguments (Ibidem: 228-30):

(1) The carrying out of new combinations is a difficult task, only accessible to people with certain qualities. During periods of stagnation only a few people can succeed in this direction. However, if one or a few have advanced with success, many of the difficulties disappear. Success makes it easier for more people to follow suit, until finally the innovation becomes familiar and its acceptance a matter of free choice.

(2) As entrepreneurial qualifications will be distributed according to the 'law of error', the number of individuals who satisfy progressively diminishing standards in this respect continually increases. Hence, the successful appearance of an entrepreneur is followed by the appearance not simply of some others, but of ever greater numbers, though they may be progressively less qualified.

(3) Reality shows that every boom starts in one or a few branches of industry (railway building, electrical and chemical industries, and so forth), and that it derives its character from innovations in the industry where it begins. But pioneers remove the obstacles for others, not only in the branch of production in which they first appear but, owing to the nature of these obstacles, *ipso facto* also in other branches.

(4) The more the process of development becomes familiar and a mere matter of calculation to all concerned, and the weaker the obstacles become in the course of time, the less the 'leadership' that will be needed to call forth innovations. Hence, the less pronounced will become the swarm-like appearance of entrepreneurs and the milder the cyclical movement.

(5) The swarm-like appearance of new combinations easily and necessarily ex-

plains the fundamental features of periods of boom. It explains why in-creasing capital investment is the very first symptom of the coming boom, why industries producing means of production are the first to show super-normal stimulation.

The boom, caused by the bunching of innovations, will eventually come to an end. 'The only cause of the depression is prosperity', to use Juglar's words: the boom calls forth forces which inevitably will lead the economy into depression. The essence of disturbance caused by the boom, Schumpeter argued, lies in the following three circumstances (Ibidem: 232-35):

(a) The new entrepreneur's demand for means of production drives up their prices.

(b) The new products (innovations) come on the market after a few years and compete with the old. At the beginning of the boom costs therefore rise in the old business (argument a); later their receipts are reduced, first in those businesses with which the innovation competes, but then in all old businesses, insofar as consumers' demand changes in favour of the innova-tion. The average time which elapses before the new products appear fun-damentally explains the length of the boom. This appearance of new pro-ducts causes the fall in prices, which on its part terminates the boom, *may* lead to a crisis, *must* lead to a depression, and starts all the rest.

(c) The appearance of the results of the new enterprises leads to a credit de-flation, because entrepreneurs are now in a position to pay off their debts; since no other borrowers step into their place, this leads to the disappear-ance of the recently created purchasing power just when its complement in goods emerges.

Also, the boom has altered the data of the system, upset its equilibrium and thus started an irregular movement in the economic system, which we conceive as a struggle towards a new equilibrium position. This makes accurate calculation im-possible in general, but especially in the planning of new enterprises (Ibidem: 235-36).

Thus, the boom creates out of itself an objective situation which brings an end to the boom, leads *easily* to a crisis, *necessarily* to a depression, and hence to a period of relative steadiness and absence of development. The depression as such we may call the 'normal' process of resorption and liquidation (Ibidem: 236). It is a struggle towards a new equilibrium position; depression will not stop until it has done its work, i.e. accomplished this equilibrium (Ibidem: 243). But apart from the digestion of innovations the period of depression does something else: it fulfils what the boom promised. This effect is lasting, while the phenom-ena felt to be unpleasant are temporary. The stream of goods is enriched, pro-duction is partly reorganized, costs of production are diminished, and what at first appears as entrepreneurial profit finally increases the permanent real in-comes of other classes (Ibidem: 245).

When Schumpeter first wrote the theory which we have cited so profusely, the economic cycle he had in mind was apparently the 7-11 year business cycle, with which all 19th century economists were familiar. Schumpeter saw this as an investment cycle, but one in which investment was induced by innovative activity. Innovation was incorporated in new products, the introduction of which upset equilibrium by changing the data of the system. After the carrying through of new combinations, therefore, the system would have to find its way towards a new equilibrium, at a higher level, but through depression. Innovation was therefore linked with the business cycle in a model which then had only two phases: prosperity and depression.

In his monumental *Business Cycles* (1939; see especially Chapters 3 and 4), Schumpeter restated and expanded his theory. The relation between innovations and cyclical fluctuations was applied to all cycles, including that in which we feel that the link between innovation and fluctuation is most essential, i.e. the Kondratieff cycle. The phases distinguished were also further elaborated. Instead of two phases, Schumpeter now recognized four: prosperity, recession, depression and recovery (Figure 6.1). Prosperity would give way to recession, before depression would set in; the recovery phase was the finding of a new equilibrium position. A simpler two-phase cycle, suggested by Schumpeter as a first approximation, would consist of only the first two phases: prosperity and recession. The latter phase would then be a period of adaptation, in which the system would draw toward equilibrium.

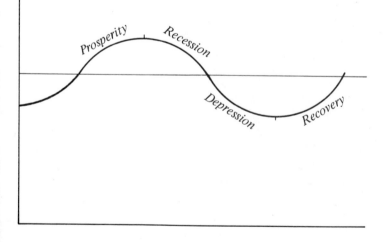

Figure 6.1. *Schumpeter's Four-Phase Cycle*

In Chapter I we have referred to Schumpeter's three-cycle scheme: 1 Kondratieff consisting of 6 Juglars, and 1 Juglar consisting of 3 Kitchins. Schumpeter was quick to add that he had found this scheme only 'useful' in his work; it did not necessarily follow from his model. Theoretically, the number of cycles could be indefinite. Schumpeter, however, contented himself with just three classes of cycles, those 'discovered' by Kitchin, Juglar and Kondratieff (Ibidem: 169). His main argument was, that 'if innovations are at the root of cyclical fluctuations, these cannot be expected to form a single wavelike movement, because the periods of gestation and of absorption of effects by the economic system will not, in general, be equal for all the innovations that are undertaken at any time' (Ibidem: 166-67). The long wave can be associated with a number of such basic innovations:

> Historically, the first Kondratieff covered by our material means the industrial revolution.... We date it from the eighties of the eighteenth century to 1842. The second stretches over what has been called the age of steam and steel. It ran its course between 1842 and 1897. And the third, the Kondratieff of electricity, chemistry, and motors, we date from 1898 on. These datings do not lack historical justification. Yet they are not only tentative, but also by nature merely approximate. A considerable zone of doubt surrounds most of them, as will be seen more clearly later on (Ibidem: 170).

A more detailed long-wave chronology is given in Table 6.2, which uses Schumpeter's four phases and was constructed by Kuznets on the basis of Schumpeter's historical analysis in his *Business Cycles*. The dates given are equilibrium points, rather than cycle troughs or peaks. For the first and second Kondratieff they were established from the discussion for Great Britain; those for the third were derived from the discussion for the United States.

Table 6.2. *Schumpeter's long-wave chronology*

	prosperity	recession	depression	recovery
1. Industrial Revolution Kondratieff: cotton textile, iron, steam power				
	1787-1800	1801-1813	1814-1827	1828-1842
2. Bourgeois Kondratieff: railroadization				
	1843-1857	1858-1869	1870-1884/5	1886-1897
3. Neo-Mercantilist Kondratieff: electricity, automobile				
	1898-1911	1912-1924/5	1925/6-1939	

Source: Kuznets (1953: 109).

Schumpeter's theory of economic development can be briefly summarized in a number of propositions:

1. Innovation is the fundamental impulse which sets and keeps the capitalist engine in motion (see also Schumpeter 1952: 83).
2. Innovations are an essentially discontinuous phenomenon: they appear in swarms.
3. Therefore economic development is a cyclical process: 'cyclical "waves" [are] essentially the form "progress" takes in competitive capitalism' (Schumpeter 1928: 383).
4. Innovations have different impacts. That is why, simultaneously, cycles of different length exist. The long wave is caused by such basic innovations as railroadization, electrification and motorization.

Schumpeter's theory has not been generally accepted. He has never been a mainstream economist. To some extent, this may have been due to the timing of his books. The first to be published after his arrival at Harvard University in 1932, *Business Cycles*, came in the wake of Keynes's *General Theory* and somehow became lost in the ensuing Keynesian revolution. When the postwar growth era apparently made the business cycle obsolete, the neoclassical growth theory, with its exogenous technological change, became popular. So the two central themes of Schumpeter's work, innovation and cyclical growth, disappeared into the background. Whatever interest remained in his work was restricted solely to his *Capitalism, Socialism and Democracy*. Interest was aroused again only after the long wave had gone down. But Schumpeter's theory was not accepted even by all those who did give it serious consideration. A long-wave theory, such as Schumpeter's, has to provide answers to at least three questions: (a) why do innovations appear in clusters? (b) why does the innovation impulse work itself out as a four-phase cycle? (c) why does it generate a cycle, i.e. a self-repeating process, in which every phase is necessarily followed by the next one, so that recovery is inevitably followed by a new bundle of innovations? Above, we have seen Schumpeter's answer to the first question, but this has not been satisfactory to many. The four-phase cycle has been described, but is it also clear how the demarcation points between the various phases can be determined? And does prosperity necessarily follow recovery? Could not the long wave end in secular stagnation, as some of Schumpeter's contemporaries thought?

The explanation of cyclical processes comes down to the explanation of the turning points of a cycle. In Schumpeter's four-phase approach, the upper turning point is formed by the transition from prosperity to recession. We have to assume that this point is reached when entrepreneurial profits, made with the introduction of innovations, melt away. In terms of market organization, Schumpeter seems to think of the transition towards (near-)perfect competition, with new products being supplied at a price equal to the minimal cost per unit product. The arrival of new entrepreneurs would change the market from a monopolistic one into a more competitive one ('The introduction of new methods of production and new commodities is hardly conceivable with perfect −

and perfectly prompt – competition from the start'; Schumpeter 1952: 105). Schumpeter does not appear to consider market saturation; when he refers to the limitations of an innovation, he has in mind the lower limit of the price of a commodity. But can the transition towards perfect competition be seen as an upper turning point? Not necessarily, since it does not have to imply a retardation in economic activity. Possibly the upper turning point should be interpreted in a rather special way, i.e. as the cessation of entrepreneurial activity; 'Therefore, along with new products streaming into markets, and with repayments increasing in quantitative importance, entrepreneurial activity tends to slacken, until finally it ceases entirely' (Schumpeter 1939: 136). We have to assume that the weakening of the innovation impulse will eventually lead to a slowdown of growth. When this will happen, however, is not so clear.

Nor is it clear when the lower turning point of the long wave is reached. In Schumpeter's scheme this is the transition from depression to recovery: 'When depression has run its course, the system starts to feel its way back to a new neighbourhood of equilibrium. This constitutes our fourth phase. We will call it Recovery or Revival' (Ibidem: 149). This image of the course of a depression may be found in other places, with expressions such as 'the depression has to spend itself', 'the process of depression cannot stop until it has done its work', etc. Only when this has happened, can the economy get ready for a new innovation impulse. During depression 'there is necessarily uncertainty about what the new data will be, which makes the calculation of new combinations impossible and makes it difficult to obtain the cooperation of the requisite factors' (Schumpeter 1961: 243). This connection between the old and the new cycles is not satisfactory if it concerns the explanation of the Juglar, but is even less so if the cyclical character of the Kondratieff has to be explained. Our conclusion has to be, therefore, that Schumpeter has not managed to provide a convincing explanation of the swarm-like appearance of basic innovations prior to long-wave expansion.

Kuznets, in his thorough and oft-cited review of Schumpeter's *Business Cycles* (Kuznets 1940, reprinted in Kuznets 1953), argued that Schumpeter had failed to forge the necessary links between his primary factors and concepts (entrepreneur, innovation, equilibrium line) and the observable cyclical fluctuations in economic activity. What precisely was the connection between the distribution of entrepreneurial abilities and the bunching of innovations? If we take for granted that these abilities are scarce, why would their operation be discontinuous over time? Kuznets could think of only one plausible explanation of the bunching of innovations, and that is that the opportunities for major innovations, i.e. those that bear upon Kondratieff cycles, are not necessarily continuous over time. 'For example, we may say that electricity did not become available sooner because it had to wait until the potentialities of steam power were exhausted by the economic system and until the attention of inventors and engineers was ready to be diverted to the problems of electricity' (Kuznets 1953: 113). Kuznets refers here to the possible discontinuity in the appearance of inventions; others would argue that it is not invention but innovation which is unevenly distributed over time.

Despite any serious doubts one may have about the connections between Schumpeter's key variables of entrepreneurial ability, innovation and economic fluctuations, he has provided us with insights whose relevance has continued and even increased in recent years. We may not agree with his monocausal explanation of all classes of cycles; we may have doubts about his explanation of the two turning points of the cycle; we may find his account of the transition from phase to phase in his four-phase model unsatisfactory. Nevertheless, his works remain a rich source of inspiration, indispensable for anyone who, like Schumpeter, is puzzled by the alternation of periods of prosperity and depression which have been manifested since the Industrial Revolution.

Schumpeter has now been rediscovered in two ways. Firstly, the growing dissatisfaction with the neoclassical approach to technological change has given rise to new theories, which draw heavily upon the viewpoints sketched by Schumpeter in his *Theory of Economic Development*. Secondly, Schumpeter's notion of swarms of innovations has been incorporated in various modern long-wave theories.

The Schumpeterian model is now recognized as an attractive alternative to the neoclassical growth model. It awards a major role to concepts such as innovation and imitation; it explains how market structure can change within an industry; and it allows for technological change to be more than mere cost-reducing process innovations. Its main drawback may be its lack of susceptibility to formal modelling. More recently, however, Nelson & Winter (1974) have developed what they call 'an evolutionary theory of economic growth', a framework for a Schumpeterian analysis of economic development, in which innovation is perceived as 'change of existing decision rules', and which assumes firm behaviour to be 'satisficing' rather than optimizing. Their theory is microeconomic; using Markow processes, they can simulate changes in an 'industry state', which consists of the finite list of the states of firms, all producing a homogeneous product by employing two factors – labour and physical capital. Nelson & Winter consider the outcomes of their simulation runs as 'quite successful' if compared with historically observed trends.

In another development, a post-Keynesian alternative has been offered to neoclassical macroeconomics; this, too, focusses on concepts that are central to Schumpeterian economics: innovation, entrepreneurship, unbalanced growth. 'Unlike neoclassical macrodynamics [post-Keynesian macrodynamics] strives to encompass the real world of uncertainty, oligopolies, new products and technologies, a world in which the "human element" is reflected in the quality of the entrepreneurial class' (Cornwall 1979: 29-30).

Modern long-wave theorists have also gone back to Schumpeter. Mensch is one of them; others include Freeman (1979a, 1979b), Clark, Freeman & Soete (1981a, 1981b), Hartman & Wheeler (1979), Graham & Senge (1980), and Kleinknecht (1981). Of these authors, Clark, Freeman & Soete have suggested a number of clarifications of Schumpeter's theory (see the discussion on Mensch's theory below). Hartman & Wheeler, oddly enough, have taken patent activity as a proxy for the measurement of clusters of innovations. They find that, in Britain at least, the growth rate of patents sealed is highest during Kondratieff downswing periods. Kleinknecht, a former co-worker of Mensch, has tested the swarming hypothesis, while Graham & Senge have followed in the footsteps of Forrester (see Chapter VII), arguing that innovative activity is determined by fluctuations in the output of the capital-goods producing sector.

MENSCH'S THEORY

Mensch was one of the first to sense that something was wrong with innovation. The original German version of his *Stalemate in Technology* (Mensch 1979) was published in 1975; exercises on the same theme had been published even earlier (Mensch 1971, 1972). He has also been a leader and inspirator of the Kondratieff-revival. His analysis is Schumpeterian, his purpose to demonstrate and explain the clustered appearance of major or basic innovations prior to a long-wave upswing. The importance of his contribution is that he has supplied some of the missing parts in Schumpeter's explanation of the long wave.

Mensch distinguishes different types of innovations. Basic innovations are those that give rise to the creation of entirely new industries. Improvement innovations are seen as the further development in established areas of activity. A third category is formed by so-called pseudo-innovations: innovations that in reality are not innovations at all. Mensch is concerned with the appearance of basic innovations, for these are responsible for the periods of upswing, also known as the expansion phases of the long wave. Yet Mensch does not subscribe to the wave model that Kondratieff and others employed. In his words 'the wave model incorporates a deterministic recurrence of phase transition' (Mensch 1979: 73). Instead, his instrument is 'the metamorphosis model of cycles of structure change', which holds that 'the economy has evolved through a series of intermittent innovative impulses that take the form of successive S-shaped cycles (Ibidem: 72-73) (see Figure 6.2).

Mensch's reasoning is as follows: basic innovations generate new industries. Assuming for the moment that they do indeed appear in clusters, this simultaneous creation of new growth industries will boost economic growth. In the course of the life cycles of the growth industries, new improvement innovations will be made but eventually individual industrial branches will stagnate

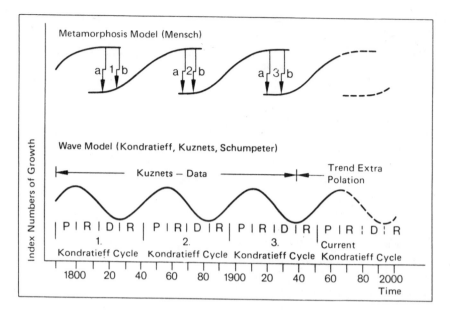

Figure 6.2. *Mensch's metamorphosis model of industrial evolution*

Reprinted with permission from G. Mensch: *Stalemate in Technology* (Cambridge, Mass., Ballinger Publishing Company, 1979).

Because of the exhaustion of further possibilities for technological improvements, either because all of the new expertise has already been put into practice or because improvement innovations are no longer worthwhile in a saturated market or both.... Stagnation in what until now were the most flourishing areas of the economy causes the slower tempo of activity in the other branches to slacken even further. Reaching the upper limits to growth in individual industrial sectors has repercussions that affect the economy as a whole (Ibidem: 66).

Growth thus ends as the former growth industries, more or less simultaneously, reach the saturation levels of their respective life cycles. Pseudo-innovations may be tried to postpone stagnation, but they will not prevent it. What follows is a 'stalemate in technology': there is an abundance of technological knowledge waiting to be transformed into new innovations, but the actual implementation of new technologies only occurs if investors become desperate enough to assume the higher risks associated with the introduction of basic innovations, rather than continue with the old activities. Stagnation is nothing but lack of basic innovations (Mensch 1979: xvii, calls this the main thesis of his book). Only

'Innovationen überwinden die Depression' ('innovations overcome the depression'), as the subtitles of his German and English books proclaim. Firms will only innovate if the potential of the old batch of basic innovations has been exhausted, the economy has slid into stagnation, and the only way to get out of it seems to be through new innovations.

Even though Mensch does not see his own perception of long-term economic development as a wave model, he has clearly attempted to explain upper and lower turning points in long-term development. The upper turning point is explained as the saturation of former growth industries, the lower turning point is reached when firms start to transform technological knowledge into new basic innovations. Between upper and lower turning points lies the technological stalemate.

Lack of innovation is the main cause of depression. Had major innovations taken place evenly and continuously through time, the industrial world would not have gone through the long depressions that occurred after 1825, 1873, 1929 and 1973. Basic innovations are only introduced after depression has set in: 'Erst in der Talsohle der Konjunktur, wenn die Gewinne mit den abgegrasten Technologien unerträglich gering sind, überwindet das Kapital die Risikoscheu und stürzt sich auf die Möglichkeiten der Basisinnovationen, die dann habhaft sind' (Mensch 1975: 180). This statement, which did not appear in the English version of Mensch's book, can be translated as follows: 'Only in the trough of the cycle, when the profits of used-up technologies are unbearably low, will capital overcome its aversion to risk-taking and throw itself upon the possibilities of available basic innovations'). In other words, basic innovations will appear in bunches during long-wave depression phases, i.e. in the decades following 1825, 1873, and 1929. Mensch supports his claim by presenting series of basic innovations which, if taken together for ten-year periods, yield a time distribution as given in Figure 6.3. Peaks are shown for the decades of the 1760s, 1830s and 1840s, 1880s, and 1930s.

Mensch's work has met with mixed reactions. He has been commended for his attempts to fill in that which was clearly missing in Schumpeter's analysis, and for the host of other ideas brought forward in his books (often presented as 'theories'). But he has been criticized for the shakiness of his empirical support and therefore for the validity of his hypotheses. The sharpest criticism has come from three British long-wave researchers (Clark, Freeman & Soete 1981b), whose own work is very much in the Schumpeterian tradition and who, therefore, have a keen interest in any attempts to find empirical support for Schumpeter's swarms of innovations. As Schumpeter's long-wave expansion phases were clearly carried by the type of major innovations which Mensch has labelled as 'basic innovations', empirical validation of the cluster-hypothesis would have to start with a list of basic innovations. But the compilation of such a list is no easy matter. Firstly, which innovations should be included, and secondly, what should be

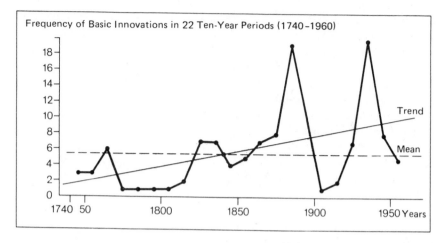

Figure 6.3. *Swarms of basic innovations, according to Mensch*

Reprinted with permission from G. Mensch: *Stalemate in Technology* (Cambridge, Mass., Ballinger Publishing Company, 1979).

taken as the date of innovation? We shall face this problem later in this book (Chapter X). Every list, however conscientiously drawn up, can be objected to, but we shall postpone a discussion of the problems involved and how to deal with them until Chapter X. Here, it suffices to remark that Clark, Freeman & Soete had a number of reasons to find Mensch's list unsatisfactory, and as a result could not regard his empirical evidence as adequate; however, they did not deny that some bunching of innovations over time was likely to have occurred.

If Mensch did not validate his hypothesis satisfactorily, then what about the hypothesis itself? Two opposing views exist. One is that innovation only takes place in a favourable economic climate, as during periods of expansion. This is the Schmookler hypothesis (Schmookler 1966, 1972), according to which the effect of a depression would be to slow down the flow of innovations. The other view is that of Mensch, who contends that depression forces firms to innovate. To cite Mensch (1979: 178-79) once again: 'Under pressure from high unemployment and underutilized capital, opposition to and reservation about untried, risky new ideas appear with a sense that relief might come from anywhere. This situation produces a surge of basic innovation that ends the stagnation gripping the economy in the technological stalemate and ushers in the recovery phase.' Here Mensch uses Schumpeter's four-phase model to argue that the 'surge of basic innovations' marks the end of the depression phase and the beginning of the recovery phase. Innovative surges have occurred around 1764, 1825, 1886, and 1935, when the frequency of innovations (number of basic innovations introduced) and the speed of innovative change (the reduction of lead time from invention to innovation) were at their highest points, according to Mensch. He labels them 'radical years'.

It is true that 1825 and 1886 roughly coincide with Schumpeter's transition from depression to recovery; 1935, however, is well before the end of Schumpeter's third Kondratieff depression (see Table 6.2).

Does this mean that 'depression is the motor of basic innovation', as Mensch contends, and not that a favourable economic outlook is necessary for innovations, as Schmookler and also Schumpeter argued? We shall not try to resolve this issue here, but will postpone the discussion until Chapter VIII, where we shall present our own views on the timing of basic innovations. It will then prove important to distinguish between different types of innovations, e.g. product innovations on the one hand and process innovations on the other hand, rather than putting them all into one heap and attempting to interpret peaks in time of heterogenous basic innovations. Some innovations may be most likely to occur during depression, while for other types recovery or even prosperity appears to be the most probable time of introduction.

Another issue, raised by Clark, Freeman & Soete (1981b) in their review of Mensch's book, concerns the concept of innovation swarms. In Mensch's view, these swarms are a disparate set of basic innovations introduced during a very short time span, as during 'radical years'. He uses the term 'wagon train effect' or 'band-wagon effect' to describe the course of events: 'First only a few wagons move into gear; then as the train gradually grows larger, the speed accelerates, and thus when the last stragglers join the group, it is moving at full speed. This is precisely how the swarm of basic innovations appears in an economy during a technological stalemate' (Mensch 1979: 162). Freeman et al. have taken serious objection to this view: 'It is very hard to see in what sense the original quite separate launch of helicopters, television, tetra-ethyl lead, titanium, etc. in the mid-1930s could constitute a "band-wagon" in any normal meaning of the term.' And they continue: 'We do think the band-wagon effect is extraordinarily important – in our view it is the main explanation of the upswings in the long waves, but we see it as the steepest part of the "S-curves" characteristic of many diffusion processes, not the relatively flat piece of the curve which often follows the basic innovation for a few years' (Clark, Freeman & Soete 1981: 153). In other words, the swarming process is Schumpeterian, not Menschian. High profits in one innovative sector invite imitators to join that sector, but the introduction of the magnetic taperecorder in 1935 had nothing to do with the first application of catalytic oil cracking, also in 1935. We agree with Freeman et al. Only when the success of an innovation becomes apparent – often not until a number of years after its introduction – do others jump on the bandwagon. Take, as a recent example, the video cassette recorder, introduced by Philips in 1970. The date of the innovation, i.e. the first commercial application, is 1970.

Yet the VCR picked up speed only in the second half of the 1970s. We would not go so far as to deny the existence of any cross-sectoral effects of innovation (neither did Schumpeter). But it would seem that these effects are important only during recovery or early prosperity, when the success of innovation has a positive effect on the overall economic climate and may evoke further innovative activity in all kinds of fields. It is very difficult to picture such a cross-fertilization around 1935, in the middle of the Great Depression. Depression may force firms to move into new directions — we believe it does, and this necessity to innovate may pose itself more or less simultaneously in a number of sectors, all faced with saturation. A resulting cluster of innovations, however, could not be seen as the 'wagon train effect' which Mensch writes about.

Notwithstanding this dispute on the nature of the Schumpeterian swarm and its timing, Mensch's work has proved an important stimulus for further research on the determinants of innovation. In this respect, mention should be made of Kleinknecht's contributions on the link between basic innovations and growth industries (Kleinknecht 1979), and on the timing and statistical significance of innovations (Kleinknecht 1981). Furthermore, Graham & Senge (1980) have drawn on Mensch's theory to explain the fluctuations in basic innovations as a result of fluctuations in the production of the capital goods sector. Finally, we have also found Mensch's stalemate in technology to be a source of inspiration, as will become apparent in Chapter VIII.

VII

FLUCTUATIONS IN INFRASTRUCTURAL INVESTMENT

INFRASTRUCTURAL INVESTMENT AS A CAUSE OF LONG WAVES

One of the most striking features of the economic decline that has occurred since 1973/74 has been the excess capacity in such sectors as steel, oil refining, construction, shipbuilding, and motor vehicles. Take, for instance, *steel*. Capacity utilization in the steel industry has historically been rather low. The growth of productive capacity takes place in big lumps. If world demand for steel approaches capacity limits, the reaction of producers is to invest in new plants simultaneously. Consequently, the industry as a whole suffers from excess capacity again until demand catches up with that capacity. The latest of these investment booms occurred in the early 1970s. Capacity growth even accelerated during the 1974/75 depression, the result of decisions taken several years earlier. While capacity utilization in the Western world averaged 79 per cent between 1967 and 1974, after 1974 the stagnation in steel demand on the one hand, and the continued growth of capacity on the other hand, created an enormous gap, resulting in a capacity utilization rate of only 61 per cent in 1977. Not all the existing capacity can be considered effective – some of it is technologically obsolete; nevertheless, 1977 production was no more than 76 per cent of this effective capacity.

Steel has been called 'perhaps the sickest major industry in the world' (*Management Today*, January 1981: 54). Its fortunes depend very much on the world economy. If the industrialized countries are in a state of depression, their steel industries probably are also depressed. In the European Community, for instance, steel production in 1980 was seven per cent below its 1970 level, and even 18 per cent below its 1974 peak. North America did not do much better. With productive capacity in the Western world still growing slightly, and that in the newly industrializing and developing countries growing rapidly, even under the most rosy demand forecasts, normal capacity utilization rates are not foreseen until 1985.

World *shipping* is another sector which is faced with considerable excess capacity. Here, too, capacity continued to grow long after the bottom had fallen out of the market in 1973. The world tanker fleet finally stopped growing in 1978, a growth which had begun in 1945, but by 1978 capacity utilization had

Table 7.1 *Output growth in a number of basic sectors, 1975-1980*

	Iron & Steel	Petroleum refineries	Shipbuilding	Automobiles
United States	96	106	108	107
Canada	120	76	84	85
Japan	125	102	39	170
Germany	108	115	78	122
France	111	105	–	121
Italy	121	93	41	125
United Kingdom	67	97	68	86

Numbers shown are 1980 indices (1975=100).

Source: OECD: *Indicators of industrial activity*, 1982-I.

dropped to 57 per cent. The shipping slump has had severe consequences for the shipbuilding industry. Consider, for instance, the 1980 production indices (with 1975=100) shown in Table 7.1. If steel was in crisis, the shipbuilding industry virtually collapsed in the second half of the 1970s. As with steel, only the newly industrialized countries have managed to prosper in the post-1973 years. Other than with steel, where the crisis was totally unexpected (in 1975 the International Iron and Steel Institute still predicted continued capacity shortages), the tanker glut was foreseen by the shipbuilders who, in 1972, predicted 'that by 1975 about half the capacity for building the giant tankers which increasingly dominate the industry will be idle' (*The Economist*, 22 July 1972). Even in successful Japan, excess capacity rose to 35 per cent in 1978.

Yet another sector with excess capacity and slimming problems, is *oil refining*. Again, problems are most severe in the older industrialized countries and, again, new capacity was still added well after 1973. In Europe, oil-refining capacity has risen from 920 million tonnes a year in 1973, to a billion tonnes a year in 1981, with over-capacity running at about 40 per cent. The closure of some refineries is inevitable. By 1985, Europe's capacity may have shrunk to about 700 to 800 million tonnes a year. The capacity utilization rate of Japanese oil refineries fell to 56 per cent in 1981.

In the *aluminium* industry excess capacity is expected to increase, despite the reduction of capacity in Japan and some European countries. World capacity is still growing faster than world demand, so that by 1988 a capacity utilization rate of only 78 per cent is expected.

This list may easily be extended by adding yet other sectors where productive capacity has outgrown demand. In each case the story would be the same: world capacity in the basic sectors, reacting with long lags to changes in world demand, has been over-expanded, and would have been even if world demand had continued to grow at its pre-1974 pace. Excess capacity is highest in the older industrial countries, including Japan, and lowest in the newly industrialized countries, which have more modern plants and lower labour costs. Excess capacity will continue to be a problem at least until 1984/85.

The sectors of the economy discussed so far can be called 'basic sectors', in the sense that they produce the industrial and transportation infrastructure necessary to accommodate a growing world economy. If economic growth is seen as propelled by a few leading sectors, then during the growth phase of these leading sectors two kinds of infrastructure are required: infrastructure for the leading sectors themselves, and a general infrastructure to serve the economy as a whole. Take, for instance, the postwar chemical industry. For its own growth it needed first of all industrial and harbour complexes. These sprung up everywhere in Europe, Japan, North America and, later on, in newly industrialized countries such as South Korea and Taiwan. But chemicals and the other growth sectors of the postwar era also needed a general transportation and communication infrastructure: roads, waterways, trucks, ships, airplanes, telephone facilities, energy, and so on, the production of which occurs within our basic sectors.

As with agriculture and raw material production, the productive capacity of basic industries can only react with considerable lags to demand increases. The lags are similar to those discussed above in Chapter V:

(1)   a recognition lag – demand increases have to be perceived as structural for capacity expansions to be considered;

(2)   an appropriation lag – funds have to be appropriated before construction of capital goods can begin;

(3)   a gestation lag – the lag caused by the construction time of capital goods.

Here too, the indivisibility of large, long-lasting capital goods leads to lumpiness in the way that capital stocks are increased. The essence of every economic cycle, caused by fluctuations in investment, is the overshooting and undershooting of capital-goods production. It takes too long before production gets under way, but once it is going it tends to overshoot the long-term needs. Excess capacity results and, as a reaction, fewer capital goods are produced for a while, until technical and economic obsolescence reduces the capital stock to a point where it is insufficient to meet the needs. If this mechanism holds for infrastructural investment as well as for the other forms of capital goods production, direct and indirect effects taken together could cause a wave-like fluctuation in aggregate output.

Let us take a look at postwar crests of this wave for three typical infrastructural variables, i.e. civil transport aircraft produced, completed miles of highway, and tonnage of launched merchant vessels (Figures 7.1–7.3). The first two are United States series; vessels completed represent world totals. Transport aircraft production in the USA reached a peak in 1968, well before the oil crisis of 1973. Actually, two peaks are shown, the first occurring in 1958. This could indicate the existence of a Juglar cycle around the long-term movement. Construction of the United States highway system had earlier reached its all-time peak, in 1959. Highway construction, used as a tool of anti-depression policy during the 1930s, was reduced sharply during World War II but resumed again after the war. This is

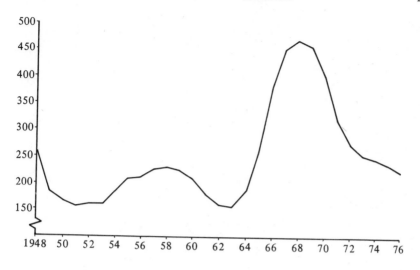

Figure 7.1 *Civil transport aircraft produced, United States, 1948-1976
(five year moving averages)*

Source: *Historical Statistics of the U.S.* and *Statistical Abstract of the U.S.*

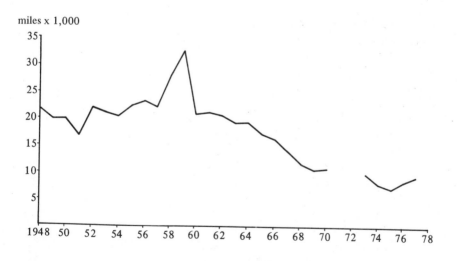

Figure 7.2 *Miles of highway completed, United States, 1948-1977*

Source: *Historical Statistics of the U.S.* and *Statistical Abstract of the U.S.*

tonnage (in mlns)

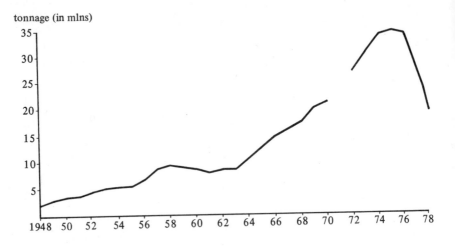

Figure 7.3 *Gross tonnage of merchant vessels launched, world, 1948-1978*

Source: *Historical Statistics of the U.S.* and *Statistical Abstract of the U.S.*

a typical case of an investment in infrastructure which cannot continue in-definitely at the same high level. The U.S. highway system has been more or less completed – as the railway system once was – and number of miles added consequently fell sharply in the late 1960s and 1970s. Present capacity is suffi-cient to meet the needs of the economy. For world merchant shipping output the timing of the peak differs, but the story is essentially the same. Tonnage-added peaked in 1975, after the first oil crisis. Clearly, however, long-term shipping needs were over-estimated and production dropped sharply after 1976.

A single postwar peak, of course, does not prove the existence of a long wave of infrastructural investment. To demonstrate the plausibility of such a long wave, longer series would be needed. Fortunately, for a number of basic sectors products, U.S. series can be extended back to the 1870s, so that two long waves can be covered. Rather than presenting graphs, we give annual average growth rates for long-wave upswing and downswing periods (Table 7.2). In this way, we cannot locate peaks and troughs, but we can see whether growth rates go up and down in conformity with the long wave.

All four series shown in Table 7.2., with the exception of steel, show the same growth pattern: the 1895-1913 ('La Belle Époque') growth rate is higher than the preceding 1873-95 ('The Great Depression') growth rate; and also higher than the following 1913-29 and 1929-48 rates. After 1948 growth rates go up again, albeit only slightly for iron and steel. The latter sector's growth rate for 1873-95 is very high, signalling the beginning of its life cycle.

Table 7.2 *Annual growth rates, trend periods, United States*

	1873-95	1895-1913	1913-29	1929-48	1948-73
Pig iron	6.1	6.7	2.0	1.4	1.7
Raw steel	16.8	9.4	3.8	1.9	2.1
Cement	6.4	13.8	4.2	1.0	3.4
Capacity of vessels entered	2.3	5.5	3.1	0.5	5.5

Source: Van Duijn (1980a: 25-26)

The four series thus display a long-wave pattern, although this observation does not tell us which is cause and which is consequence. Do our basic sectors follow aggregate economic activity, or do they cause economic activity at large to fluctuate? Figures 7.1-7.3 would suggest that the creation of excess capacity certainly compounds the problem of lack of investment once a depression phase has set in. They also suggest, however, that infrastructural investment downturns may occur well before the aggregate growth rate drops to depression levels. This earlier downturn is not peculiar to the USA. In a long-wave study, using Dutch data, we have obtained similar results (Van Duijn 1979a). It is only that the problem of excess capacity becomes apparent during a depression; investment growth may have slowed down before the depression sets in.

The series reported on so far all pertain to particular products. We assume that there will be little disagreement as far as the relation of these series to infrastructural investment is concerned, even though products such as iron and steel have many applications other than in investment goods. In verifying the relation between capital formation and the long wave, we would prefer to use direct estimates of infrastructural investment, but the problem is that most historical investment data are aggregated. Investment in machines and equipment, in buildings, in transportation goods, and in transportation infrastructure, are usually put together in one statistic. In Chapter IX we shall present a number of calculations concerning long-term trends in capital formation and capital stock growth, based on such aggregate data. Clearly, however, these are no more than indications of the possible bunching of infrastructural investment during long-wave expansions.

Long-wave theorists have always been interested in the role of investment. Kondratieff and De Wolff linked the useful life of 'basic' capital goods to the length of the long wave. Later in this chapter we shall see that even investment in capital goods with an average life of some 15 years can generate long waves. Colin Clark, whose remarkable book *The Economics of 1960* was written in 1941, argued that 'the most deep-seated motive force of these long period changes lies in capital movements. The world's fields of investment seem to pass, with long alternations, through capital-hungry and capital-sated phases' (Clark

1944: 89). His periods of capital scarcity (1850-75 and 1900-30) and abundance (1875-1900 and 1930-45) coincide roughly with the long-wave periods usually distinguished in the literature. His hypothesis, as Clark himself admits, is based on *a priori* considerations. No theoretical model is offered. A confirmation of the hypothesis is found through an investigation of British and U.S. investment data, international capital movements, world trade, terms of trade, and gold production. Subject to some qualifications, Clark concludes: 'the hypotheses seem to have been on the whole proved' (Ibidem: 104). What about the length of these capital-hungry and capital-sated phases? Clark sticks to a 25-year length for each phase, and argues that

> the period of a world war, which lengthened the capital-hungry period of 1900-1930, should have the effect of shortening the capital-sated period, whose normal duration might have been from 1930 to 1955.... [The] shortening effect [of the present war] may probably be put at ten years instead of five years. This indicates that the capital-hungry period would begin about 1945, or in effect at the conclusion of the present war (Ibidem: 106).

Extending Clark's arithmetic yields 1970 as the end of the postwar capital-hungry phase, a prediction which has proved remarkably accurate.

Following the 1973/74 downturn, economists have again begun to look at capital abundance as its possible cause. Thus, it was argued that long waves were to be seen as cycles of the transportation industry. In the U.S. case, the first Kondratieff cycle (peaking in the 1810s) could be explained by the massive investment in harbour and canal development; the second (peaking after the Civil War) by the building of the national railroad system; the third wave occurred after World War I, as the automobile industry built up its productive capacity and the states built their road systems; while the fourth Kondratieff cycle could be explained by the suburbanization of the post-Korean War period, resulting in the Interstate Highway system and the two-car family (Cherry 1980: 257-58).

While this explanation does not sound particularly convincing (e.g. the expansion of the federal highway system continued into the 1930s, and indeed reached peak levels during that decade), it quite rightly points at the significance of infrastructural investment during long periods of expansion.

Hartman & Wheeler (1979) have also looked at a number of infrastructural data for the USA and Great Britain (increase in canal miles, miles of highway, and kilometers of railroad, plus numbers of commercial aviation). Unfortunately, however, they fail to distinguish between long waves in aggregate economic activity and Rostow's price cycle, mix up the different trend periods and, as a result, conclude that infrastructural development reaches high levels during Kondratieff downswing periods!

Van der Zwan (1976) has discussed the increase in capital intensity of production during the 1870s, 1920s and 1960s. This increase, he argues, was induced by rising labour costs, and in many cases took the form of production on a larger scale, allowing firms to reduce unit costs by profiting from scale economies. Van der Zwan postulates that the expansion of productive capacity through scale increases was ultimately not met by sufficient expansion of market demand, thus leaving firms with excess capacity. The interesting part of Van der Zwan's contribution is that he describes a mechanism through which excess capacity of other than infrastructural capital stock can be explained. This is the second of the two kinds of capital stocks distinguished earlier in this chapter. It is most likely that the industries Van der Zwan had in mind were former growth industries such as the chemical and electrotechnical industries – which had long hoped that the reduction of unit costs through scale increases would be awarded by a product-absorbing market.

The most outspoken modern representative of the view that fluctuations in capital goods production cause long waves – even without any major disturbances in the consumer goods sector – is Jay Forrester. Forrester is best known for his system dynamics models: large, long-term, non-linear simulation models, which include social and psychological as well as economic variables. Since 1956, when he started to work on the system dynamics approach, Forrester has applied his methodology of studying social systems to a whole range of areas, from industrial dynamics, to urban dynamics, and to world dynamics (the well-known Club of Rome study on the *Limits of Growth*). Work on a System Dynamics National Model started after 1972. With his national model Forrester was able to generate Kondratieff-cycles (Forrester 1975a, 1975b, 1976, 1977).

Although the fully developed national model is said to have 15 industrial sectors, long waves can be simulated with a model that distinguishes only a consumer goods sector and a capital equipment sector (Figure 7.4). The former orders capital goods from the capital equipment sector. The latter also needs capital equipment as a factor of production, but has to order it from its own output. Under conditions of full capacity, therefore, demand for capital equipment stemming from the consumer goods sector can only be met if the capital equipment sector first increases its own productive capacity, i.e. produces its own input in order later to meet the needs of the consumer sector. This 'bootstrap' structure has a highly destabilizing effect and is responsible for substantially lengthening the periods of fluctuation.

Labour is freely available to both sectors in the simple version of the Forrester model. If low mobility of labour is assumed, however, this would be another factor which would increase the length of the period of fluctuation. Prices are held constant.

A typical simulation of the system dynamics model, over a 200-year period, is shown in Figure 7.5. Output in the capital sector clearly displays a long fluctuation of some 50-65 years duration. In addition to this long wave, shorter cycles

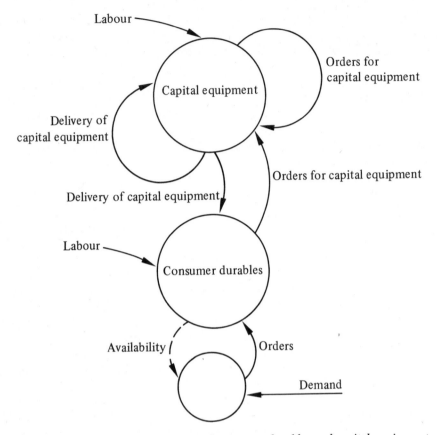

Figure 7.4 *The two-sector structure of consumer durables and capital equipment in Forrester's model*

Source: Forrester (1977: 527), with permission

of some three to seven and 15 to 25 years are generated for the consumer goods sector. The only exogenous input that drives the system is demand for consumer goods, rising at about one per cent per year, on which is superimposed a small, very short-term randomness.

Forrester believes his long wave to be an unstable oscillation. In his model the cycle grows until restrained by a number of non-linearities which constrain ordering, manufacturing, and deliveries. The fundamental causes he sees to be the bootstrap structure around the capital sector, the perception delays in human decision making, and the life of the capital plant. The latter factor is of importance, yet the cycle generated is not an echo wave, for the average life of

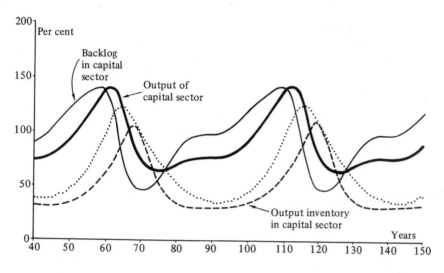

Figure 7.5 *Kondratieff cycle appearing in the capital goods sector*

Source: adapted from Forrester (1975a: 16)

capital equipment in his model is only 15 years. The actual length of the cycle is determined far more by the bootstrap structure of the capital equipment sector, which 'creates the 50-year cycle out of what would otherwise be a 20-year medium cycle in capital acquisition' (Forrester 1977: 534).

How does a typical long wave unfold? Starting from the depression years at the bottom of the cycle, Forrester (1975a: 18) distinguishes the following phases:

(1)   slow growth of the capital sector of the economy;
(2)   gradual decay of the entire capital plant of the economy below the amount required, while the capital sector is unable to supply even replacement needs;
(3)   initial re-circulation of output of the capital sector to its own input whereby the capital sector initially competes with its customers for capital equipment;
(4)   progressive increase in wages and development of labour shortage in the consumer sectors which encourage capital-intensive production and still higher demands for capital equipment;
(5)   over-expansion of the capital sector to a capacity greater than that required for replacement in order to catch up on deferred needs;
(6)   excess accumulation of physical capital by consumer (housing and durables) and by durable manufacturers (plant and equipment);

(7)   developing failure of capital equipment users to absorb the output of over-
        expanded capital sectors;
(8)   sudden appearance of unemployment in the capital sectors;
(9)   relative reduction of labour cost compared to capital to favour a shift back
        to more labour-intensive production which further diminishes the need for
        new plant;
(10)   rapid collapse of the capital sector in the face of demand below the long-
        term average needed by the economy; and
(11)   spreading discouragement and slow decline of excess capital stock through
        physical depreciation.

We do not know what actually goes on in Forrester's long-wave model. The
computer print-outs shown in the various publications about the System Dynamics National Model are not accompanied by a presentation of the mathematical
model itself, not even of a simple version thereof. We therefore have no knowledge of its complexity, the lag structures used, or the values of the various parameters (such as capital and labour productivity, depreciation rate, adjustment
coefficients).

Yet it is quite clear that a long cycle can be generated with the type of two-
sector model used by Forrester. It is essentially a multiplier-accelerator model
with an added specification for the way that the output of the capital equipment
sector is allocated. As this latter sector has to expand first before it can deliver
capital goods to the consumer goods sector, this bootstrap structure amounts to
the specification of a capacity constraint, lengthening the cycle.

Demand for consumer goods, growing at one per cent per annum, reduces
instability and puts a bottom in the economy. Capacity constraints provide the
ceiling. The bootstrap mechanism allows us to distinguish two types of investment: the capital goods produced for the capital equipment sector itself will include the more durable capital goods such as infrastructural investment, transportation, and buildings; those produced for the consumer goods sector will include buildings, but also – and especially – machines and equipment. In a more
elaborate model, the different types of investment activity, along with the factors determining them, could be more precisely distinguished.

An attractive feature of the capital goods explanation of the long wave is its
analogy with the shorter cycles. Volatile inventory investment produces the
short inventory cycle, investment in machines and equipment yields the 'old'
7-11 year business cycle, investment in buildings creates a building cycle, while
infrastructural investment gives rise to a long wave. The differences in length of
the various cycles stem from the difference in average life of the associated
capital goods, from the lag structures governing their production, and from the
lumpiness characterizing the growth of the various capital stocks.

A second attractive feature of the capital goods explanation is the strictly
endogenous character of the cycles it produces. A model that generates divergent

oscillations which are kept in bounds by a capacity ceiling and a floor in demand, without having to rely on exogenous shocks of whatever nature, is attractive indeed. It can explain lower and upper turning points with equal ease, and this is important considering the problems that most long-wave theorists have had with the lower turning point.

A third attraction of this explanation is its simplicity: only a few mathematical equations are needed to demonstrate the workings of the model. Even without assumptions on variations in risk-taking behaviour, expectations, changes in (relative) prices, technological change, or on labour mobility, it can generate cycles in the Kondratieff-range.

Simplicity has both a positive and a negative side. For instance, the super-multiplier-accelerator model assumes synchronized behaviour on the part of the capital goods-acquiring firms. In other words, the model assumes that individual firm behaviour, if aggregated, will yield macro-behaviour of the same form. There are reasons to believe that this assumption is fairly realistic, especially if the role of expectations is brought into the analysis. Firms may expand their productive capacity more or less simultaneously, if that expansion is based on a common economic outlook.

In the case of infrastructural investment, however, another kind of synchronization is needed: i.e. between the private and the public sectors of the economy. Large-scale increases in an economy's industrial and transportation infrastructure will require government action and government funds, and the existence of a long wave in infrastructural investment would assume that governments behave cyclically rather than counter-cyclically. It assumes that they do not manage to expand the economy's infrastructure at an even pace. Whether this assumption is true or not has to be determined on empirical grounds. A second comment on the capital goods explanation relates to the relative size of the capital equipment sector. The output of this sector may well exhibit a long-wave pattern, but are its direct impact and the indirect effects on the economy large enough to produce a macroeconomic long wave? During the age of the railroad the impact may have been large enough to determine macroeconomic growth as such, but can the same be said of the building of a network of motorways during the 20th century? Care should be taken not to underestimate the indirect effects of such investment projects, both in terms of the measurable input-output and Keynesian multiplier effects, as in terms of difficult to measure effects on economic outlook in general. Even so, it is questionable whether this 'basic' investment can be seen as the prime force behind the macroeconomic long wave.

This brings us to a third point. In its simple form, the capital goods explanation is a rather mechanistic explanation of the long wave. The whole area of technological change, with the new production techniques that it brings and the new products and sectors that it spawns, is left out of the analysis. The cycle repeats itself without any impulse from what is widely held to be the fundamental cause of growth: technological change, or better, innovation. Could a pervasive movement, such as the long wave, be explained solely by so simple a mechanism as the multiplier-accelerator model?

While working on his long-wave model, Forrester apparently encountered similar questions. Thus, he states: 'in [Figure 7.5] a long wave is being created without technological change. On the other hand, it seems inescapable that successive upswings in the long wave have embodied different technologies. The explanation appears to lie in the ability of the long wave to bunch technological change into specific time periods' (Forrester 1977: 539). Even though a long wave can be generated in a rather mechanical way, the role of technological change is brought in to add some life to the system.

In a later article, Forrester has stated his position more precisely: 'I do not see innovation as causing the long wave. Rather, I believe that the long wave strongly influences the climate for innovation by compressing technological change into certain time intervals and altering the opportunities for innovation' (Forrester 1979: 32). How exactly innovation is affected by the long wave, which causal relations operate, and whether innovation acts to amplify the long wave, he does not clarify. Yet Forrester too seems to view his own super-multiplier-accelerator as too narrow an explanation for the long wave. Two other economists of the System Dynamics Group at MIT, Graham & Senge (1980) have taken a position similar to that of Forrester. They, too, argue that 'although long waves can be explained without new innovations as an explicit causal factor, the long-wave theory has important implications for innovations.' These authors attempt to integrate Forrester's model with Mensch's depression-trigger hypothesis, but unfortunately fail to see that these two explanations of the long wave are mutually exclusive: either the capital-stock adjustment mechanism causes the downswing to turn into upswing, or innovations overcome depression. Graham and Senge seem to favour the first, Forrester-explanation, when they state: 'As a new upswing begins, investors begin to exploit new technologies that have gone untapped for decades' (Graham & Senge 1980: 309).

There is no doubt that the explanation of long-run investment behaviour has to be an integral part of any theory dealing with the long wave. Both major depressions of the 20th century (post-1929 and post-1973) have been characterized by deficient investment outlays. The boom periods of the 20th century (before 1913 and the 1948-73 episode) saw the contrary: an abundance of investment. Whether or not fluctuations in investment are the ultimate cause of the long wave, they need to be explained.

A SIMPLE LONG WAVE MODEL

Long waves of (infrastructural) investment can be generated by using a simple capital-stock adjustment model. This can be a model with a consumption goods sector and a capital goods sector. One can also follow Forrester's approach by distinguishing two segments of the capital goods sector: one that produces capital goods for the consumption goods sector, and one that produces capital goods to bring the own productive capacity to the desired level. The latter approach is preferable, as it deals more satisfactorily with the way in which capital stocks are built up in growing economies: the consumption goods sector can only expand if the capital goods sector has enough capacity to allow for this expansion. This time sequence can be most clearly exemplified by the way the centrally-planned economies and the newly industrialized countries have grown: they first built up their basic sectors (steel being a prime example), before moving on to (durable) consumer goods.

The model presented in this section is a very simple illustration of this mechanism. It is simple because it focusses on the capital goods sector only, omitting the labour market and the frictions that result from shifting labour resources from one sector to another. It is also simple because, as is the case in all simple capital-stock adjustment models, prices do not play a role. Furthermore, the demand for capital goods stemming from the consumption goods sector is assumed constant. In the long run this implies a zero-growth economy, in which a constant portion of the capital stock of the consumption goods sector has to be replaced each year. Of course, as cycles are generated and the actual output of the capital goods sector changes from year to year, the income-generating effect of investment might be expected to cause fluctuations also in the demand for consumption goods. We do not allow this effect to disturb the even pace at which capital goods are ordered by the consumption goods sector. It might be said that we separate the multiplier from the accelerator: the Keynesian multiplier is not allowed to amplify the cycle caused by the accelerator.

Our model has seven equations:

(1) $P_t^* = \gamma B_t$

(2) $K_t^* = \kappa P_t^*$

(3) $P_t = \text{Min}\,[P_t^*, K_t/\kappa]$

(4) $I_t^k = \text{Max}\,[0, \beta(K_t^* - K_t)]$

(5) $I_t^c = P_t - I_t^k$

(6) $K_{t+1} = K_t + I_t^k - \delta K_t$

(7) $B_{t+1} = B_t + C_t - I_t^c$

Here the variables are defined as follows:

B = order backlog of the consumption goods sector
C = demand for capital goods from the consumption goods sector
I^c = investment goods produced for the consumption goods sector
I^k = investment goods produced for the capital goods sector
K = capital stock of the capital goods sector
K* = desired capital stock
P = production volume of the capital goods sector
P* = desired production
The subscript t denotes time. Each time period represents one year.

Seven of the variables are endogenous; only the eighth, C, is exogenous. Equation (1) relates the desired production of capital goods to the order backlog stemming from past demands from the consumption goods sector. The intention is to work away a fraction γ of that order backlog each year. To fulfill this intention a certain capital stock, K*, is needed. The relation between production and desired capital stock is given by the capital-output ratio, κ (2). Actual production is equal to desired production or, if that desired production requires a larger than existing capacity, by full-capacity output (3). The production of the capital goods sector consists of investment goods, which are delivered to the consumption goods sector, and/or to the capital goods sector. If more capital stock is needed than is actually present, a fraction β of the gap between the two is eliminated (4); if capacity is sufficiently large to meet the needs of the consumption goods sector, all investment output goes to that sector (4 and 5). Whatever is produced is added to the capital stock, or subtracted from the order backlog respectively (6 and 7). The capital stock is depreciated at a rate of 100δ per cent.

Our model can be simulated and solved analytically. The analytical solution, consisting of two parts, is presented first.

Solution A: $P^*_t < K_t/\kappa$ (existing capacity is sufficient to produce the desired investment goods)

If $P^*_t < K_t/\kappa$, then $P_t = P^*_t$ (3). Also, $K^*_t < K_t$, so that $I^k_t = 0$ (4), and $I^c_t = P_t = \gamma B_t$ (5, 3, and 1).
Therefore:
(8) $K_{t+1} = (1-\delta)K_t$, and
(9) $B_{t+1} = (1-\gamma)B_t + C_t$.

In words: the capital sector has excess capacity, which is gradually reduced by depreciating the existing stock by 100δ per cent each year. The order backlog is reduced by a fraction γ, but each year new orders, worth C, are placed. This process will continue until idle capacity has been scrapped to the point where the desired capital stock exceeds actual stock.

Solution B: $P^*_t > K_t/\kappa$ (existing capacity is not sufficient to produce the desired investment goods)

If $P^*_t > K_t/\kappa$, then $P_t = K_t/\kappa$ (3). Also, $K^*_t > K_t$ (2, 3), so that $I^k_t = \beta(K^*_t - K_t)$ (4) and $I^c_t = K_t/\kappa - \beta\kappa\gamma B_t + \beta K_t$ (5, 3, and 1).

Therefore:

(10) $K_{t+1} = (1-\beta-\delta)K_t + \beta\kappa\gamma B_t$

(11) $B_{t+1} = -(1/\kappa+\beta)K_t + (1+\beta\kappa\gamma)B_t + C_t$

Equations (10) and (11) form a system of simultaneous first-order difference equations, which can very easily be solved. The characteristic roots, x_1^- and x_2, can be determined from the equation:

(12) $x^2 - (2-\beta-\delta+\beta\kappa\gamma)x + (1-\beta-\delta+\beta\gamma[1+\kappa-\kappa\delta]) = 0$.

The equilibrium values for K and B, $\bar{K}$ and $\bar{B}$ respectively, assuming $C_t = C_{t+1} = \ldots = C_{t+n}$, are

(13) $\bar{K} = \dfrac{\kappa}{1-\kappa\delta} C$, and

(14) $\bar{B} = \dfrac{\beta+\delta}{\beta\gamma(1-\kappa\delta)} C$.

As an example of a computer simulation run of the model, the following parameter values are used:

$\kappa = 3$
$\delta = .05$
$\beta = .05$
$\gamma = .4$

This means that each year the capital stock is depreciated by five per cent, and that the capital goods sector attempts to produce 40 per cent of the existing backlog. If the desired capital stock exceeds the existing one, however, only five per cent of that gap can be produced each year. The different percentages for β and γ reflect the different nature of investment for the capital goods sector (infrastructural investment) vis-à-vis investment for the consumption goods sector (buildings, machines and equipment).

As initial values were chosen $K_0 = 300$ and $B_0 = 500$. Furthermore, $C_t = C_{t+1} = \ldots = \bar{C}$ was set equal to 100. Figure 7.6 shows a 48-year cycle in output of the capital goods sector. It is a damped cycle, with the equilibrium values being equal to $\bar{K} = 352.94$ (and therefore $\bar{P} = 117.65$), and $\bar{B} = 588.24$. In this particular run, $P^*_t > K_t/\kappa$ for all t, so that the analytical solution B can be applied to determine the equilibrium values as well as the convergent character of the time path (the modulus is less than one) and the cycle length (equalling 48.77 years).

In general, explosive cycles can be generated with higher values for β and γ. A more rapid elimination of the capital stock gap and order backlog will lead to periods in which solution A applies; it will also shorten the cycle.

Models such as this are simple illustrations of a long-wave mechanism. They

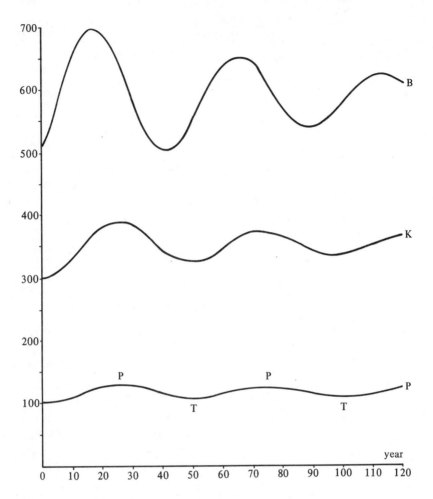

Figure 7.6 *Computer simulation of a long wave*

can be made more elaborate by expanding the consumer goods sector, e.g. by including a feedback from income generated in the capital goods sector, to total
income and therefore to consumption, and to the investment demand originating
from the consumption goods sector. This would have the effect of increasing the
amplitude of the cycle. Also, the capital goods sector can be made more elaborate than it now is. Furthermore, a price mechanism could be included. Extensions such as this have been made by Eelkman Rooda (1978). Moreover, a very
similar model to that presented here has been used by long-wave researchers at
Central Management Services of ICI (Britain).

VIII

INNOVATION, INNOVATION LIFE CYCLES, AND INFRASTRUCTURAL INVESTMENT

Having reviewed the major long-wave theories, we have now arrived at the point where we can present our own explanation of forces which have determined the long-cyclical development of the industrial economies since the Industrial Revolution. Our explanation contains three major building blocks. These are: the concepts of innovation, innovation life cycles, and infrastructural investment. Innovations and the life cycles that emerge from them form the long-wave engine on the output side of the growth process: infrastructural investment required by innovation is an output factor as well as an input factor. It reinforces growth during the upswing and is also a determinant of the supply-side of the economy. We see other variables, which also fluctuate in a long-wave fashion, as dependent variables. That is, we do not see the growth of money supply, the distribution of income over labour and capital, the attitude towards risk taking, or even war and war preparation as autonomous forces. Rather, their fluctuations seem to us to be derived from the forces mentioned earlier.

Our long wave is a long wave in production growth. We attach great theoretical and empirical significance to the Kondratieff price cycle as explained in Rostow's theory (Chapter V), but this cycle and the long wave in production growth are different waves, with different underlying mechanisms and different timing. The two have moved in synchrony during some historical periods but not since World War I.

Let us proceed now by discussing the three building blocks of our long-wave explanation. First of all *innovation*. If the number of major or basic innovations fluctuates over time, there must be fluctuations over time in the strength of innovation-impeding and innovation-promoting factors, all of which may be examined at various levels of aggregation. In Table 8.1 we have summed up a number of innovation-impeding factors, as seen by an *existing firm* with a particular product line. Only innovation-impeding factors are listed, on the assumption that forces which exert a negative influence on innovation will generally be stronger than those with a positive influence This assumption is anything but new, and may frequently be found in the innovation literature. The key argu-

---

A note to this chapter may be found on p. 144.

ment is always the risky nature of innovative behaviour. The risk increases as the innovations to be developed become more novel, differing more strongly from existing products and production processes. This explains why, at any moment, improvement innovations are more likely than basic innovations. Firms cannot reasonably be expected to become involved in the development of fundamentally new products and processes if there is no compelling reason for them to do so.

From Table 8.1 it is possible to derive which conditions are innovation-promoting: a flexible organizational structure, product markets which approach saturation, favourable macroeconomic prospects. Such conditions could reduce resistance to change on the part of existing firms. But even if hindrances to innovation are overcome, three necessary and ever present conditions have to be met: market demand, technological knowledge, and financial means. Of these three conditions the presence of unmet needs, expressed in market demand, is without doubt the most essential.[1]

Apart from the innovation impediments that existing firms have to overcome, a niche in the market is the most important impulse for the establishment of a *new* firm. The presence of technological knowledge is a necessary condition, but not a sufficient one: witness the long time-lags between invention and the moment of introduction of most major innovations (see Chapter X), and also the duplication which has often occurred when the presence of market demand for a new product has become evident.

Financial constraints rarely form a bottleneck factor in the innovation process. Research and development have to be financed, of course, but many innovations reach the market with only a moderate financial input. The financial requirements for innovation have certainly increased over time, but here, too, the priority of market demand reveals itself: it is recognition of demand potential for the innovation to be developed which induces financiers to back a project.

The nature of the wants to be satisfied helps to distinguish innovations which are substitutes for existing products or processes from those which are entirely new consumer or capital goods or production processes. In this context it is perhaps better to speak not of commodities as the relevant variables, but, after Lancaster (1971a), of consumption activities or production activities which require goods and production processes as inputs. The Lancaster approach also demonstrates the arbitrary character of a division between 'new' products on the one hand, and substitutes on the other hand. The meaning of the term 'substitution' can be stretched. For a consumption activity such as 'visiting foreign countries', bicycle, car, train and airplane would certainly be substitutes. They are all means of transportation. But bicycles, cars, trains and airplanes each have a number of strictly unique properties for which no substitutability exists. Television was an innovation because of other unique traits. But an evening spent watching TV can be a substitute for listening to the radio or going to the movies.

Table 8.1 *Reasons for not innovating*

A. *Internal organizational structure of the firm*
   1. Organizational structure   – bureaucratic organization: inflexibility, risk-aversion, resistance to change

B. *Product mix of the firm*
   1. Technology   – indifferent attitude with respect to technological change
    – orientation towards small improvements rather than fundamental research, in view of the lower risks and better short-term payoff of the first
   2. Sales   – rapid growth (growth phase of the life cycle)
   3. Buyers   – resistance to change on the part of buyers
    – low success rate of new products
    – failure to recognize unmet needs
    – lack of articulation of new wants and needs (e.g. by the government)
   4. Market share   – large market share
   5. Market structure   – oligopolistic and monopolistic markets
   6. Costs   – need to protect investments in existing technology
    – costs of research and inquiry
    – switch-over costs
    – costs of financing
   7. Profitability   – high profitability of existing product line

C. *Macroeconomic conditions*
   1. Overall economic outlook   – unfavourable economic environment (as in long-wave depression phases)
    – lack of government support for innovation
   2. Purchasing power   – lack of purchasing power

Innovations will often retain certain characteristics of existing products or processes while adding or improving others. The gyro-compass was in that sense an improvement of the magnetic compass; Gillette's safety razor an improvement of the hitherto used razor; the pneumatic tyre of the solid tyre. As the new product borrows more properties from the old, it is more likely to be called an improvement innovation; also, its sales potential will be more predictable. If new properties predominate in the perception of users, the term basic innovation is more suitable. To launch a basic innovation, however, is a more risky venture.

The main demand impulse behind a basic innovation sometimes lies in the circumstance that the properties of the product are not much different from what is already on the market, but are available at lower cost. It is well-known that improvements of basic innovations are usually cost-reducing; in a few instances, however, cost reduction has been the prime mover behind innovation. The development of synthetic materials such as rayon, bakelite, neoprene (synthetic rubber) and detergents can be explained in this way. War conditions (absolute scarcity due to blockades; autarchic policies) have sometimes speeded-up a particular innovation. If cost reduction is the primary goal, the properties of the new product may be initially inferior to those of its natural counterpart (inflammable rayon versus silk; the first synthetic rubbers). A low price is then the prime demand-creating factor.

The distinction between cost-reducing innovations and property-adding innovations, however, is very often a matter of accentuation. The telephone has certainly reduced the cost of communications, but most people will be inclined to see the telephone in terms of its unique properties (and less as a substitute for other means of communication).

In the above we have been concerned mainly with product innovations. In introducing process innovations, the primary objective is usually to reduce the costs of producing a certain commodity — which itself may be a recent innovation. Whether the innovation is to be labour-saving or capital-saving will be dependent on relative changes in the price of production factors.

Innovation-impeding and promoting factors may differ from firm to firm, and may change over time. There is a considerable body of literature on the relation between innovation and firm size, and on innovation and market structure (on the latter, see e.g. Kamien & Schwartz 1975). Table 8.1 gives a first indication of the variables which play a role in the relation between innovative behaviour and firm size.

Smaller firms usually have the advantage of a more flexible organization and lesser weight of vested interests. Their disadvantages are the usually restricted financial means available for research and development, and their equally restricted technological knowledge. While small firms have fewer impediments to cope with, therefore, it is often more difficult for them to meet the necessary conditions for innovation. Nevertheless, the opinion (with which Schumpeter and Galbraith are associated) that in our day and age the innovation process would be largely confined to large-firm innovation, has not proved correct.

In Chapter II above it has been argued that growth is an S-shaped process. Product innovations, if successful, give rise to such S-shaped curves, i.e. to product life cycles or, in some cases, to industry life cycles. Wherever growth can be traced back to a particular innovation, it is possible to speak of *innovation life cycles*. This concept has been used in earlier publications (Van Duijn 1977b, 1979a), but was developed even earlier by Kuznets (1972: 450-51) who speaks of 'a life-cycle model of a major innovation', and, in a rudimentary form, by Schmookler in an article written in 1967 but published posthumously (Schmookler 1972: 70-84). The life cycle of a major innovation indicates how an innovation develops over time, measured as the output accounted for by that innovation.

Life cycles are usually assumed to be S-shaped, up to their decline phase, with gradually decreasing growth rates of output. While various interpretations and applications of the S-shaped growth curve exist, they can be reduced to two main types: the limited possibilities for further technical improvements given a certain state of technology, versus the limited possibilities for further market penetration given a certain rate of penetration. Both interpretations are applicable to an innovation life cycle, the two aspects usually being interrelated: cost-reducing improvement innovations can increase the rate of penetration of a product; market saturation will be a strong incentive for product improvements in order that a decline in sales can be prevented or postponed. The strongest force, however, would seem to be the market.

The simple four-phases model presented in Chapter II illustrates the course of an innovation life cycle. The phases are characterized by demand structure and type of innovative activity:

Introduction: there are many product innovations as different technological options exist, and little is known about the nature of demand.

Growth: there is increasing acceptance by customers, with a decreasing number of product innovations. Sales growth leads to standardization of technology, and there are cost-reducing process innovations.

Maturity: the output ratio slows down, and competition through product differentiation increases; innovations concern improvements. Process innovations are labour saving.

Decline: declining sales. Attempts are made to escape saturation through changes in technology, and the use of labour-saving process innovations continues.

The decline phase should in fact be considered as an open-ended phase. Absolute decline, resulting in complete replacement, is but one possible course of an innovation following its maturity. Several variations to the standard life cycle pattern exist (Figure 2.3), representing the different ways in which industries may react when faced with saturated markets. From empirical observation, it would appear that very few of the late 19th and early 20th century major innovations have been completely replaced by substitutes. Even those that face prolonged decline are fairly limited. This may imply something about the length of life cycles of major innovations, though it should be realized that population growth has been an important intervening factor, which has increased the size of markets considerably (even in fairly closed economies such as that of the USA).

Little can be said about the length of the various phases of the innovation life cycle. Innovations are too diverse in nature and area of application to allow for generalizations with respect to the length of their lives. Also, market conditions at the time and place of introduction will vary considerably. Compare, for instance, the introduction of television in the USA with the introduction of the motor car. The latter innovation needed an introduction phase of approximately 15 years before the growth phase set in; television sales, on the other hand, reached their peak a few years after introduction. Since 1950, a slightly decreasing trend has even set in. The quick growth to maturity of television can be attributed to pent-up consumer demand which had no outlet during World War II.

Kuznets (1979: 64) mentions a time span of about 20 years for what corresponds roughly to our introduction phase, and much more than 20 years for the diffusion phase, so that, even if the obsolescence phase is disregarded, life cycles tend to be half-a-century or longer. This is obviously a matter which can only be resolved through detailed studies of particular innovations, and by being very specific about geographical market area (should the life cycle of television be studied in the USA or on a world-wide basis?).

Despite our limited knowledge of the duration of innovation life cycles, the question of their length is very important. Innovations contribute to growth, but the size of that contribution will depend, among other things, upon the phase of the life cycle. Insight into the duration of various phases would give us some understanding of the growth potential of an economy.

Innovations could conceivably appear at random, in which case and at any point in time, innovation life cycles would be observable at various stages of development, some in their early phases, others experiencing rapid growth, and still others facing maturity and decline. History shows that this is not quite the case, however. If a narrow definition of innovation is taken, of course, they can at any moment be found in various stages of progress. For basic innovations, however, the story is different. Their rapid growth phases have often developed in synchrony, their combined power giving rise to what we have come to call long-wave expansion phases.

Rostow has used the term 'leading sectors' to express the motor function of basic innovations in their growth phase:

Old sectors may be declining, others may be stagnant, others may be moving forward at about the average rate of industrial production as a whole (like raw material production); but there will be one or more leading sectors, reflecting the introduction of major new technologies, moving ahead more rapidly than the average, absorbing a disproportionate volume of current investment and able entrepreneurs, stimulating requirements to sustain it, and, quite often, bringing about accelerated urban growth in new regions (Rostow 1978: 104-5).

The proposition made here is that a long-wave expansion concurs with, and is determined by, the rapid growth of a number of basic innovation-incorporating sectors. In other words, macroeconomic growth is determined by sectoral growth. This statement may sound trivial, but it is the key towards understanding the long wave. If a number of basic innovations can carry the economy during the growth phases of their life cycles, what will happen when these cycles enter their maturity phase? It would mean that macroeconomic growth would slow down and recession would set in.

In Chapter VI we presented Schumpeter's four-phase cycle (Figure 6.1): prosperity, recession, depression, recovery. That terminology seems appropriate to describe the different phases of a long wave, with three provisos:

1. We agree with Schumpeter that long waves can be divided into Juglars ('business cycles'); however, we would use cycle peaks rather than neighbourhood-of-equilibrium-points as mark-off points.
2. We would not necessarily let one Kondratieff-cycle be equal to six Juglars. The various phases of the long wave could, in our view, last for one or two Juglars. Wars could interrupt the phase sequence.
3. We would view the trend underlying the long wave as an upward one, so that a modified Schumpeter-scheme would result (Figure 8.1), with prosperity and recession together making up the upswing phase, and depression plus recovery the downswing phase of the long wave.

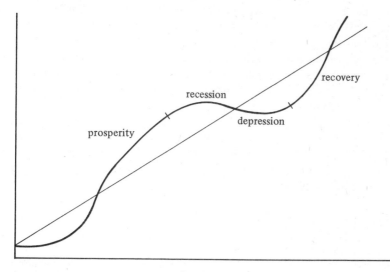

Figure 8.1 *A four-phase long wave with upward trend*

The main macroeconomic characteristics for each phase are summarized in Table 8.2. With this scheme we are running ahead of things. A more complete description and explanation of the four long-wave phases is yet to follow. If the long wave is perceived as a succession of life cycles of leading sectors, it would be tempting to match long-wave phases with life-cycle phases:

— prosperity — growth,
— recession — maturity;
— depression — decline, and
— recovery — introduction.

Table 8.2 *Macroeconomic characteristics of long-wave phases*

Characteristic	Depression	Recovery	Prosperity	Recession
Gross national product	Little or no growth	Increasing growth rates	Strong growth	Decreasing growth rates
Investment demand	Excess capacity; rationalization	Increase in replacement investment	Strong expansion of capital stock	Scale-increasing investment
Consumer demand	For a while continued growth at the expense of savings	Purchasing power seeks new outlets	Expansion of demand in all sectors	Continued growth of new sectors

Although it cannot be denied that periods of prosperity are carried by the strong growth of one or more leading sectors, phases do not coincide so smoothly. An important deviating pattern can be observed: leading sectors can survive macroeconomic depressions (i.e. continue to grow during depressions, albeit at a reduced rate), and resume expansion again during the next upswing. The U.S. motor car and aircraft industries are cases in point: both resumed growth after World War II. Micro-electronics is an innovation-packed sector that continues to grow throughout the present depression.

Major innovation life cycles may therefore be stretched over more than one long wave, but growth rates are not nearly as high 'the second time around'. In the case of the motor car industry, initial demand led to rapid expansion in the 1920s. As this demand became saturated, excess capacity resulted, thus starting a negative multiplier-accelerator effect.

There is therefore no simple match between long wave phase and innovation life cycle phase. Long waves are also caused by fluctuations in industrial infrastructural investment; major innovations, while being diffused at gradually decreasing growth rates, can extend their potential over more than one long wave expansion phase. Yet every expansion phase has coincided with the introduction of new clusters of innovations. What, then, determines the timing of these innovations?

Before attempting to answer this question, a distinction should be made between various types of innovation:
— major product innovations which create new industries;
— major product innovations in existing industries;
— process innovations in existing industries; and
— process innovations in basic sectors (such as steel or oil refining).
To the first category belong such innovations as the motor car, the airplane, radio, synthetic fibres, plastics, or the electronic computer — to name but a few. Their introduction often gave rise to new firms which eventually became industries, although in some instances existing firms have been responsible for prin-

cipal innovations (as in chemicals), with new firms joining in. All these innovations have in common the creation of completely new markets.

The second category contains innovations introduced by firms in answer to the market saturation of their existing product line. Such firms experience strong pressure to innovate in the maturity phase, and even more so in the decline phases of their industry life cycles. Current examples are television production and the gramophone record industry. We assume that, for some industries at least, saturation will coincide with, and partly cause, a long-wave downturn. This would be true at present not only for the two just mentioned, but also for the European car industry, synthetic fibres, and some household durables.

Process innovations that improve the production process in existing industries constitute the third category. These will most likely be a response to two different forces: demand increases pushing firms to increase labour and capital productivity; and cost increases pressuring firms to reduce their requirements for their most expensive input factors (labour, energy).

The final category is formed by innovations in basic sectors, of which steel and oil have so far been the most important. Increased demand will be a strong impetus to innovate in these sectors.

In Table 8.3 we hypothesize how strong the propensity to innovate is likely to be during each of the four phases of the long wave, for each of these four categories of innovations. Major product innovations, which create new industries, are possible during a depression phase. It is much more likely, however, that they will be introduced during the recovery phase, when increasing demand for replacement investment will turn the pessimism of the depression phase into a more optimistic economic outlook. Projects which carry major risks are only undertaken in a favourable economic climate. Prospects are even better during the prosperity phase, although the presence of new growth sectors will make the introduction of still more radical innovations less urgent.

Table 8.3 *The propensity to innovate during different phases of the long wave*

Type of innovation	Depression	Recovery	Prosperity	Recession
Product innovation (new industries)	+	++++	++	+
Product innovation (existing industries)	+++	+++	+	+
Process innovations (existing industries)	+++	+	++	++
Process innovations (basic sectors)	+	++	+++	++

In existing industries, the majority of innovations are likely to be introduced during the depression and recovery phases. These industries can respond more quickly to a long-wave downturn, provided that this coincides with demand saturation for existing products. One reason for this quicker response is that existing industries are more aware of the life cycle phases of their own products; another is that changing the technological base of a product is less risky when it continues to serve the same market (i.e. to meet the same need). As soon as the new generation of products (e.g. gramophones, or records) has gained acceptance by the public, the need for further and more radical product innovations decreases.

Process innovations in existing industries are seen as the reaction to two kinds of forces: market demand increases, and cost increases. While the effects of process innovations are more noticeable during long-wave downturns (through increases in unemployment), these innovations may be implemented equally well during long wave expansion. Innovations in basic sectors (oxygen steel making, catalytic cracking) usually occur as responses to final demand increases. Demand-induced innovations in producer goods sectors will be mainly introduced during long wave expansion.

As Table 8.3 shows, the overall propensity to innovate is highest during the recovery phase, and lowest during the recession phase. It also illustrates the contradiction that is apparent in present discussions on innovation. On the one hand, the lack of innovation is emphasized (as witnessed by the many government memoranda on the subject); on the other hand, expressions such as 'the chip revolution' and the 'information explosion' suggest an abundance of innovations. Table 8.3 shows both: there is indeed a lack of (employment-creating) product innovations in new sectors, but there is equally no lack of (labour-saving) process innovations in existing sectors. The table offers a stylized picture of the propensity to innovate as determined by meso- and macroeconomic factors. In reality, of course, several other forces affect this propensity. War conditions, for instance, have historically been a major force in bringing about innovations and this should be borne in mind when confronting the hypotheses of Table 8.3 with empirical evidence.

This explanation of the long wave needs to be completed with an assessment of the role of infrastructural investment. Innovation life cycles show how growth can slow down because of demand saturation, but we have also seen that some innovations continue to prosper during depression. There must therefore be something more in the macroeconomic conditions which causes prolonged depression; something which could not be overcome by, say, the radio, rayon and aircraft industries in the 1930s or the micro-electronic industries in the 1970s. That 'something more' is the alternation of capital-hungry and capital-sated periods, to use Colin Clark's words, an alternation which leaves strong marks on the economy.

In Chapter VII two kinds of infrastructural investment have been distinguished: one which more directly serves the growth of leading sectors, in the form of industrial complexes, harbour complexes and the like; and another which provides the transportation and communication infrastructure for the economy as a whole. When innovation life cycles enter their growth phase, demand for both categories of infrastructural investment will increase, output in the first responding rather more quickly than output in the second. Long-wave prosperity phases will therefore be characterized by rapid leading-sector growth as well as by rapid infrastructural investment growth. The only force which will slow down overall output growth is productive capacity constraint. Resources have to be mobilized; they also have to be diverted to those sectors which need them. During the recession phase the economy's infrastructure will approach completion, but the multiple lags that are characteristic of investment projects of long duration will make overshooting likely.

Projections of future demand for infrastructure will be based on an extrapolation of the prosperity phase. It is not recognized that growth in this phase is much higher than average growth over a complete long wave. As far as the role of infrastructural investment is concerned, therefore, the seeds of depression are sown during prosperity. Sector-related infrastructural investment during the recession phase will be scale-enlarging investment. Economies of scale are striven after in an attempt to solve the problem of retardation of growth of market demand on the one hand, and increasing (labour-)costs on the other hand. If firms become engaged in a race to increase their market share by being the first to reduce unit costs, the outcome of that race will be excess capacity.

The immediate cause of the long-wave downturn should be sought in the volatility of investment behaviour rather than in the saturation of markets. Saturation is a gradual process. It explains why economies, once in depression, do not recover quickly. But it cannot by itself explain a downturn. A complete explanation of the long wave therefore has to rely on the interplay of innovation life cycles and infrastructural investment. Investment behaviour is very much determined by expectation. Once expectations change, whether for real reasons (e.g. because it becomes abundantly clear that overcapacity is in the making) or for imagined reasons, it is difficult to turn them around. The downturn may take on the appearance of a crisis (stock market crash, oil crisis); however, this should not be mistaken for the cause of the downturn.

The ensuing depression will tend to prolong itself. Initially, it may seem that the economy will be able to work itself out of it very quickly, but gradually it will become evident that time is necessary in which to dispose of excess capacity. It will also become obvious that the former bunch of growth industries has too limited a potential for the future. In such an unfavourable economic environment the propensity to innovate will be low. In the same way that prosperity was extrapolated to give too rosy a future, depression will now be extrapolated to make the economic outlook unnecessarily gloomy. Governments, by nature slow to react, may well be instrumental in prolonging a depression. While they have the means to shorten it, their tactics are likely to be too dilatory. Nevertheless, each time a depression occurs the government will be called upon to provide a way out.

Investment behaviour could be seen as the immediate cause of the downturn; in the absence of any aggressive innovation-promoting government strategy, investment behaviour will also have to provide the incentive for recovery. The day will come when excess capacity will be eliminated, and even if new growth industries are lacking, the existing infrastructure will need to be renewed. The basic industries may then take the lead, giving rise to what might be called a 'technical' recovery. In itself, this cannot sustain prolonged macroeconomic growth, but the important function of the investment surge is that it will change the overall economic outlook, thus removing hindrances to innovation, and paving the way for a new cluster of growth industries.

A full explanation of the long wave therefore has to include an assessment of the important role of infrastructural investment, but it must also include recognition of the role of major innovations. The long-lasting prosperity of the past would not have been possible without leading sectors to carry the expansion; depression would have been less drastic and severe if the traditional large falls in investment had not occurred.

We have by-passed several variables which also move in a long-wave fashion. They include labour's share of income, and therefore also the profit share of income. In the 20th century, income distribution is determined much more by institutional forces than it was in the last century. This entails that actual changes in the income distribution will follow macroeconomic developments with a considerable lag. Therefore, labour's share will go up during depression – an increase that will also reflect the reduced profitability of existing product lines. During the recovery the labour share will fall, as a result of the view that is then generally accepted that the profit share has to go up in order to finance investment projects. The increase of the profit share will continue during the prosperity phase. Then wage demands will begin to catch up, actual wage increases will start to outstrip productivity increases, and the profit share will start on its long-wave decline phase. In short: profit and wage shares are determined by the varying profitability of innovations in the course of an innovation life cycle, and by the lagged response of wages to macroeconomic development.

Unemployment is another variable with a long-wave time pattern. When at its long-wave peak, unemployment is the clearest and starkest signal of depression. Its fluctuations result from the interaction of two forces: on the output side the expansion and contraction of demand; on the input side the change in relative costs of labour, capital and energy. Employment will increase during the introduction and growth phases of a typical innovation life cycle, as improvement innovations cause the quality of a product to go up and its cost to go down. Product volume increases and so does employment. As the life of a growth sector progresses, additional innovations increasingly become labour-saving process innovations, partly in reaction to wage increases which outlast productivity increases. Wage demands which exceed the productivity standard will eventually create unemployment. Unemployment will be at its lowest during late prosperity; it will be at its highest during the later years of the depression phase.

With respect to price changes and the money supply, our view is that of an agnostic. Rostow's view of the causes of the Kondratieff price cycle is a significant one, and we agree that capacity changes in agriculture and raw materials may be at the root of long price cycles, which need not be synchronous with output growth cycles. With regard to the role of money supply, we are convinced that long waves are not a monetary phenomenon, even though actual output growth and especially the severity of fluctuations may well be affected by fluctuations in money supply.

Our interpretation of the long wave is summarized in Table 8.4. Table 8.5 shows a long-wave chronology which, as far as the second, third and fourth Kondratieff are concerned, has been derived from industrial production data for the United Kingdom, the United States, Germany and France (the core countries, as they are sometimes called), and from estimates of world industrial production (see Chapter IX). We have added a first Kondratieff to this table but, as Chapter IX will show, British industrial production data (the only reliable data available for that period) provide no support for the existence of a first long wave in production. While the Napoleonic Wars may have created a price cycle, it has not been possible to establish a cycle in industrial production growth. Our attitude with respect to this first industrial long wave is therefore one of agnosticism: perhaps the wave would show up in world output data, and perhaps not.

The prosperity phases in our chronology have lasted for two Juglars, while the length of the other three phases has historically been limited to one Juglar only. This is not the result of some a priori consideration but of experience, which shows that prosperity phases, during which the leading sectors of a particular long wave are in the growth phase of their life cycle, have lasted approximately 20 years. Another six to ten years may be added for the recession phase, when growth sectors are reaching maturity. It may well be that the time in which basic innovations are absorbed will become shorter in future. In the past, however, expansions have lasted about a quarter-of-a-century, if not interrupted by war. Downswings have historically lasted about 20 years, with the depression covering some eight to 11 years. The length of the current depression phase may well fall within this range.

Table 8.4 *A summary of characteristics of long-wave phases*

Characteristics	Depression	Recovery	Prosperity	Recession
Gross national product	little or no growth	increasing growth rates	strong growth	decreasing growth rates
Investment demand	excess capacity; rationalization investment; unfavourable economic outlook	increase in replacement investment; start-up of new sectors	strong expansion of capital stock; emphasis on infrastructural investment	scale-increasing investment; gradual shift towards rationalization
Consumer demand	for a while continued growth at the expense of savings	purchasing power seeks new outlets	expansion of demand in all sectors	continued growth of new sectors
Propensity to innovate:				
Product innovation (new industries)	+	++++	++	+
Product innovation (existing industries)	+++	+++	+	+
Process innovations (existing industries)	+++	+	++	++
Process innovations (basic sectors)	+	++	+++	++
Employment	massive unemployment due to rationalization and stagnating demand	unemployment rates going down as replacement investment and new product demand goes up	(near) full employment, as leading-sector growth affects economy at large	increase in unemployment because of labour displacement
Labour's share in national income	going up as real wage increases outstrip productivity increases	going down as high unemployment brings down wage demands	going down during early prosperity, then going up again	going up, as real wage increases outstrip productivity increases
Market structure	monopolistic and oligopolistic market structure; high bankruptcy rate	new markets with few competitors are shaping up	competitive markets during early prosperity, then concentration	diversification mergers

Long waves are an *international* phenomenon. As we shall show in Chapter IX, long waves are more visible in international production data than in those of individual countries. The reason is simple: national economies have their own

Table 8.5 *A long-wave chronology*

1st Kondratieff	2nd Kondratieff	3rd Kondratieff	4th Kondratieff
Prosperity 1782-1792	prosperity 1845-56	prosperity 1892-1903	prosperity 1948-57
Prosperity 1792-1802	prosperity 1856-66	prosperity 1903-1913	prosperity 1957-66
(war 1802-1815)		(war 1913-1920)	
Recession 1815-1825	recession 1866-72	recession 1920-1929	recession 1966-73
Depression 1825-1836	depression 1872-83	depression 1929-1937	depression 1973-
Recovery 1836-1845	recovery 1883-92	recovery 1937-1948	

'life cycle of development'. Depending on their take-off date, countries may perform strongly during depression (as do newly industrialized countries such as Taiwan and South Korea during the present depression), or they may do rather poorly during a long-wave expansion (as did the two oldest industrialized countries, i.e. the UK and the USA during the 1948-73 upswing). In the world economy as a whole, the effects of extra rapid and extra slow growth cancel each other out, but the fundamental causes of long waves remain. Over the years, basic innovation life cycles have become international phenomena. This applies also to the build-up of infrastructure, where the relevant variables are worldwide stocks and capacities rather than national stocks. This may explain why so far we have failed to demonstrate the existence of a first industrial production long wave. British data do not show a marked slowdown between 1825 and 1845, but the British industrial economy was then young and vigorous, capable of outgrowing the downswing, just as the U.S. economy to some extent outgrew the second Kondratieff downswing (still a reason for some scepticism with respect to the long wave on the part of U.S. economists). The fact is that we lack reliable evidence to show that the 'world' economy was depressed after 1825, although some European countries (e.g. France) were certainly in such a state.

The long wave is but one of many forces which determine the actual performance of an economy, but it is a very fundamental one. Our reading of history is that it is gaining in importance, as national economies become more and more interwoven. The shortening of transportation and communication channels makes the world the relevant area for most growth markets, rather than an individual country. In that respect, the worldwide competition for micro-electronics gives some indication of what is to come in the decades ahead. More countries will be going up and down together than in the past. This is the result of the realignment brought about by the fourth Kondratieff upswing. Increased international trade has given rise to greater wealth; it also will bring stronger fluctuations. Despite the degree of freedom which each industrialized country will retain, no one will be able to escape the impact of the long wave entirely.

NOTE

1   For a critical review of empirical studies supporting the demand-pull view, see Mowery &
Rosenberg (1979).

PART III

EMPIRICAL EVIDENCE

IX

LONG WAVES IN PRODUCTION

FLUCTUATIONS IN INDUSTRIAL PRODUCTION

If one thinks of long waves as being generated by clusters of basic innovations which create new industries and cause long expansions in the production of capital goods, the Kondratieff cycle should manifest itself first of all in the development of the *index of industrial production*. National income or product is less adequate as a measure, since it contains other components besides industrial production (e.g. agriculture, trade, domestic services), the development of which is not quite clear in a long wave context. In addition, valuation problems are most severe with national product or income. Ideally, the industrial production series should be transformed into series on a per capita basis in order to neutralize the effects of internal population growth and migration (e.g. the pre-1920 transatlantic migration waves!).

Another problem which has to be coped with is that of trend elimination. If there is a secular movement of higher order than the Kondratieff, it must be the S-shaped life cycle of economic development of Rostow's stage theory (Rostow 1960). The long-term economic development of a country cannot be expected to be represented adequately by a constant rate of growth. If a particular country's take-off occurs during the expansion phase of a particular Kondratieff, the same high rates of growth should not be expected to recur in the next Kondratieff. This implies that to fit a log-linear trend to an industrial production time series will typically not yield a Kondratieff-cycle in the residuals.

Take the case of Great Britain, for instance. If a log-linear trend is fitted to Hoffmann's industrial production index for Britain over the 1700-1950 interval (Hoffmann 1955), only two turning-points result: a trough around 1782 and a peak around 1873. This is an interesting result, both in terms of the long wave hypothesis and in terms of Rostow's stages theory: the years around 1782 can be regarded as the beginning of the first Kondratieff and as the time at which the British economy took off; 1873 marks the upper turning-point of the second Kondratieff and the completion of Britain's drive to maturity.

Whether the addition of a quadratic term to the log-linear equation will solve

---

Notes to this chapter may be found on p. 172.

this problem is questionable; the results will be affected by the nature of the time period covered. Our experience is that the pattern of residuals is very sensitive to the trend assumption that is made. It is not difficult to find the low values of the Durbin-Watson coefficients, but the blocks of negative and positive residuals are situated differently from case to case. In terms of $\bar{R}^2$ it is difficult to prefer one trend specification to another, while the combination of empirical and theoretical knowledge indicates only that there is no reason to prefer a log-linear trend to any other trend specification. If it is still intended to use a log-linear trend to test for the existence of a long-wave pattern, other requirements must be imposed. A procedure which presumes log-linear trend estimation, is presented in Appendix D to this chapter.

Next there is the problem of the long wave turning points. There are a few on which virtually all authors agree: those around 1848, 1873, and 1896, but others are subject to debate. Should 1913 or 1920 or 1929 mark the end of the third Kondratieff upswing? Did the first Kondratieff turn down in 1815 or in 1825? The reason these turning points are debated lies in the varying behaviour of price series and physical production series. Prices fell after 1815 and after 1920, but these declines followed war-related price increases and should not be seen as indications of an economic slowdown, but as adjustments to more normal price levels.

Similarly, going by price movements alone would produce an upswing phase which started in 1932 and is still continuing. Such a result would deny both the previous and the current depression. Rostow (1978) has interpreted price changes since 1932 in relative terms by arguing that 1951-72 were years of falling raw material prices which, in his theory, make this an interval of Kondratieff contraction. Innovation and investment theories of long waves, however, should focus on real production series and not derive turning points from price series, certainly not from 20th century price series.

But how, then, are turning points determined? They are clearly needed in order to demonstrate that periods of growth acceleration and retardation have alternated since the Industrial Revolution. Turning points mark the transition from rapid to slow growth and vice versa. One way by which this problem of periodization may be approached, without prejudging the issue, is to divide the time that has elapsed since the Industrial Revolution into Juglars, i.e. into investment cycles of 7-11 years in length. By measuring the average annual growth rate of industrial production for each of these Juglars, it is possible to determine whether the hypothesized acceleration and retardation of growth has indeed occurred, and the extent to which the Kondratieff periods thus found conform with those mentioned in the literature. In Schumpeter's view a Kondratieff cycle consisted of six Juglars, but there is no theoretical reason why Kondratieffs should not last for five or seven Juglars. In fact, we shall argue later that five Juglars is a more likely length for a Kondratieff cycle than Schumpeter's six. The

Table 9.1 *Juglar peak years for Great Britain and the United States*

Great Britain			United States		
1782	1857	1920		1856	1920
1792	1866	1929		1864	1929
1802	1873	1937		1873	1937
1815	1883	1948		1882	1948
1825	1890	1956		1895	1957
1836	1903	1965	1836	1903	1966
1845	1913	1973	1845	1913	1973

length of a Juglar can be measured in two ways: from trough to trough, or from peak to peak. For purposes of calculating growth rates, peak to peak measurement is most appropriate, since output peaks are bound by capacity constraints, while troughs may occur at various degrees of under-utilization of capacity. Table 9.1 lists Juglar peak years for Great Britain and the United States. In the literature all these years are recognized as major business cycle peaks – as opposed to peaks of the minor or inventory cycle – although there is some debate as to whether 1907 rather than 1903 should be seen as the culmination of the business cycle expansion which started in 1895/96 (see Hansen 1964).

Schumpeter's long waves consisted of four phases: prosperity, recession, depression and recovery, and Juglars might be labelled accordingly. Obviously, if a Kondratieff cycle lasts for five or six Juglars, one or two of these phases would cover two rather than one Juglar. In fact, prosperity periods caused by the establishment of new leading sectors, have historically lasted two Juglar cycles, before a minor slowdown (recession) has set in. In addition, major wars have interrupted growth during long wave expansions, causing long waves to extend to six Juglars. It should be emphasized, however, that there are no theoretical arguments which compel us to set the length of 'normal' Kondratieff cycles as equal to five Juglars. Their length depends entirely on the nature of the major innovations responsible for the expansion phases, and on the nature of the infrastructural investment needed to accommodate these innovations.

Assuming, for the time being, five Juglars to a long wave, the following hypothesis with respect to the course of Juglar growth rates γ could be formulated:

$$\gamma_{P_1} > \gamma_{P_2} > \gamma_R > \gamma_D ,$$
$$\gamma_D < \gamma_r , \qquad\qquad (1a)$$
$$\gamma_r < \gamma_{P_1} \text{ (next Kondratieff)}$$

Here, the subscripts indicate the different Kondratieff phases: P = prosperity; R = recession; D = depression; and r = recovery. Taking into account the long time lag by which the production of (basic) capital reacts to innovation impulses, an alternative hypothesis might be:

$$\gamma_{P_1} < \gamma_{P_2},$$
$$\gamma_{P_2} > \gamma_R > \gamma_D, \tag{1b}$$
$$\gamma_D < \gamma_r,$$
$$\gamma_r < \gamma_{D_1} \text{ (next Kondratieff)}$$

Hypotheses (1a) and (1b) state that Juglar growth rates change in time according to a long-wave pattern, with the growth rates of the first and/or second prosperity-Juglar *ex hypothesi* exceeding those of the subsequent recession- and depression-Juglars, and also exceeding those of the preceding depression- and recovery-Juglars. A test of this hypothesis will have to show whether a long-wave pattern in growth rates actually exists.

Let us turn now to the empirical record. Below, average annual growth rates of industrial production are presented for the four core countries of the 19th century industrial world: Great Britain, the United States, France and Germany. In addition, available estimates of world industrial production have been used to calculate growth rates for the whole industrialized world. Peak years may differ from country to country (as Table 9.1 has already shown). In the case of the four core countries, we have used business cycle chronologies to determine peak years (see, e.g. Burns & Mitchell 1946 for reference dates); world industrial production peaks have directly been determined by looking at output fluctuations. Average annual growth rates have been calculated by applying the compound growth rate formula. In this way, only output data for (initial and terminal) peak years are required.

First of all the series for Great Britain (Table 9.2). Two sources were employed: Hoffmann (1955) referring to Great Britain, and Feinstein (1976) referring to the United Kingdom. For the years between 1857 and 1929, Feinstein's series show a clear pattern of declining and increasing rates of growth. The Great Depression of the 1930s, however, does now show up in the British data. Postwar developments are as expected, with decreasing rates during each subsequent Juglar. A completion of the post-1973 Juglar (in 1984?) will not change this picture.

A comparison of Feinstein's and Hoffmann's growth rates shows rather remarkable differences, which can hardly be attributed to the difference in area covered (United Kingdom as opposed to Great Britain). At any rate, they call for some caution in the interpretation of outcomes based on such historical series. Considering the whole time span between 1782 and 1948, the overwhelming impression is one of gradually decreasing growth rates, an impression which would not conflict with the notion of the S-shaped life cycle of economic development. If industrial production is split into consumer goods and producer goods, a long-wave pattern can be recognized in the latter. Those who claim that the long wave is the result of fluctuations in the production of producer goods can trace these fluctuations in the fourth column of Table 9.2. The historical

Table 9.2 *Juglar growth rates, Great Britain, 1782-1979*

Juglar	Ind. prod.[a]	Ind. prod.[b]	Cons. goods[c]	Prod. goods[d]
1782-1792		4.8	5.0	3.1
1792-1802		2.4	2.2	3.0
1802-1815		2.1	2.1	2.1
1815-1825		3.9	3.8	4.2
1825-1836		3.7	3.7	3.8
1836-1845		3.3	2.9	4.0
1845-1857		3.3	2.3	5.0
1857-1866	3.2	2.1	1.0	3.7
1866-1873	2.3	3.6	3.5	3.7
1873-1883	2.2	2.0	1.0	3.3
1883-1890	1.6	1.3	1.4	1.2
1890-1903	1.8	1.3	0.9	1.6
1903-1913	2.3	2.6	2.1	3.0
1913-1920	-0.0	-1.4	-0.8	-1.9
1920-1929	2.8	1.7	0.8	2.6
1929-1937	3.3	2.7	1.6[e]	1.0[e]
1937-1948	1.2	0.8		
1948-1956	3.7			
1956-1965	3.2			
1965-1973	2.5			
(1973-1979	-0.6)			

a Total industrial production, in Feinstein (1976); plus own computations (1965-79).
b Total industrial production, excluding building, in Hoffmann (1955).
c Industrial production, consumer goods industries, in Ibidem.
d Industrial production, producer goods industries, in Ibidem.
e Period 1929-35.

Source: S.K. Kuipers & G.J. Lanjouw (eds): *Prospects of Economic Growth*, Chapter 20. Reproduced with permission.

development of British industrial production, however, as represented by Hoffmann's index, provides only meagre support for the long wave hypothesis. For one thing, a depression phase in the first Kondratieff (1782-1845) is lacking. After the war-Juglar of 1802-15, growth recovered and only gradually decreased during following Juglars. This lack of a depression between 1825 and 1845 is due to the railway boom. In Phyllis Deane's words: 'If there was a period when the rate of capital formation shifted up at all sharply, it was in the railway age, i.e. in the period between 1830 and 1850. This was when the community built up its basic overhead capital, its essential infrastructure' (Deane 1973: 200). The expansion of the two leading sectors of the Industrial Revolution, cotton textiles and iron, was not followed by a period of slowdown. Instead, railroadization took over in the 1830s, giving rise to the railway age which can be seen as a continuation of the Industrial Revolution. After the 1845-57 Juglar producer goods growth rates decreased, only to rise again briefly at the beginning of the 20th century.

The extended nature of the British Industrial Revolution becomes even clearer if annual growth rates are calculated for what are commonly held to be the Kondratieff upswing and downswing periods. The following sequence then results:

| 1782-1825 | 3.2 | 1845-1873 | 3.0 | 1890-1913 | 1.9 |
| 1825-1845 | 3.5 | 1873-1890 | 1.7 |

The 1825-45 growth rate, which should be lower than both preceding and following upswing growth rates, proves to be the highest of any 19th century Kondratieff period.

It would seem fitting, then, to forget about a first Kondratieff in Great Britain. Price decreases in the second quarter of the 19th century were not matched by a slowdown in industrial production growth. Britain, the first country to industrialize, expanded for over 90 years, then slowed down. From 1873 onwards its industrial production has followed the international rhythm (see Table 9.5).

Table 9.3 *Juglar growth rates, United States, 1864-1979*

Juglar	Ind. prod.[a]	Manuf. prod.[b]	Per capita GNP[c]
1864-1873	6.2	5.8	
1873-1882	5.8	5.6	
1882-1895	4.0	3.9	
1895-1903	6.4	5.7	2.8
1903-1913	5.3	4.9	1.8
1913-1920	3.1 ⎫ 4.0		-0.4 ⎫ 1.3
1920-1929	4.8 ⎭		2.7 ⎭
1929-1937	0.4		-0.7
1937-1948	5.0 ⎫ 4.8		3.1 ⎫ 2.8
1948-1957	4.4 ⎭		2.3 ⎭
1957-1966	5.3		2.4
1966-1973	3.9		2.3
(1973-1979	2.8)		

a   Industrial production index (NBER and FRB) in US Dept. of Commerce (1973), plus Survey of Current Business, US Dept. of Commerce for years after 1970.
b   Index of production for manufacture, in Frickey (1947).
c   Per capita GNP, 1958 prices, in US Dept. of Commerce (1975).

Source: as Table 9.2.

The next country to consider is the United States (Table 9.3). The industrial production index clearly shows a pattern of increasing and decreasing growth rates. Trough rates are reached in the 1880s and again in the 1930s. In addition to long wave fluctuations, the U.S. sequence exhibits a gradual slowdown of growth, similar to the British. Frickey's series (in the second column) confirms the pattern found in the first column, but is too short. In the column showing the growth of per capita GNP a clear Kondratieff pattern is discernible. For testing purposes, however, industrial production should be preferred to GNP. The third column is therefore included only because it gives per capita data.

The French series of Juglar growth rates (Table 9.4) shows a depression (1824-36), followed by railroadization. The 1856-66 growth rate is an anomaly, but from then on a very clear Kondratieff pattern unrolls.

Table 9.4 *Juglar growth rates, France (1815-1979) and Germany (1850-1979)*

France Juglar	Ind. prod.[a]	Germany Juglar	Ind. prod.[b]
1815-1824	1.4		
1824-1836	0.5		
1836-1847	2.3		
1847-1856	2.8	(1850-1857	3.4)
1856-1866	0.6	1857-1866	3.9
1866-1872	2.1	1866-1872	5.9
1872-1882	1.9	1872-1882	1.2
1882-1890	0.4	1882-1890	5.0
1890-1903	1.6	1890-1903	3.8
1903-1913	3.5	1903-1913	4.4
1913-1920	-6.7 ⎫ 1.4	1913-1920 ⎫ 1.1	
1920-1929	8.1 ⎭	1920-1929 ⎭	
1929-1937	-2.6	1929-1937	3.0
1937-1948	0.3		
1948-1957	6.6	1948-1957	15.4
1957-1966	6.1	1957-1966	5.8
1966-1973	5.8	1966-1973	5.2
(1973-1979	2.1)	(1973-1979	1.5)

a   Mitchell (1975); plus *Annuaire Statistique de la France* (INSEE) for postwar years.
b   Mitchell (1975); plus *Statistisches Jahrbuch für die Bundesrepublik Deutschland* for postwar years.

Source: as Table 9.2.

The picture for Germany (Table 9.4) shows other peculiarities. High growth rates until 1872, a depression-Juglar, but then a resumption of growth. In Germany, as in Britain, the 1929-37 growth rate is higher than that of the preceding Juglar. In Hitler's Germany, war preparations quickly undid the production decline of the depression.

So far the four core countries have been examined, but what if they are lumped together? Irregularities might disappear and a clearer picture of international long waves could emerge. Even better: we could employ estimates of total *world* production. There are a number of such aggregate measures. Lewis (1952) developed indices of world production and trade for 1870-1950 and 1881-1950 respectively; Lewis (1978) constructed an index of industrial production for the four core countries during the 1865-1913 interval. Kuczynski (1980) presents indices of industrial production and agricultural production, 1859-1976. Rostow (1978) gives composite indices for world industrial production, 1700-1971, and the volume of world trade, 1720-1971, though with only a few benchmark years. Finally, Maddison (1977) has calculated year to year, percentage changes in aggregate GDP of 16 capitalist countries. Juglar growth rates, derived from these sources, are presented in Table 9.5.

The results are striking. *What emerges from this table is a near-perfect long-wave pattern*: peak growth (1866-72), followed by depression (1872-83), recovery (1883-92) and new prosperity (1892-1903 and 1903-13). Then the interruption of war and renewed growth (1920-29), followed by the Great Depression of the 1930s and World War II. After the war, strong growth continued up to 1973.

Table 9.5 *Juglar growth rates, aggregate industrial production and GDP*

Juglar	World ind. prod.[a]	Idem, excl. USSR[b]	16 capitalist countries[c]	4 core countries[d]
(1850-1856	7.6)			
1856-1866	2.8			
1866-1872	4.5			4.3
1872-1883	2.7	2.8	2.4	3.2
1883-1892	3.4	3.3	2.7	3.1
1892-1903	4.3	4.2	2.9	3.5
1903-1913	4.1	4.0	3.0	3.6
1913-1920	−1.0 ⎫		0.3	
1920-1929	5.1 ⎭	2.8	3.8	
1929-1937	1.6	1.4	1.3	
1937-1948	1.8	2.9[e]	1.8	
1948-1957	5.9		4.8	
1957-1966	5.9		4.8	
1966-1973	5.1		4.8	

a   Industrial production, world economy, in Kuczynski (1980).
b   World production manufactures (incl. USA, excl. USSR), in Lewis (1952).
c   Aggregate GDP of 16 capitalist countries, in Maddison (1977).
d   Industrial production core countries (USA, Great Britain, Germany, France), in Lewis (1978).
e   1937-1950.

Note: Average annual growth rates are compounded rates, measured from Juglar peak to Juglar peak, except in series for 16 capitalist countries, where arithmetical averages of year-to-year growth rates are given.

What makes these findings especially valuable is that they demonstrate that the national peculiarities of the four core countries are precisely that: national peculiarities. Great Britain, the USA, Germany and France each have their own histories, in which the S-shaped life cycle of economic development may be more conspicuous than long wave fluctuations. The industrialized world as a whole, or even the four core countries taken together, moves forward along a long wave path.

It is now possible to present, with a fair amount of confidence, a long wave

chronology which starts in the middle of the 19th century. For the years preceding 1845, there is little indication of a major depression which should have
followed the first stage of the Industrial Revolution. For the quarter-of-a-
century following 1845 few data are available with which to confirm growth
rates based on the Kuczynski-index. Yet, with due allowance for negative effects
on world production stemming from the American Civil War, the long wave
chronology, presented in Table 9.6 could well be defended with the data available.[1] As Table 9.6 shows, we dismiss the first Kondratieff altogether.

Table 9.6 *A long wave chronology of world industrial production*

Juglar	2nd Kondratieff	3rd Kondratieff	4th Kondratieff
Prosperity 1	1845-1856	1892-1903	1948-1957
Prosperity 2	1856-1866	1903-1913	1957-1966
(war)		1913-1920	
Recession	1866-1872	1920-1929	1966-1973
Depression	1872-1883	1929-1937	1973-
Recovery	1883-1892	1937-1948	

With the long wave chronology thus obtained, hypotheses (1a) and (1b) can
now be tested with a small sample sign test, based on the binomial distribution.
World production series should do well in such a test, individual country series
are expected to do less well. Counting the number of correct order relations
between adjacent Juglars in Tables 9.2-9.5 the following right-hand tail cumulative binomial probabilities hold for $\pi = 0.5$:[2]

	(1a)	(1b)
United Kingdom, Feinstein	.1937	.1937
	(8 of 12)	(8 of 12)
Great Britain, Hoffmann	.9104	.9104
	(3 of 9)	(3 of 9)
United States, NBER/FBR	.1134	.1134
	(8 of 11)	(8 of 11)
France	.0461	.1334
	(10 of 13)	(9 of 13)
Germany	.2745	.1134
	(7 of 11)	(8 of 11)
World ind. prod., Kuczynski	.0059	.0328
	(10 of 11)	(9 of 11)
World ind. prod., Lewis	.0156	0.1094
	(6 of 6)	(5 of 6)
16 capitalist countries, Maddison	0.0899	0.0196
	(7 of 9)	(8 of 9)

Cumulative probabilities of less than five per cent are only found for the
world production series of Kuczynski and Lewis (hypothesis 1a), and for the
Kuczynski and Maddison series (in case of hypothesis 1b). All individual country

series fail to pass this sign test with the exception of France (hypothesis 1a). One problem with these series is that they are rather short. At $\pi = 0.50$ one miss out of six signs (as in the test of hypothesis 1b for the Lewis-series) already has a probability of 11 per cent. Nevertheless, this statistical test confirms that *world industrial production follows a long wave pattern*: a pattern which cannot convincingly be found in the industrial production series of our four core countries, with the exception of France.

So far we have spelled-out Kondratieff waves with a fair amount of detail: five or six Juglars, and four different phases. Most long wave economists, however, have only distinguished upswing and downswing phases. The simple requirement then is that the average growth rate of a downswing phase is lower than that of preceding and following upswing phases. In Table 9.7 we have summarized the development of industrial production for a number of countries in these terms. Only the third Kondratieff expansion has been split into two parts, before and after World War I. In Table 9.8 the same is done for total output, with the use of Maddison's (1977) data. Growth rates are again calculated from initial and terminal Juglar peak years. Individual country phases may differ because of Juglar peak differences.

Table 9.7 *Long wave upswing and downswing growth rates, industrial production*

	United Kingdom		United States		Germany[a]	
2nd Kondratieff						
Upswing	1845-1873	3.0	(1864-1873	6.2)	(1850-1872	4.3)
Downswing	1873-1890	1.7	1873-1895	4.7	1872-1890	2.9
3rd Kondratieff						
Upswing	1890-1913	2.0	1895-1913	5.3	1890-1913	4.1
	1920-1929	2.8	1920-1929	4.8	1920-1929	.
Downswing	1929-1948	2.1	1929-1948	3.1	1929-1948	.
4th Kondratieff						
Upswing	1948-1973	3.2	1948-1973	4.7	1948-1973	9.1
	France		Italy		Sweden	
2nd Kondratieff						
Upswing	1847-1872	1.7				
Downswing	1872-1890	1.3	1873-1890	0.9	1870-1894	3.1
3rd Kondratieff						
Upswing	1890-1913	2.5	1890-1913	3.0	1894-1913	3.5
	1920-1929	8.1	1920-1929	4.8	1920-1929	4.6
Downswing	1929-1948	-0.9	1929-1948	0.5	1929-1948	4.4
4th Kondratieff						
Upswing	1948-1973	6.1	1948-1973	7.9	1948-1973	4.7

a 1948-73: West Germany.

Sources:
United Kingdom: Hoffmann (1955) for 2nd Kondratieff (GB data); Feinstein (1976) for 3rd and 4th Kondratieff.
United States: US Dept. of Commerce (1973) plus own update.
Germany, France, Italy and Sweden: Mitchell (1981).

Table 9.8 *Long wave upswing and downswing growth rates, total output,*
1870s-1973

	2nd Kondratieff downswing 1870s-90s[a]	3rd Kondratieff upswing 1890s-1913[a]	3rd Kondratieff downswing 1920-29	1929-48	4th Kondratieff upswing 1948-73
Australia	2.9	3.9	2.3	2.2	4.8
Belgium	2.0	1.9	3.4	0.3	4.2
Canada	3.4	4.4	4.0	3.1	5.1
Denmark	2.8	3.5	2.1	1.7	4.1
France	0.8	1.8	4.9	0.0	5.3
Germany	2.3	3.2	4.9	-0.0	6.8
Italy	0.7	2.2	3.0	0.6	5.6
Japan		2.4	3.4	-0.2	9.4
The Netherlands	1.4	2.3	3.9	1.5	4.9
Norway	1.4	2.5	3.2	2.9	4.2
Sweden	1.8	3.3	4.8	2.5	3.9
United Kingdom	1.9	1.8	1.9	1.6	2.9
United States	4.2	4.0	4.0	2.3	3.8

a Kondratieff periods are 1872-90 (Belgium, France, Germany), 1873-90 (Italy, UK), 1873-95 (USA), 1873-96 (Canada), 1874-96 (Australia), 1876-95 (Japan), and 1874-91 (Denmark, Norway, Sweden). With only a 1870 estimate available, 1870-90 is taken as the downswing phase for the Netherlands.

Source: Maddison (1977).

All countries listed in Table 9.7 satisfy the long wave requirement stated above (insofar as data are available), *at least if we split the 3rd Kondratieff upswing into two parts* − 1890s-1913 and 1920-29. We find then that the downswing of the latter quarter of the 19th century brought lower annual growth rates than preceding and following upswing phases (up to 1913), and that the 1929-48 interval gave lower rates than preceding (1920-29) and following (1948-73) upswings. World War I has to be omitted in order to save the pattern of alternating acceleration and deceleration. The disruption of production caused by World War II is not needed to produce low growth rates for the 3rd Kondratieff downswing. Only in the case of the United Kingdom did the depression years 1929-37 yield a higher average growth rate than the preceding 1920-29 Juglar. With the same split of the 3rd Kondratieff upswing being applied to total output data (Table 9.8), the same long wave pattern results. Only Belgium, the United Kingdom and the United States do not manage to top the downswing growth rate of the 1870s-90s during the following 'belle Epoque'. Moreover, nine out of 13 countries grew more rapidly during the 1920s than during the 'belle Epoque'. There thus seems very little reason to see the 1920s as part of a long wave downswing, as many authors do. If one annual growth rate is calculated over one long 3rd Kondratieff upswing (1890s-1929), France, Germany, Italy, the Netherlands, and Sweden still satisfy the alternation requirement.

Although less conspicuously, and only by excluding the World War I impasse, most countries for which we have long time series available have grown according to a long wave pattern. With the exception of the earliest entrants (UK, Belgium, USA), for all other countries listed in Table 9.8 *long wave growth is an adequate typification of the development pattern during the past century.*

FLUCTUATIONS IN CAPITAL FORMATION

Many long wave theories include hypotheses on fluctuations in capital formation. These should occur alongside, or as a result of, fluctuations in general economic activity. In some theories, in fact, fluctuations in investment are seen as the ultimate cause of long waves. This position has recently been defended by Forrester, but its history goes back to the writings of the early Marxist proponents of long waves in capitalist development, such as Van Gelderen and De Wolff. This is not surprising as all types of cyclical fluctuations can be linked with particular types of investment, from inventory investment (the inventory cycle), via investment in machines and equipment (the Juglar), and investment in buildings (the Kuznets cycle), to investment in infrastructure or basic capital (the long wave). The more durable the investment involved and the longer the lags between demand impulse and actual construction of the capital good, the longer will be the generated cycle.

If investment fluctuations are indeed the key to long wave fluctuations, the level of investment activity might be expected to be low during long wave downswings, and high during long wave expansions. A more detailed look could reveal whether these investment lows occur during depression phases rather than during recovery phases, and whether investment demand is higher during the first or second prosperity-Juglar (see Table 9.6), etc. A major problem in testing this investment hypothesis lies in the nature of the investment data. Firstly, investment time series cover a shorter time span than industrial production series. Secondly, prewar data rarely distinguish between the various investment categories mentioned above; instead, they are presented as aggregate investment data, making impossible any test of the relationship between the fluctuations in infrastructural investment (road construction, harbour works, industrial complexes, etc.) and long waves. Thirdly, investment data are usually less reliable than other economic statistics. Fourthly, its volatility makes it difficult adequately to typify the level of investment activity during a relatively short time span such as a Juglar. Compounded growth rates from Juglar-peak to Juglar-peak, and estimates of annual growth rates are of little use. An alternative measure is to express the level of investment as a percentage of national product and to average these percentages over a Juglar. This has been done in Table 9.9. Instead of focussing on investment, a direct look can also be taken at capital stock, the development of which is characterized by far less volatility, and which enables compounded

Table 9.9 *Capital formation as a percentage of national product.*

	United Kingdom[1]	United States[2]	Germany[3]	Italy[4]	Sweden[5]
1825-1836	3.8a				
1836-1845	5.4				
1845-1857	7.0		8.9b		
1857-1866	7.1		10.8	9.1c	
1866-1873	6.8		12.8d	8.9	
1873-1883	7.8		11.1e	8.4f	10.8g
1883-1890	5.5	22.0h	11.5i	10.8i	9.1j
1890-1903	7.7	17.9k	12.9	9.3	12.0l
1903-1913	6.5	17.2	15.3	14.8	12.1
1913-1920	4.4	11.6	.	5.9	12.1
1920-1929	8.4	14.6	11.9m	15.2	13.0
1929-1937	9.1	6.1	5.3	15.5	15.1
1937-1948	7.1	7.7	.	15.3	18.8
1948-1957	14.0	16.3	14.7n	18.0	21.4
1957-1966	16.8	15.3	19.6	19.5	23.8
1966-1973	18.5	15.5	17.2	18.2	23.3
1973-1979	18.4	15.1	12.3		21.4
1845-1873	7.0		10.7o	9.0p	
1873-1890	6.8		11.3q	9.6	9.9r
1890-1913	7.2	17.5s	13.9	11.7	12.1t
1920-1929	8.4	14.6	11.9m	15.2	13.0
1929-1948	7.9	7.0	.	15.3	17.3
1948-1973	16.3	15.7	17.4u	18.6	22.8

Percentages are arithmetic averages of annual rates.

Notes
1 Gross capital formation, excluding stocks, as percentage of GNP.
2 Gross private domestic investment, excluding stocks, as percentage of GNP.
3 Net capital formation, including stocks, as percentage of NNP.
4 Gross capital formation, including stocks, as percentage of GNP.
5 Gross capital formation, excluding stocks, as percentage of GDP.

a 1830-1836   b 1850-1857   c 1861-1866   d 1866-1872   e 1872-1882
f 1873-1882   g 1870-1881   h 1890-1895   i 1882-1890   j 1881-1894
k 1895-1903   l 1894-1903   m 1925-1929   n 1950-1957   o 1850-1872
p 1861-1873   q 1872-1890   r 1870-1894   s 1895-1913   t 1894-1913
u 1950-1973

Sources: United States, Kendrick (1961) for 1890-1948; *Economic Report of the President* (1980) for 1948-79. All other countries, Mitchell (1981).

growth rates to be calculated again. Measurement problems, however, prevent many countries from having, or publishing, capital stock time series. We have calculated capital stock growth rates for the United Kingdom, the United States and Germany (Table 9.10).

In Table 9.9 investment shares in national product are presented for five countries, per Juglar, and per Kondratieff upswing and downswing phases. A sixth country, France, could not be included for lack of data over a longer period. The investment shares per Juglar show little if any tendency to fluctuate

Table 9.10 *Capital stock growth rates*

United Kingdom		United States			Germany	
			(a)	(b)		
1857-1866	1.2				1857-1866	2.4
1866-1873	1.2				1866-1872	2.5
1873-1883	1.7				1872-1882	2.7
1883-1890	1.2	1890-1895	4.7		1882-1890	2.8
1890-1903	2.5	1895-1903	3.5		1890-1903	3.2
1903-1913	2.0	1903-1913	3.1		1903-1913	3.4
1913-1920	0.9	1913-1920	2.4		1913-1920	.
1920-1929	1.3	1920-1929	3.1		1924-1929	2.3
1929-1937	1.4	1929-1937	-0.3	-0.7	1929-1937	1.4
1937-1948	1.3	1937-1948	1.3	0.9	1937-1948	.
1948-1956	3.3	1948-1957	3.3	3.5	1950-1957	4.9
1956-1965	4.0	1957-1966		3.3		
		1966-1973		4.4		
		1973-1979		3.7		
1857-1873	1.2				1850-1872	2.2
1873-1890	1.5	1890-1895	4.7		1872-1890	2.8
1890-1913	2.3	1895-1913	3.3		1890-1913	3.2
1920-1929	1.3	1920-1929	3.1			
1929-1948	1.3	1929-1948	0.6	0.2		
(1948-1965	3.7)	1948-1973	3.7			

Growth rates are compounded annual growth rates, measured from Juglar peak to Juglar peak.

Sources and definitions:
UK: Gross reproducible capital stock at constant replacement cost, plant & machinery + vehicles, ships and aircraft (Feinstein 1976: Table 43).
USA: (a) real capital stock, national economy (Kendrick 1961: Table A-XV);
(b) constant dollar gross stock of fixed non-residential private capital (*Survey of Current Business*, February 1981: 59).
Germany: Net capital stock, 1913 prices (Hoffmann 1965: 253-54).

according to a long wave pattern. The least that might be expected is that these shares are relatively low during long wave depression phases. Minor decreases occurred in Germany and Italy during the 1873-83 Juglar; a relative low was reached during the following Juglar in the United Kingdom and Sweden. Without a long wave chronology in mind, however, one would not be detected in these individual country sequences. The Great Depression of the 1930s only shows up in the data for the United States and Germany. In the United Kingdom, Italy and Sweden (countries with very different political constellations at that time) the average investment share even increased after 1929. A relative investment decrease does occur after 1973, but for some countries it is much smaller than might have been expected.

In Germany, Italy and Sweden the overall tendency has been for investment shares to increase over time, a tendency which is clearly shown in the graphs in Rostow's *World Economy* (1978), and which suppresses any long wave fluctuations which might have occurred in aggregate investment activity. In the United

Kingdom, on the other hand, a clear step-up occurred only after World War II. Previously, investment had fluctuated but without a recognizable pattern. In the United States, by contrast, the tendency for the investment share has been to decrease, with a huge drop between 1929 and 1948, and a recovery after the war.

To summarize investment tendencies by calculating average shares for the much longer Kondratieff upswing and downswing periods, gives results that are somewhat more compatible with the long wave view. All five countries reviewed have a number of outcomes in common:

1. Investment shares were higher during the 1890s-1913 upswing than during the preceding Kondratieff downswing (if only marginally so in the case of the United Kingdom).
2. Investment shares were higher during the 1948-73 upswing than during the 1929-48 downswing.
3. Post-1973 shares are lower than 1948-73 upswing shares, even if in some cases the drop is only minor.

The capital stock growth rates shown in Table 9.10 confirm our earlier findings: no *prima facie* evidence of growth fluctuations of the long wave type in the Juglar growth rate sequence; modest support for the long wave view if Kondratieff upswing and downswing periods are compared. United Kingdom capital stock growth reached peak levels between 1890 and 1913, and again after 1948. The same applied to Germany. There is no evidence of an investment boom in these countries before 1872/73, however, relative to the following Kondratieff downswing. The Great Depression of the 1930s shows up in the United States and German data, but not in the United Kingdom, where growth slowed down earlier.

Those who see long waves as caused primarily by investment fluctuations are therefore likely to be disappointed by what the investment and capital stock data reveal. If a small sample sign test were applied to the Juglar data in Tables 9.9 and 9.10, only Germany would pass such a test (hypothesis 1b) at the five per cent level. Does this mean that the investment hypothesis has to be rejected? A qualified answer is in order:

1. The sign test applied to industrial output growth of individual countries led to a rejection of the long wave hypothesis for all countries, with the exception of France. Nevertheless, world production data unmistakeably showed long wave fluctuations. A similar result is conceivable for the time pattern of world investment.
2. Long waves are intertwined with even longer term secular tendencies. Thus, Rostow's country histories (Rostow 1978) show a gradual increase of the investment/GNP-ratio for the United Kingdom (up to 1870/1900), the United States (up to 1870), France (up to 1900) and Germany (up to 1913), and a decrease thereafter. In all cases, the postwar years brought new highs for this ratio.

3. There is no doubt about the decline in the investment/GNP-ratio after 1973. This may have had several causes (the oil crisis, uncertainty, high interest rates), but one of these was the excess capacity built up during the preceding growth years.
4. Our data pertain to all investment activities, but the investment hypothesis refers specifically to investment in capital goods of long duration.[3]

Fluctuations in investment may not be the ultimate cause of long waves, but its role should not be underestimated, whether in bringing an end to a Kondratieff upswing, or in bringing about a recovery. In the latter respect, the present call for a step-up of investment expenditure, which can be heard in all Western countries, is of significance.

A LONG WAVE CHRONOLOGY

In the first section of this chapter a long wave chronology was given based on fluctuations in world industrial production. With the additional outcomes of the preceding section in mind, we shall now compare our dating of the long wave with that of other authors. It should be remembered throughout that our focus is on production, not on prices.

Table 9.11 does not list all existing long wave chronologies (for a more complete listing, up to the 1950s, see Imbert 1959: 38). Many datings are based exclusively on price fluctuations, a survey of which would be merely repetitious.

Let us now look at each of the turning-points in Table 9.11. Most authors locate the beginning of the first 'industrial' long wave at around 1790. Schumpeter mentions 1787, but all of his turning points are chosen in such a way that they represent 'neighborhoods of equilibrium' rather than Juglar peak or trough years.[4] There is some disagreement on the timing of the first Kondratieff upper turning point. Most authors take 1815; the two Marxists, De Wolff and Mandel, opt for 1825.

The dating of the first long wave is mainly, if not exclusively, determined by price movements. Indeed, 1789/90 represents a price minimum, 1815 a price maximum. Kondratieff himself had no physical quantity series at all for this first wave. Had he been able to use Hoffmann's estimates of industrial production in Great Britain in this period, he would have seen that 1782 was a more likely starting point for the first long wave, but also that no slowdown in economic activity occurred after 1815, nor after 1825. The fall in the price level following the Napoleonic wars was not matched by a retardation of economic growth.

The years that are taken to mark the beginning of the 2nd Kondratieff range from 1842 to 1851. Here again, it would seem that most authors have been guided by price movements. The wholesale price level in Britain and the United States bottomed out in 1849, but for other price series 1844 was a trough year,

Table 9.11 Long wave chronologies according to various authors

	1st Kondratieff		2nd Kondratieff		3rd Kondratieff		4th Kondratieff	
	lower	upper	lower	upper	lower	upper	lower	upper
1. Kondratieff (1926)	ca. 1790	1810/17	1844/51	1870/75	1890/96	1914/20		
2. De Wolff (1929)	–	1825	1849/50	1873/74	1896	1913		
3. Von Ciriacy-Wantrup (1936)	1792	1815	1842	1873	1895	1913		
4. Schumpeter (1939)	1787	1813/14	1842/43	1869/70	1897/98	1924/25		
5. Clark (1944)	–	–	1850	1875	1900	1929		
6. Dupriez (1947; 1978)	1789/92	1808/14	1846/51	1872/73	1895/96	1920	1939/46	1974
7. Rostow (1978)	1790	1815	1848	1873	1896	1920	1935	1951
8. Mandel (1980)	–	1826	1847	1873	1893	1913	1939/48	1967
9. Van Duijn	–	–	1845	1872	1892	1929	1948	1973

while the value of British foreign trade reached a low as early as 1842. The business cycle peak for this period fell in 1845, the trough occurred in 1848.

There is little disagreement among economic historians about the expansive nature of the world economy between 1845 and 1872/73, but output data are still less than complete, in that they do not cover the entire period for most countries (see Table 9.7). There was an unmistakeable slowdown in production growth after 1872/73, however, which coincided with a fall in the general price level. Authors who list years other than 1872 or 1873 as the upper turning point, do so for reasons explained earlier (Schumpeter), or because dating accuracy is not their first concern (Clark). Of all turning points, this 2nd Kondratieff peak is the one most agreed upon.

The 3rd Kondratieff upturn occurred sometime during the 1890s. Wholesale prices bottomed out in 1896, world industrial output growth accelerated after the 1892 peak, while according to Schumpeter a new prosperity phase started after the 1890 European Juglar peak. Yet this range in dates is small compared with the range in 20th century turning points. Should the 3rd Kondratieff peak be located at 1913, 1920 or 1929? The two Marxists together with Von Ciriacy-Wantrup chose 1913 (the end of la belle Epoque); Dupriez and Rostow examined price fluctuations and picked 1920; but output growth clearly recovered after World War I and on that basis 1929 should be taken to mark the end of the 3rd Kondratieff upswing.

From here on, price and output movements diverge, and so do the datings of turning points. Rostow, who sees the long wave strictly as a price cycle, consistently looks at price turning points, notably at those in the ratio of raw material and industrial prices. In his view the 5th Kondratieff upswing started with the raw material and foodstuffs price explosion of 1972. Dupriez and Mandel see World War II as separating the 3rd and 4th Kondratieffs. In their view, as in ours, the 4th long wave did not start until after the end of World War II. Finally, Mandel views 1967 as the beginning of a recession phase; a clear drop in output growth did not occur until after 1973.

Our own long wave chronology given in Table 9.6 is to be interpreted as the dating of a long-term industrial output growth cycle, with Juglar peaks taken as mark-off points. Variances with the datings of other authors result mainly from their reliance on price movements. In that respect, Schumpeter's chronology has our preference (despite one differently located turning point and our denial of a first Kondratieff cycle). Mandel also views the growth of industrial output as a key indicator, but we disagree on his choice of upper turning points for the 3rd and 4th Kondratieffs. Our emphasis on the role of innovation life cycles in generating long wave expansions leads us to reject Mandel's peaks.

APPENDIX D

Testing the long wave hypothesis after trend elimination with a log-linear trend*

J.J. van Duijn & R.L. Vellekoop

In this appendix a method is presented to test for a long-wave pattern in production time-series, after trend elimination through the estimation of a log-linear trend. In principle, there are three estimation methods with which to test the long wave hypothesis: (1) one may assume that the long wave does not exist, estimate a log-linear trend, and see whether the regression residuals exhibit a long wave pattern; (2) an attempt can be made to explain the long wave in such a way that the long wave no longer shows up in the residuals; or (3) a combination of both methods can be applied, for instance by estimating some kind of quadratic function. Here, we shall deal only with the first method.

We wish to stress that our assumption of a log-linear trend does not imply that this trend specification is theoretically correct. Furthermore we assume *a priori* knowledge of Kondratieff turning points.

We assume a log-linear specification

$$\ln y_t = \alpha + \beta t + u_t \qquad\qquad t = 1, \ldots, n \qquad (A.1)$$

If a long-cyclical pattern exists this could show up as a long wave in the regression residuals e_t, where

$$e_t = \ln y_t - \ln \hat{y}_t = \ln y_t - \hat{\alpha} - \hat{\beta} t \qquad\qquad t = 1, \ldots, n \qquad (A.2)$$

At first glance, the tendency would seem to be to demand that the long wave should manifest itself as an alternation of blocks of positive and negative residuals. This will only be the case, however, if, given the presence of a Kondratieff cycle, the underlying trend has been specified correctly. If this is not so, other residual patterns can result which a long wave test should be able to cope with. With some patterns, it would make little sense to look only for positive and negative residuals.

The test we propose is based on the property of the cycle to decrease from peak to trough and to increase from trough to peak. We assume that turning points are known. A peak year is indicated by t^+ and a trough year by t^-.

As test statistic we propose

$$T = \sum_{t=t^1}^{t^2} (e_t - e_{t-1}) \quad 1 < t^1 < t^2 < n, \qquad (A.3)$$

where

---

* This appendix was originally written as a response to Van der Zwan (1980).

$T < 0$, if $t^1 = t^+$ and $t^2 = t^-$, and

$T > 0$, if $t^1 = t^-$ and $t^2 = t^+$.

There is a simple expression for T. If $t^1 = t^+$ and $t^2 = t^-$ (measurement from peak to trough), then

$$T = \ln y_{t-} - \ln y_{t+} - (t^- - t^+)\hat{\beta} \qquad (A.4)$$

Mutatis mutandis the expression for T can be determined if we measure from trough to peak.

The long wave test becomes:

H_0 (no long wave) : $T = 0$ for all phases
H_i (a long wave exists): $T > 0$ from trough to peak
                                     $T < 0$ from peak to trough.

The test proposed above has been applied to four sources, viz. Frickey's industrial production series for the USA (1860-1914), Hoffmann's index of industrial production in Britain (1700-1950), Mitchell's series of industrial production in France between 1815 and 1970, and Lewis's series of world production and trade 1870-1950.

A. *Frickey's industrial production series for the USA, 1860-1914*

Series investigated (as by Van der Zwan 1980):

1. index of production for manufacture;
2. idem, durable commodities;
3. idem, non-durable commodities;
4. idem, transportation and communication;
5. index of industrial and commercial production.

Estimation of a log-linear trend gives the following results (bracketed numbers are standard errors; $t = 1, \ldots, 55$):

1. ln (manufacture)   = 2.668 + 0.04824t   DW = 1.17 $\bar{R}^2$ = 0.988
                          (0.023) (0.00071)

2. ln (durables)   = 2.287 + 0.05719t   DW = 1.05 $\bar{R}^2$ = 0.966
                          (0.047) (0.000147)

3. ln (non-durables) = 2.828 + 0.04449t   DW = 0.88 $\bar{R}^2$ = 0.985
                          (0.017) (0.00052)

4. ln (transp. & comm.) = 2.394 + 0.05660t   DW = 0.54 $\bar{R}^2$ = 0.994
                          (0.019) (0.00060)

5. ln (ind. & comm.)   = 2.535 + 0.05236t   DW = 0.90 $\bar{R}^2$ = 0.993
                          (0.019) (0.00060)

Application of this test to Van der Zwan's turning points yields:

	Manufacture	Durables	Non-durables	Transp. & comm.	Ind. & comm.
1861-1873	0.04973	0.26923	0.01819	0.21874	0.17403
1873-1896	-0.11259	-0.39002	-0.04250	-0.16013	-0.11672
1896-1913	0.09868	0.33138	0.02434	0.14812	0.13671

Conclusion: the residuals are in conformity with the pattern that could be expected on the basis of the existence of a Kondratieff cycle. We disagree with Van der Zwan's statement that the interval 1873-96 was not followed by an interval of prosperity.

B. *Hoffmann's index of industrial production in Britain, 1700-1950*

The estimated trend is (t = 1, …, 239, 247, …, 251):

$$\ln(\text{ind. prod.}) = -0.366 + 0.02223t \qquad DW = 0.10 \quad \bar{R}^2 = 0.970$$
$$(0.035)\ (0.00025)$$

We use Kondratieff turning points obtained from Table 9.2: 1782, 1825, 1845, 1873, 1903, 1929 and 1948. In addition, we have divided the 1903-29 expansion phase into two segments: 1903-13 and 1920-29.

Applying the test to these turning points yields T values:

1782-1825	0.39232
1825-1845	0.25132
1845-1873	0.19411
1873-1903	-0.21436
1903-1913	0.03647
1920-1929	-0.04923
1929-1948	-0.12013

Conclusion: the contraction phase of the first Kondratieff cannot be demonstrated in Britain. The expansion phase of the third Kondratieff is restricted to the 1903-13 Juglar; the 1920s show no revival in Britain.

C. *Mitchell's index of industrial production in France, 1815-1970*

The following log-linear trend was estimated (t = 1, …, 99, 105, …, 124, 132, …, 155):

$$\ln(\text{ind. prod.}) = 2.895 + 0.01497t \qquad DW = 0.31 \quad \bar{R}^2 = 0.941$$
$$(0.028)\ (0.00032)$$

Using the Kondratieff turning points obtained in Table 9.4 the following values
for T result:

1824-1847	-0.03509
1847-1872	0.05886
1872-1903	-0.02852
1903-1929	0.04682
1929-1948	-0.46184

Conclusion: in the case of France our test affirms the existence of a Kondratieff
cycle. All signs are in conformity with the long wave hypothesis.

D. *Lewis's time-series of world production and trade, 1870-1950*

Series investigated (as by Van der Zwan):
1. world production of manufactures (incl. USA, excl. USSR);
2. world production of manufactures (excl. USA and USSR);
3. world trade of primary products (value);
4. world trade of primary products (quantity).

Estimation of a log-linear trend resulted in the following equations ($t = 1, \ldots$,
$44, 52, \ldots, 69, 81$ and $t = 1, \ldots, 33, 41, \ldots, 58, 70$ respectively):

1. $\ln(\text{manuf., incl. USA}) = 3.037 + 0.3084t \quad DW = 0.51 \quad \bar{R} = 0.969$
   $(0.028)\,(0.00070)$

2. $\ln(\text{manuf., excl. USA}) = 3.211 + 0.02693t \quad DW = 0.59 \quad \bar{R} = 0.968$
   $(0.025)\,(0.00062)$

3. $\ln(\text{prim.pr., value}) = 3.559 + 0.02154t \quad DW = 0.24 \quad \bar{R} = 0.608$
   $(0.083)\,(0.00241)$

4. $\ln(\text{prim.pr., quant.}) = 3.692 + 0.2139t \quad DW = 0.50 \quad \bar{R} = 0.928$
   $(0.029)\,(0.00084)$

To determine long wave turning points we have consulted Table 9.6. The follow-
ing Juglar-peaks were used: 1872, 1892, 1929 and (for lack of other data) 1950.
In addition, we have taken 1881 as starting point for the trade series.
Application of the test to these turning points yields:

	Manuf. incl. USA	Manuf. excl. USA	Prim. prod. value	Prim. prod. quantity
1872-1892[1]	-0.02151	-0.04838	-0.12528	0.07762
1892-1929	0.14452	0.14473	0.61479	0.19169
1929-1950	-0.16711	-0.19935	-0.35540	-0.33730

1 1881-1892 for the trade series.

Conclusion: all signs are in conformity with the long wave hypothesis, with the
exception of the sign for the shortened contraction phase (1881-92) of the trade
volume series.

APPENDIX E

Testing the long wave hypothesis by means of spectral analysis

Spectral analysis is a method by which to discover hidden periodicities in a given time series. Time series can be represented as a collection or 'spectrum' of independent sine curves whose frequencies are multiples of a certain basic frequency. Each may have a different amplitude. By estimating a sample spectrum it is possible to show each frequency's contribution to the total variance of a series. The sample spectrum thus provides information on the relative strengths of cycles with a frequency f (or, which is the same, with length 1/f). A nine-year business cycle should show up in the spectral density function as a concentration of variance – called a spectral peak – at frequency bands around 1/9th cycle per year. Long waves would have to produce peaks at bands around 1/50th cycle per year. The advantage of spectral analysis is that it estimates simultaneously the relative importance of cycles of different frequencies, thus eliminating the need to smooth a series of its shorter cycles.

In economic cycle analysis, spectral analysis has been widely applied for the purpose of testing for the existence of the 15-25 year Kuznets cycle (Harkness 1968, Klotz 1973, Klotz & Neal 1973, Soper 1975). Its use for verification of the long wave hypothesis is of more recent date: the renaissance of the long wave has naturally led to a renewed interest in the application of statistical techniques to time series which might follow a long wave pattern. The use of spectral analysis in this field, however, is not without danger. It is even questionable whether spectral analysis should be applied to time series which cover at most four times the cycle to be investigated. Series about three cycles long are considered to be the absolute minimum (Klotz & Neal 1973), but some authors mention seven cycles (Granger & Hatanaka 1964), or even ten (Soper 1975) as the minimum length. Adherence to such criteria would make spectral analysis unsuitable for the verification of a theory which so far has recorded only four long waves.

A second problem in the application of spectral analysis is that the observed time series are assumed to be stationary, i.e. trend-free in mean and variance. Most economic time series, however, have strong trends in their mean values; some have trends in their variance as well. So trends have to be removed, e.g. by taking first differences of the original data or first differences of the logarithms of the original series. Removing trend (and seasonality) is a form of what is called 'pre-whitening'. Pre-whitened data yield a smoother spectrum, which then has to be 'recoloured' to estimate the spectrum of the raw data. The transfer functions used for 'pre-whitening' and 'recolouring' may affect the location of cyclical peaks.

An example of the difficulties created by the use of transfer functions is given by Klotz & Neal (1973), who cite research on the Kuznets cycle in the USA, where spectral analysis applied to growth rates implied cycles of only 10 to 12 years in duration. If levels instead of growth rates were taken, however, cycle frequencies shifted toward Kuznets wave-lengths. If different filters are combined (e.g. by calculating moving averages and then transforming the data by taking first differences of the logarithms) some frequencies will be blown up while others will be depressed.

At this point we may conclude that spectral analysis is not suited for testing long wave hypotheses. The Kondratieff cycle is too long in comparison with the length of the time series available, while the series are so evidently non-stationary that filters have to be applied in order to make them stationary. These filters in turn will yield the wrong spectral peaks. The results which thus far have been obtained should therefore be viewed with considerable scepticism.

Kuczynski (1978) applied spectral analysis and cross-spectral analysis to the residuals of a world industrial production time series, after trend elimination with a log-linear trend. Trends were similarly eliminated from series giving the ratio of industrial production to total production, world exports, and the ratio of world exports to total production. In addition, Kuczynski constructed time series of basic innovations and basic inventions. Cross-spectral analysis looks for a correlation between cycles of the same length in two series. In addition to a degree of coherence it establishes the lag relationship between the two series.

Kuczynski found a cycle in the 60-year range (which had a very large band width due to the shortness of the time series — for industrial production only 127 years) which went from changes in the ratio of industrial to total world production, to changes in the level of industrial production (two year lag), to changes in the export production ratio and the export level (both eight year lags), and finally, to changes in innovative (nine years) and inventive (23 years) activities. Coherence in the 60-year cycle band is shown in the table below, where i = industrial production to total production ratio, I = industrial production, e = export-production ratio, E = exports, B = innovative activity, C = inventive activity. The time lag between industrial production, innovation and invention is interesting. Innovation appears to be dominated by changes in the i-ratio (with a lag of nine years), while innovation itself generates inventive activities. This result provides some support for the Mensch hypothesis (see Chapter VI), except that the lag between innovation and industrial production seems to be too short, but also for the Schmookler hypothesis (inventive activity is stimulated during upswing). But whereas the supposed 60-year cycle 'explains' about one-sixth to one-fourth of the residual variance of the production and exports series, only some five per cent of the residual variance of the invention and innovation series is explained.

A further disturbing outcome of Kuczynski's analysis is the appearance of an

i	I	e	E	B	C
i	–	.626	.217	.268	.797	.714
I		–	.470	.653	.623	.463
e			–	.955	.108	.091
E				–	.199	.157
B					–	.924
C						–

unknown 13-year cycle. This cycle may have been caused by the crises of 1918/ 19, 1931/32 and 1944/45, together with the troughs of 1866/67, 1892/93 and 1957/58. Kuczynski does not exclude the possibility that both the 60 and 13-year cycles are random events.

Haustein & Neuwirth (1982) have followed-up on Kuczynski's analysis by extending his index of world industrial production from 1850 back to 1740, using Hoffmann's (1955) index of British production, and UN statistics from 1976 to 1979. The result is an industrial production time series with 240 observations. They have also constructed quite ingenious indices of invention and innovation. The invention series runs from 1738 to 1979; the innovation series starts in 1764. The authors do not mention which transformations have been applied to the non-stationary series.

Using spectral and cross-spectral analysis, Haustein & Neuwirth find various cycles, the longest of which is a 50-year cycle showing up in industrial production, which is influenced by the innovation index with a lag of 21 years (coherence 0.40). This may be compared with Kuczynski's 60-year cycle with a nine-year time lag between innovation and industrial production. Haustein & Neuwirth's results in this respect would seem to be more plausible. Yet their analysis also shows unexplained cycles with lengths of 40, 32, 20, 13 and 7 years, most of which are unknown in the cycle literature. The seven-year cycle could possibly be the Juglar, but Haustein & Neuwirth confess to difficulties in explaining the others. And the question arises: if cycles of all kinds of lengths are generated, is it surprising to find one or more in the long-wave range?

Van Ewijk (1981) has applied spectral analysis to wholesale prices of the core countries (Great Britain, France, Germany and USA) and to a number of British and French volume series. His volume series have been converted by taking first differences of the logarithms of the original series. To cope with non-stationarity in the price series, Van Ewijk has reduced the observation period to 1770-1930, cutting the last 50 years of rising price levels. He is aware of the methodological problems involved: 'Strictly one should have to wait one or two centuries before applying spectral analysis to the long wave thesis. The length of the present observation period does not allow for a rigorous test of the Kondratieff-cycle' (Van Ewijk 1981: 13). Although the existence of a long wave in prices cannot be verified, therefore, Van Ewijk does at least find spectral peaks which are not inconsistent with the long wave hypothesis if the period of observation is restricted to

1770-1930. No trace of a long wave is found in the volume series. The spectral density functions for Britain show a 12-13-year cycle (see Kuczynski, and Haustein & Neuwirth!), plus a small concentration of power at frequencies corresponding to a 25-30-year cycle. This 'cycle' should be treated with suspicion, however. Its length equals the period between the two world wars, and it disappears if war data are replaced by intrapolated data.

Spectral analysis cannot prove or disprove the existence of long waves. While it is tempting to apply the technique to the long wave hypothesis, its usefulness in this field is extremely limited for the reasons mentioned above: the time series are too short and do not satisfy the stationarity requirement. While this latter requirement makes spectral analysis less well suited for application in the area of economics in general, the relative shortness of time series makes it particularly unsuited for application to the economic long wave. But an even more important objection to the use of spectral analysis in this area may be the underlying assumption that the long wave is a regular cycle. It is not. The lengths of the upswing and downswing phases of the long wave have varied greatly over time, with wars being but one major factor causing these lengths to differ. Technological changes and structural changes in human behaviour in economic affairs are two other factors.

NOTES

1. In Van Duijn (1979a: 91) a long wave chronology is presented, which uses Juglar troughs as benchmarks. Only for that reason does the time table presented there differ from that given in Table 9.6. Also, the first Kondratieff has been included in Van Duijn (1979a).
2. The 1913-20 and 1920-29 growth rates are combined into one recession growth rate for 1913-29. The 1973-79 period has been treated as a depression-Juglar.
3. Hoffmann (1965) gives subdivisions for German capital stock. Growth rates of railways plus water- and roadworks were:

1850-57	2.6	1882-90	1.7	1929-37	1.8
1857-66	3.4	1890-03	2.3	1950-57	3.0
1866-72	3.8	1903-13	2.9		
1872-82	4.0	1924-29	1.7		

This sequence shows a build-up of the German infrastructure, admittedly well into the depression of the 1870s, but with a considerable slowdown in the 1880s, and a recovery thereafter.
4. A re-phasing of Schumpeter's dates would yield the following Juglar-peak turning points: 1792, 1815, 1845, 1873, 1899, and 1929.

X

FLUCTUATIONS IN INNOVATIONS

A SURVEY OF BASIC INNOVATIONS

Do major or basic innovations appear in swarms, as Schumpeter and his follow-ers have suggested, or are they evenly distributed over time? Is the propensity to innovate higher under certain macroeconomic conditions than under others? To determine the dynamic pattern of major innovations, a list of such innovations would first have to be drawn up. This is easier said than done. The problems of listing and dating major innovations are well-known.

1. *Innovations are heterogeneous in character.* There are product innovations and process innovations; there are innovations in old industries and innova-tions that have established new industries. Adding all these for certain time-periods would amount to adding up apples and pears.

2. *Innovations are heterogeneous in area of application.* For instance, product innovations may be consumer goods, or producer goods, or sometimes both. Consumers may consider the innovation of the vacuum cleaner as very basic, but have no notion of the significance of the innovation of the gyro-compass.

3. *Innovations are heterogeneous in impact.* The development of the motor car spawned a major industry; the impact of the zip fastener was much smaller. Yet each would count as only one innovation.

4. *Seminal innovations versus subsequent improvements.* Should only Bessemer steel – the beginning of the modern steel industry – be listed or also sub-sequent improvements in the steel industry? Or, to take another example, should only the original transistor of Shockley et. al. be mentioned, or also its successors such as the silicon and the planar transistor?

5. *Competing technologies.* The introductory phases of some industry life cycles have been characterized by the co-existence of and competition between different technologies. Examples are the cylindrical record and the flat disc (the flat disc won); the internal combustion engine-driven motor car versus the electric car (the first won); and, more recently, the three different video-cassette recorder systems (VHS, Betamax and Philips) and the three video-disc systems (Philips, RCA and the Japanese). Should all be mentioned, or only that which survives?

6. *Innovation versus invention.* The moment of innovation is the moment of

market introduction of the new product or process. For most 20th century innovations the timing and the name of the innovator(s) are fairly well recorded. With most early 19th century innovations this is not the case. Often only the name of the inventor is known, and assumptions have to be made about the rapidity of application of an invention.

7. *Recent innovations.* The success of an innovation, and therefore its 'basic' character, can only be assessed after some time has passed, usually at least a decade. This implies that lists necessarily get thinner towards the date of compilation. Drop-offs in numbers of basic innovations thus do not necessarily mean reduced innovativeness. DNA-recombinant analysis, fibre optics, holography, the compact disc and kevlar may well appear on future lists, but not on the present ones. And how should recent developments in microelectronics be assessed? Should the hand-held portable calculator and the home computer be seen as basic innovations?

8. *Innovations past and present.* In retrospect, some of the older innovations may not seem as important as they once were. We may include the arc lamp on our list as the predecessor of the incandescent lamp, but other innovations are likely to be omitted which at one time might have been considered large leaps forward. In that sense, our current perspective could well lead to an under-representation of innovations before, say, 1870.

Despite these difficulties, we have ventured to draw up a list of 160 major innovations introduced during the 19th and 20th centuries (Table 10.1). This is a compilation of the *communis opinio* of various experts, from whose publications we have drawn (see list of sources at the bottom of Table 10.1). We have relied heavily on Baker (1976), De Bono (1974), Jewkes et. al. (1969), Landes (1969), Mahdavi (1972) and Robertson (1974), using the other sources mentioned for additional information and support. As a general rule we have excluded innovations that were mentioned in one source only.

The advantage of the innovation records used is that they were written without an eye towards possible long-wave bunching effects. The authors, with the exception of Freeman (but perhaps not the Freeman of that time), have no interest in the long wave and could not be accused of having devised their lists with an intended time pattern in mind. We could perhaps be accused of having intentionally omitted certain innovations, but the reader who is familiar with our sources can easily verify that virtually all these were single-source innovations. Some researchers (e.g. Kleinknecht 1981: 295) have argued that a compilation of innovations from different sources, as made here, would not produce a 'random' sample. Apart from the inappropriateness of the world 'random' in this connection, it should be clear that for long-wave testing purposes any list from a single outside source will have even more deficiencies than our list, which represents the opinions of various experts. This is mainly due to the fact that sources which are often used, including Mahdavi, and Jewkes, Sawers & Stillerman, are incomplete. Mahdavi's purpose was to investigate the efficiency of R&D, and more particularly the extent to which innovations are duplicated or delayed. His coverage of 20th century innovations is much better than of those of the 19th century. Consequently, his sample of 120 innovations can only be used to test for bunching effects in the 1930s and 1940s. Even there, however, his list is incomplete. For instance, Mahdavi omits black and white television, discussing instead the introduction of colour television in 1953. Jewkes, Sawers & Stillerman did not intend to be complete in any sense. While the information contained in their book is extremely important for long-wave researchers, there- fore, Clark, Freeman & Soete (1981a) have convincingly demonstrated that their 2nd edition list is deficient for testing purposes. Our list will of course also be subject to criticism. Some readers would prefer to omit certain innovations, others to add some. In our opinion, the overall picture would be little affected by such minor changes; most readers will probably agree on the basic character of the innovations listed, even though the coverage of some sectors might be im- proved.

It should be emphasized, however, that even the most conscientious listing of major innovations is of limited value. Firstly, what significance should be attached to the moment of innovation? Is it really important that television was innovated in 1936, or is it more important to know that its economic signifi- cance came only after World War II, when it took off in the USA but not in Britain, the country of innovation? In other words, is the diffusion of an innova- tion not more important than the moment of innovation? In view of the fact that the 'basic' character of an innovation can only be assessed after successful diffusion, the answer to this question has to be in the affirmative. Some innova- tions have been instantaneous successes but others have been slow starters. This holds for some of the depression-innovations of the 1930s whose success came only during postwar recovery, raising doubts as to whether much significance should be given to their timing.

Nevertheless, the moment of introduction is important. Firms or governments innovate when they have a reason to do so. Mahdavi's case studies (1972) have shown clearly that innovations have frequently been delayed until the moment that outside forces (market demand, political pressure, competition, lack of demand for existing products) have provided the incentive to speed-up the devel- opment of the new product or process. Mahdavi found delays for 83 out of 120 innovations. This implies that the moment of innovation is important, even if it takes time for the innovation to gain wide acceptance. Moreover, a long intro- duction phase is often inevitable. The high price of a new product restricts the number of its users; technical deficiencies may be reason to postpone purchasing until starting-up problems have been ironed-out. Despite such problems, how- ever, the innovators must have felt that sufficient demand existed for their pro- duct when they introduced it on the market.

FLUCTUATIONS IN INNOVATIONS

Table 10.1 *160 major innovations, 19th and 20th centuries*

	invention	innovation	innovator
crucible steel	1740	1811	Krupp (Germany)
street lighting (gas)	1801	1814	National Light & Heat Co. (GB)
mechanical printing press	1811	1814	*The Times* (GB)
sulphuric acid			
(lead chamber process)	1740	1819	Ringkuhl (Germany)
quinine	1790	1820	Pelletier-Ceventan (Fr)
portland cement	1756	1824	Great Britain
coke blast furnace	1713	1829	Neilson (GB)
steam locomotive	1769	1830	Liverpool & Manchester Railway (GB)
puddling furnace	1784	1832	Hall (GB)
electric motor	1821	1837	Davenport (USA)
steamship (Atlantic crossing)	1783	1838	Sirius (GB)
photography	1727	1839	Giroux (France)
electric telegraph	1793	1839	Paddington-Hanwell (GB)
vulcanized rubber	1839	1840	Goodyear (USA)
arc lamp	1810	1841	Paris, France
rotary press	1790	1846	Hoe Rotary (USA)
anaesthetics	1799	1846	Massachusetts Gen. Hosp. (USA)
steel (puddling process)	1840	1849	Lohage & Bremme (Germany)
sewing machine	1790	1851	Singer (USA)
safety match	1805	1855	Lundström (Sweden)
Bunsen burner	1780	1855	Bunsen (Germany)
Bessemer steel	1855	1856	various countries
elevator	1818	1857	Otis Elevator (USA)
lead battery	1780	1859	Planté (France)
drilling for oil	1859	1959	Pennsylvania Rock Oil Co. (USA)
internal combustion engine	1853	1860	Société des Moteurs Lenoir (Fr)
sodium carbonate	1791	1861	Solvay (Belgium)
Siemens-Martin steel	1857	1864	various countries
aniline dyes	1771	1865	BASF (Germany)
atlantic telegraph cable	1851	1866	Atlantic Telegraph Co. (USA)
dynamo	1820	1867	Siemens (Germany)
dynamite	1844	1867	Nobel (Sweden)
typewriter	1714	1870	Jürgens (Denmark)
celluloid	1865	1870	Hyatt (USA)
combine harvester	1826	1870	McCormick (USA)
margarine	1869	1871	Jurgens (Netherlands)
reinforced concrete	1867	1872	Ward (USA)
sulphuric acid	1819	1875	Winkler (Germany)
four-stroke engine	1862	1876	Gasmotorenfabriek Deutz (Germ.)
telephone	1860	1877	Bell Telephone (USA)
Thomas oven	1877	1879	various countries
electric railway	1834	1879	Siemens-Halske (Germany)
water turbine	1824	1880	Pelton (GB)
incandescent lamp	1854	1880	Edison Lamp Works (USA)
half-tone process	1865	1880	*The Daily Graphic* (USA)
electric power station	1867	1881	Siemens Brothers (Germany)
punched card	1823	1884	Hollerith (USA)
cash register	1879	1884	NCR (USA)
fountain pen	1656	1884	Waterman (USA)
steam turbine	1848	1884	Clarke, Chapman & Co. (GB)

Table 10.1 *continued*

	invention	innovation	innovator
transformer	1831	1885	Stanley (GB)
bicycle	1839	1885	Starley (GB)
linotype	1884	1886	*New York Tribune* (USA)
aluminium	1827	1887	various countries
motor car	1883	1888	Benz (Germany)
cylindrical record player	1877	1888	Columbia, Edison (USA)
portable camera	1881	1888	Eastman Kodak (USA)
alternating-current generator	1856	1888	Tesla Electric Co. (USA)
mechanical record player	1887	1889	Kämmerer & Rheinhardt (Germ.)
pneumatic tyre	1845	1889	Dunlop Pneumatic Tyre Co. (GB)
rayon (nitro-cellulose pr.)	1857	1892	De Chardonnet (France)
motion picture film	1888	1894	Kinetoscope (USA)
motor cycle	1885	1894	Hildebrand & Wolfmüller (Germ.)
monotype	1887	1894	Sellers & Co. (USA)
diesel engine	1892	1895	Akroyd-Hornsby (USA)
electric automobile	1874	1895	Acme & Immisch (GB)
X-rays	1895	1896	various countries
rayon (cuprammonium pr.)	1890	1898	France
aspirin	1853	1899	Bayer (Germany)
submarine	1624	1900	US Navy
safety razor	1895	1903	Gillette Safety Razor Co. (USA)
oxy-acetylene welding	1893	1903	Fouch & Picard (France)
viscose rayon	1892	1905	Courtauld & Co. (GB)
vacuum cleaner	1901	1905	Chapman & Skinner (USA)
chemical accelerator for rubber vulcanization	1906	1906	Diamond Rubber Co. (USA)
electric washing machine	1884	1907	Hurley Machine Corp. (USA)
airplane	1903	1910	military airplanes, France
bakelite	1905	1910	Bakelite Corp. (USA)
gyro-compass	1852	1911	British, German, US navies
vacuum tube	1904	1913	AT&T (USA)
assembly line	1913	1913	Ford Motor Co. (USA)
thermal cracking	1909	1913	Standard Oil of Indiana (USA)
domestic refrigerator	1834	1913	Domelre (USA)
synthetic fertilizer (nitrogen)	1908	1913	BASF (Germany)
stainless steel	1911	1914	Th. Firth & Sons (GB)
cellophane	1912	1917	La Cellophane (France)
zip fastener	1891	1918	US Navy
acetate rayon	1902	1920	British Celanese (GB)
continuous thermal cracking	1909	1920	Texas Co. (USA)
AM radio	1900	1920	Westinghouse Co. (USA)
insulin	1921	1923	Connaught Labs, Toronto (Can.)
continuous hot strip rolling	1892	1923	Armco (USA)
dynamic loudspeaker	1906	1924	United States
Leica camera	1913	1924	Leitz (Germany)
electric record player	1908	1925	Brunswick Co. (USA)
polystyrene	1925	1930	I.G. Farben (Germany)
rapid freezing	1929	1930	Birdseye (USA)
synthetic detergents	1886	1930	I.G. Farben (Germany)
freon refrigerants	1930	1931	Kinetic Chemicals (USA)
gas turbine	1900	1932	Brown-Boveri (Switzerland)
polyvinylchloride	1931	1932	I.G. Farben (Germany)

Table 10.1 *continued*

	invention	innovation	innovator
antimalaria drugs	1932	1932	Eli Lily Co (USA)
sulfa drugs	1917	1932	I.G. Farben (Germany)
synthetic rubber	1882	1932	DuPont (USA)
crease-resisting fabrics	1926	1932	Tootal Broadhurst Lee (GB)
plexiglas	1912	1935	Röhm & Haas (USA)
magnetic tape recorder	1899	1935	Magnetophon (AEG) (Germany)
colour photography	1912	1935	Eastman Kodak (USA)
radar	1887	1935	various countries
FM radio	1902	1936	Telefunken (Germany)
television	1907	1936	Electrical & Musical Ind. (GB)
catalytic cracking	1927	1937	Sun Oil, Socony-Mobil (USA)
electron microscope	1931	1937	Siemens-Halske (Germany) Metropolitan-Vickers (GB)
nylon	1934	1938	DuPont (USA), I.G. Farben (Germany)
fluorescent lamp	1896	1938	Westinghouse, Gen. Electric, Sylvania Electric (USA)
helicopter	1907	1938	Focke-Wulf (Germany)
polyethylene	1936	1939	ICI (GB)
jet airplane	1930	1942	Messerschmitt (Germany)
penicillin	1929	1942	Kemball, Bishop & Co. (GB)
continuous catalytic cracking	1942	1942	Standard Oil of New Jersey (USA)
DDT	1874	1942	allied forces
guided missile	1903	1942	V2 (Germany)
silicones	1904	1943	Dow-Corning (USA)
aerosol spray	1862	1943	United States
high-energy accelerators	1929	1943	General Electric (USA)
ball-point pen	1938	1945	Eterpen Co. (Argentina)
streptomycin	1924	1946	Merck & Co. (USA)
phototype	1936	1946	American Intertype Corp. (USA)
orlon	1945	1948	DuPont (USA)
cortisone	1931	1948	Merck & Co. (USA)
long-playing record	1948	1948	CBS (USA)
automatic transmission (passenger cars)	1904	1948	Buick (USA)
Polaroid land camera	1937	1948	Polaroid (USA)
xerography	1937	1950	Haloid Corp. (USA)
terylene	1941	1950	ICI (GB)
radial tyre	1949	1950	Michelin (France)
sulzer loom	1928	1950	Warner & Swasey (USA)
transistor	1947	1951	Bell Telephone Labs (USA)
electronic computer	1944	1951	Remington Rand (USA)
power steering (passenger cars)	1926	1951	Chrysler (USA)
continuous casting of steel	1927	1952	Mannesmann (Germany)
oxygen steel making	1939	1953	Vöest (Austria)
colour television	1925	1953	RCA (USA)
gas chromatograph	1905	1954	Perkin-Elmer Corp. (USA)
remote control	1898	1954	Argonne National Lab. (USA)
silicon transistor	1947	1954	Texas Instruments (USA)
numerically controlled machine tools	1927	1955	United States
nuclear energy	1942	1956	Calder Hall, Great Britain

Table 10.1 *continued*

	invention	innovation	innovator
fuel cell	1885	1958	Union Carbide (USA)
polyacetates	1924	1959	DuPont (USA)
float glass	1952	1959	Pilkington Bros. (GB)
polycarbonates	1935	1960	Bayer (Germany),
			General Electric (USA)
contraceptive pill	1954	1960	Searle Drug (USA)
hovercraft	1928	1960	Saunders-Roe (GB)
integrated circuit	1959	1961	Fairchild, Texas Instruments
			(USA)
communication satellite	1957	1962	USA, USSR
laser	1954	1967	Hughes Aircraft (USA)
Wankel-motor	1954	1967	NSU (Germany)
video cassette recorder	1956	1970	Philips (Netherlands)
micro-processor	1959	1971	Intel (USA)

Sources: Baker (1976); De Bono (1974); Enos (1962); Freeman (1974); Jewkes, Sawers & Stillerman (1969); Van der Kooy (1978); Landes (1969); Mahdavi (1972);Mueller (1962); Nabseth & Ray (1974); Robertson (1974).

A second remark, meant to bring Table 10.1 into perspective, concerns the possible bunching of innovations during certain time periods. What does it mean if the flow of innovations varies over time? The coincident appearance of innovations during particular decades does not necessarily imply a common cause. In Chapter VIII it has been argued that different categories of innovations will probably have different timing patterns. To this should be added specific sector-related factors. Each sector has its own life cycle, and the stage of that life cycle will exert its own influence on innovative activity even though a sector's life is also affected by general macroeconomic influences. The role of scientific break-through has been more important for the advancement of new products and processes in some sectors than in others. Synthetic materials, for example, belong to a sector which produced many crucial innovations in the 1930s; though these clearly fulfilled hitherto unmet demands, they were induced by research programmes which had started long before.

Finally, the dates of invention are listed in Table 10.1 for each innovation. Mensch (1975, 1979) has used these dates to back up his acceleration hypothesis, i.e. the notion that lead times of invention over innovation are reduced during depressions, as firms speed up the innovation process in order to overcome the depression. If there is ambiguity in setting the date of innovation, there is even more in determining that of invention, i.e. the moment when the necessary technical knowledge became available. Much of our information is derived from Mahdavi, for whom the time lag between invention and innovation was essential. For 19th century innovations, however, the moment of invention is much harder to ascertain. For some, patent dates have been taken (often given by Baker; but see Chapter VI for the limitations of patent dates), in other cases other outside sources have had to be consulted. Invention dates have been added for illustrative purposes, showing that long lags have often existed, that efficient innovation is the exception rather than the rule, or in other words, that innovation is very much an economic activity.

FLUCTUATIONS IN INNOVATIONS OVER TIME

The time pattern of major innovations can be organized in a number of ways, but we have used the long-wave chronology presented in Chapter IX. The number of innovations can be counted for each long-wave phase, which yields a first insight into the propensity to innovate during various phases. A drawback of this approach, apart from problems associated with the adding up of disparate innovations, is that our long-wave phases are Juglars and therefore vary in length. For that reason, innovations per decade have also been counted, although as an exercise this makes little economic sense. The results of both time divisions are shown in Table 10.2. In order to cover the entire 19th century a first long wave has been added, despite the fact that in Chapter IX its existence has not been proven.

Table 10.2 shows innovation peaks: one in the recovery decade of the 1880s, another during the recovery-plus-war period following the Great Depression of the 1930s. Our hypothetical distribution of innovations over time, developed in Chapter VIII, also suggested an innovation peak during recovery. In that chapter it was also hypothesized that the propensity to innovate would be at its lowest during the long-wave recession phase. This seems to be confirmed by the distribution of innovations during the 3rd Kondratieff (1892-1948). Whether 1966-73 also represents an innovation low we do not yet know, although from the current perspective this appears to have been the case. In fact, much of the current interest in 'innovation' stems from the presumed lack of it during the late 1960s and early seventies.

It is a striking fact that many innovations were made during the 1930s, or during 1929-37. This was depression time, and this swarm of innovations must have prompted Mensch (1975, 1979) to develop his 'depression-trigger' hypothesis. The 1870s also showed an increase in innovative activity, but less pronounced than that of the 1930s. Can the preponderance of innovations in the 1930s be seen as 'proof' of the depression-trigger hypothesis? Before giving them a more qualitative examination, another interpretation of the numbers in Table 10.2 should be discussed. It has been argued above that lists such as that of Table 10.1 tend to underrepresent very recent innovations (they have not yet reached their heyday and their importance cannot therefore yet be assessed) and also very old ones (the milestones are included but some innovations whose importance seems on the wane are likely to be omitted). If Table 10.2 shows a

Table 10.2 *Fluctuations in innovations over time*

long-wave phases			Decades	
war	1802-1815	3	1801-10	0
recession	1815-1825	3	1811-20	5
depression	1825-1836	3	1821-30	3
recovery	1836-1845	6	1831-40	6
prosperity 1	1845-1856	7	1841-50	4
prosperity 2	1856-1866	8	1851-60	8
recession	1866-1872	7	1861-70	9
depression	1872-1883	9	1871-80	10
recovery	1883-1892	15	1881-90	15
prosperity 1	1892-1903	11	1891-00	10
prosperity 2	1903-1913	12	1901-10	8
war	1913-1920	6	1911-20	12
recession	1920-1929	5	1921-30	8
depression	1929-1937	18	1931-40	19
war + recovery	1937-1948	20	1941-50	20
prosperity 1	1948-1957	15	1951-60	17
prosperity 2	1957-1966	8	1961-70	5
recession	1966-1973	4	1971	1
		160		160

gradual increase in innovations per period followed by a sharp drop at the end, this outcome may be due partly to these two effects. Any statistical randomness test should therefore omit the beginning and the end of our time series.

Let us therefore take the nine decades from 1871 to 1960 as being fully covered, and examine whether the time pattern of innovations in these decades deviates significantly from what randomness would lead us to expect. A χ^2 one-sample test (of the kind used by Kleinknecht, 1981, for the same purpose) can be applied to our nine frequencies (see Siegel 1956). The result is that the null hypothesis (any observed differences in number of innovations are merely chance variations) cannot be rejected even at the 10 per cent level of significance! The values of χ^2 become even lower (and randomness firmer) if innovations are divided into categories, as has been done in Table 10.3. It then appears that only war and armament-related innovations have statistically significant peaks during and around World Wars I and II. Unlike Kleinknecht (1981: 301), we thus do not find 'strong support for the existence of a depression-trigger effect'.

If the distinction between depression and recovery is done away with, and long-wave downswings are merely separated from upswing periods, the randomness hypothesis can be rejected for these longer periods. In Table 10.4 two groupings are made: one for long-wave periods of unequal length, and the other for decades that roughly coincide with long-wave periods. For the long-wave periods the null hypothesis of chance variations in number of innovations can be

Table 10.3 *Major innovations by category, 1871-1960*

decade	cons. goods	infrastructure	other (process) inn.	war & armament-related
1871-80	3	4	3	0
1881-90	7	4	4	0
1891-00	6	0	3	1
1901-10	5	1	1	1
1911-20	5	2	2	3
1921-30	7	1	0	0
1931-40	10	1	3	5
1941-50	7	1	5	7
1951-60	6	2	7	2

Notes:
consumer goods = products that were innovated with application as consumer goods in mind;
infrastructure = innovations in 'basic' sectors such as construction, oil refining, steel and aluminium;
other (process) innovations = process innovations plus intermediate products;
war & armament-related = products and processes whose innovation was determined by war or war preparation.

rejected at the one per cent level; for the two decade periods it can be rejected at the five per cent level. This cruder test, however, provides no affirmation of the presumed clustering of innovations during depression as such.

Taking into consideration the overall increase in major innovations over time, the most striking aspect of Tables 10.2 and 10.4 is not the abundance of innovations in the 1930s and 1940s, but rather the lack of innovations between the outbreak of World War I and the crash of 1929. Those innovations that did occur between 1913 and 1929 were mainly in consumer goods, and often continuations of research programmes which had already led to basic innovations prior to World War I (cellophane, acetate rayon, AM radio, dynamic loudspeaker and electric record player). This is interpreted as a confirmation of our hypothesis that innovative activity will be lowest during long-wave recession periods due to the fact that the need for firms to innovate will then be low. During long-wave recessions, some sectors continue to grow rapidly precisely because they exploit major innovations that have been introduced earlier. As long as growth is unabated in such sectors, there is no need for further radical innovations.

Table 10.4 *Innovations and long-wave periods*

depression + recovery	1872-1892	24	1871-1890	25
prosperity	1892-1913	23	1891-1910	18
war + recession	1913-1929	11	1911-1930	20
depression + recovery	1929-1948	38	1931-1950	39
prosperity	1948-1966	23	1951-1970	22

Take, for instance, the case of Great Britain. In his history of the British economy between 1914 and 1950, Pollard (1962: 98-110) singles out the following industries as growing rapidly during the interwar period: electrical goods and electrical supply, the motor industry, aircraft production, man-made fibres, the chemical industry, oil refining, glass making, aluminium, rubber, and a number of smaller consumer goods sectors. A quick glance at Table 10.1 will show that most of these sectors were fed by one or more major innovations that were introduced before World War I. The following output indices, also given by Pollard, confirm the strength of these innovative sectors:

	1924	1930	1935
electrical goods	55	67	100
electrical supply	45	71	100
automobiles and cycles	42	61	100
aircraft	23	65	100
silk and rayon	20	47	100
hosiery	70	69	100
chemical and allied products	67	69	100
share of above, plus scientific instruments (%)	12.5	16.3	19

Low during the 1920s, innovativeness picked up dramatically in the 1930s. Was this due to the depression? The answer has to be 'no'. If the depression did anything at all it was to postpone innovations. In a few instances (FM radio and the fluorescent lamp) postponement was due to the desire to protect predecessor products (AM radio and the incandescent lamp). But the case histories drawn up by Mahdavi and Jewkes et. al. for the innovations of the 1930s do not mention depression as a reason. Innovations were frequently the outcome of research programmes that had started much earlier. From 1935 onwards, war preparation became an incentive. In all cases, market demand was a necessary condition for introduction, whether by government, industry, or consumers. It is in the latter category that postponement due to the depression was most likely. As the western economies began to recover from the mid-1930s onwards, some of the barriers to innovation were done away with.

There is no doubt that the long-wave recovery phase is characterized by a high propensity to innovate. Market demand is expected to rise, an outlook which is necessary for firms to engage in the risky and arduous process of innovation. Although Schmookler (1966) seems to have been mainly concerned with the economic motives underlying improvement innovations, his thesis (invention and innovation follow demand increases) fits in well with this observation. *Mutatis mutandis* the propensity to innovate will be lowest during a long-wave recession phase. The continued growth of new industries provides a very strong reason not to launch any radical new activities. When depression sets in, the newer industries will find it easier than the older to introduce product innovations. This is confirmed by case histories. Entirely new sectors will usually make a start in the recovery phase.

The empirical record does not allow any confirmation of the depression-trigger hypothesis. Verification has been restricted to the depression of the 1930s. Economic reasoning would lead us to extend our rejection of this hypothesis to the depression of the 1870s; unfortunately, earlier records are too scanty to allow verification to be made.

Important innovations are of course made during depressions, but their explanation requires a study of the history of the industrial sector concerned. As we have seen earlier, sectoral influences are as important as macroeconomic conditions in explaining the appearance of innovations. We shall therefore conclude this chapter with a brief examination of the innovation record of a number of important 20th century industries.

Before doing so, however, a short comment on the location of introduction of the major innovations of the 19th and 20th centuries. In a pioneering article, Vernon (1966) has argued that entrepreneurial (=innovative) activity would be highest at locations in which communication between market and producer is swift and easy, and in which a wide variety of potential types of input are easily come by. As the USA offers an excellent market for high-income and labour-saving products, Vernon asserts that the first producing facilities for such products would be located there rather than in Europe, where most U.S. companies also have production plants.

Table 10.5 *Innovations by country of origin*

	19th century	20th century	Total
United States	25	50	75
Great Britain	14	11	25
Germany	14	13	27
France	7	4	11
other countries	5	5	10
innovations in more than			
one country	5	7	12
	70	90	160

Table 10.5 shows that U.S. firms have been responsible for a disproportionately large share of the selected 160 innovations. Of the 90 20th century innovations, 50 originated in the USA. European countries, on the other hand, produced more innovations in the 19th century than in the 20th century. As the saying goes, 'the Europeans invent a product, the Americans innovate it, and the Japanese make a mass product out of it.' The Americans certainly innovate, but the first part of the phrase is no longer applicable. Of all Nobel Prizes in the sciences awarded since 1945, 51 per cent went to the USA, 40 per cent to Europe, and two per cent to Japan. The USA therefore has the edge, both in

numbers and in relation to population size. There is one peculiarity, however: almost half the European prizes went to British scientists. Great Britain does not lack inventors: on a per capita basis it wins more Nobel Prizes than the USA. But Britons apparently lack the ability to turn their inventions into innovations.

INNOVATIONS BY SECTOR

This section lists some 80 major innovations which shaped the lives of thirteen 20th century growth sectors. Classifying innovations by sector reduces the heterogeneity displayed by a list such as that in Table 10.1. Innovations can now be viewed in the light of their sector's life cycle. Basic innovations can be better distinguished from important improvement innovations. Technological changes in infrastructural industries such as oil refining and steel can now be separated from innovations in consumer goods sectors.

The following discussion provides additional verification of the innovation-timing hypothesis laid down in Table 8.3. Its qualitative character precludes it from being a rigorous test of this hypothesis, but the reader should realize that 'innovation' is first of all a qualitative notion. Formal statistical tests, a simple example of which has been applied in the previous section, cannot do away with this.

In the following we have restricted ourselves to innovations made from approximately 1850 onwards. Innovation, date of innovation and innovator are listed.

Printing	1846 rotary press	Hoe Rotary (USA)
	1880 half-tone process	*The Daily Graphic* (USA)
	1886 linotype	*New York Tribune* (USA)
	1894 monotype	Sellers & Co. (USA)
	1946 phototype	American Intertype Corp. (USA)
	1950 xerography	Haloid Corp. (USA)

It is a remarkable fact that all these innovations occurred at the beginning of, or just preceding, long-wave expansion phases, perhaps due to their cost-reducing character. For example, linotype and monotype became necessary to solve the problem of under-utilization of printing machines due to composing by hand. Photocomposing machines were introduced as a method of cutting production costs. Such cost-reducing innovations are more likely during a contraction phase than during expansion. Chester Carlson's invention of xerography in 1937 was not picked up by commercial firms until after the war, i.e. a radically new process had to wait until recovery was under way.

Oil Refining	1859 drilling for oil	Pennsylvania Rock Oil Co. (USA)
	1913 thermal cracking	Standard Oil of Indiana (USA)
	1920 continuous thermal cracking	Texas Co. (USA)
	1937 catalytic cracking	Sun Oil, Socony-Mobil (USA)
	1942 continuous catalytic cracking	Standard Oil of New Jersey (USA)

The demand for oil is a derived demand. Innovations may be expected during the expansion phases of those sectors which use oil as an input. During the 1850s, increased demand for oil as a source of illumination led to drilling for mineral oil. The arrival of the motor car brought an increase in the demand for petrol. Around 1910, both thermal and catalytic cracking were considered, but the higher research costs of the latter process proved a major stumbling block. This obstacle was overcome when air traffic became more and more important – the fuel obtained from the catalytic cracking process is better suited for airplanes.

Resins, etc.	1870 celluloid	Hyatt (USA)
	1910 bakelite	Bakelite Corp. (USA)
	1917 cellophane	La Cellophane (France)
	1930 polystyrene	I.G. Farben (Germany)
	1932 polyvinylchloride	I.G. Farben (Germany)
	1935 plexiglas	Röhm & Haas (USA)
	1939 polyethylene	ICI (GB)
	1943 silicones	Dow-Corning (USA)
	1959 polyacetates	DuPont (USA)
	1960 polycarbonates	Bayer (Germany), General Electric (USA)

Two factors are of importance for the demand for resins: they are a substitute for natural products due to their technical properties; and their demand is derived demand. The latter factor would make introduction during expansion phases probable. In view of the many innovations made during the 1930s, this apparently has not always been the case. It should be recognized, however, that:
(i)   much of the German research for resins started under the influence of World War I blockades. After introduction, World War II provided new impulses;
(ii)   other research programmes were long-term programmes of the large chemical corporations (supply-induced); despite earlier introduction, true expansion, with improvement innovations, came only after 1945.
Research for postwar innovations (polyacetates and polycarbonates) originated in the first two decades of this century. The derived character of plastics demand would seem to be a plausible explanation of their timing.

Rayon,	1892 rayon (nitro-cellulose	
Synthetic	process)	De Chardonnet (France)
Fibres	1898 rayon (cuprammonium	
	process)	France
	1905 viscose rayon	Courtauld & Co. (GB)
	1920 acetate rayon	British Celanese (GB)
	1932 crease-resisting fabrics	Tootal Broadhurst Lee (GB)
	1938 nylon	DuPont (USA),
		I.G. Farben (Germany)
	1948 orlon	DuPont (USA)
	1950 terylene	ICI (GB)

Substitutes for natural fibres had been sought since the middle of the 19th century. Due to their inflammability, the first artificial silks could not compete with natural silk. Acetate rayon solved this problem. The main innovation impulse was the demand for yarns and fibres that were cheaper than the regular textile fibres.

Despite the quality improvement of synthetic fibres after World War I, it soon became clear that there was a market for even stronger, crease-resisting fibres. The basis for the synthetic fibre industry was laid by DuPont, a producer of rayon, who discovered the polyamides (nylon) as well as the polyacrylates (orlon) and the polyesters (terylene, dacron). The order of commercial development was a matter of priority. As polyester was considered to have little commercial potential, DuPont abandoned its research. ICI then innovated the fibre in 1950. Nylon, discovered in 1934 and innovated in 1938, was in considerable demand during the war.

Medicine	1899 aspirin	Bayer (Germany)
	1923 insulin	Connaught Labs. (Canada)
	1932 antimalaria drugs	Eli Lily Co. (USA)
	1932 sulfa drugs	I.G. Farben (Germany)
	1942 penicillin	Kemball, Bishop & Co. (GB)
	1946 streptomycin	Merck & Co. (USA)
	1948 cortisone	Merck & Co. (USA)

As might be expected, innovations in medicine do not display a long-cyclical pattern. This sector, however, is characterized by long time lags between invention and innovation, explained partly by the following considerations:

(i) once a particular cause of illness or death is brought under control, other diseases will become prominent and research efforts will shift towards overcoming them, perhaps leading to duplication of innovations;

(ii) for a number of innovations (notably penicillin, streptomycin and cortisone) war conditions proved to be the major incentive.

Rubber   1840 vulcanized rubber   Goodyear (USA)
           1889 pneumatic tyre   Dunlop Pneumatic Tyre Co. (GB)
           1906 chemical accelerator for
               rubber vulcanization   Diamond Rubber Co. (USA)
           1932 synthetic rubber   DuPont (USA)
           1950 radial tyre   Michelin (France)

The growth of the rubber industry is in large measure a derivative of that of the motor car industry, even though the innovation in 1889 of the pneumatic tyre resulted from the introduction of the modern bicyle (1885). This was its second innovation: in 1845 it failed due to lack of demand. The acceleration of the vulcanization process was a reaction to the increased demand for rubber. The introduction of synthetic rubber may be explained in the same way. An additional consideration for the innovating countries (the USA, but also Germany and the USSR) was the desire to become independent of the rubber-producing countries.

Steel   1856 Bessemer steel   various countries
           1864 Siemens-Martin steel   various countries
           1879 Thomas oven   various countries
           1914 stainless steel   Th. Firth & Sons (GB)
           1923 continuous hot
               striprolling   Armco (USA)
           1952 continuous casting   Mannesmann (Germany)
           1953 oxygen steel-making   Vöest (Austria)

Economic expansion during the third quarter of the 19th century created a strong demand for steel. Steel is a 'basic' sector; its demand is derived demand, so that innovations are most likely during expansionary periods, with a possible extension into early contraction. The Bessemer, Siemens-Martin, and Thomas processes conform to this. Stainless steel and continuous hot strip rolling (demand from the motor car industry) were also innovated during a long-wave expansion. Both postwar innovations were made at the beginning of a long-wave expansion, but only became widely diffused in the course of the 1960s.

Illumination   1880 incandescent lamp   Edison Lamp Works (USA)
                 1938 fluorescent lamp   Westinghouse, General Electric,
                                              Sylvania Electric (USA)

There was demand for a substitute of the arc lamp, which could not be used in houses, but the innovation of the fluorescent lamp was delayed because the incandescent lamp manufacturers wanted to protect their own interests. When fluorescent lighting could no longer be held up, the three largest incandescent lamp manufacturers innovated it simultaneously.

Telecommuni-	1877 telephone	Bell Telephone (USA)
cations and	1888 cylindrical record player	Columbia, Edison (USA)
Related	1889 mechanical record player	Kämmerer & Rheinhardt (Germ.)
Equipment	1913 vacuum tube	AT&T (USA)
	1920 AM radio	Westinghouse Co. (USA)
	1924 dynamic loudspeaker	United States
	1925 electrical record player	Brunswick Co. (USA)
	1935 magnetic tape recorder	Magnetophon (AEG) (Germ.)
	1936 television	Electrical & Musical Industries (GB)
	1936 FM radio	Telefunken (Germany)
	1948 long-playing record	CBS (USA)
	1951 transistor	Bell Telephone Labs (USA)
	1953 colour television	RCA (USA)
	1970 video cassette recorder	Philips (Netherlands)

The innovation of the telephone in 1877 created demand for what became known as radio telephony, mainly for entertainment purposes. More or less simultaneously, the cylindrical record player was invented, but Berliner's disc proved superior to Edison's cylinder. The innovation of the radio, made possible by the vacuum tube, was delayed by World War I. Radio, in turn, necessitated the next innovation in the gramophone record industry: the electric record player. The innovation of FM radio was postponed to protect the interests of the AM radio manufacturers. The tape recorder was originally invented in order to record telephone conversations, and its further development came only when the military recognized its potential. Tape recorders for recording music, etc. were first marketed in 1947. Television research was delayed by the advent of the radio. Colour television followed black and white with only a short time lag, but the principles of electronic colour television had become known as early as 1925. The innovation of the long-playing record became urgent with the arrival of these two competing products: the tape recorder and television. Philips, the innovator of the video-cassette recorder, explained the (early) introduction of this product in 1970 as due to the need to create new sources of profit for the company. The existing line of audio-visual hi-fi equipment was losing its profitability, and Philips therefore had to start new life cycles.

A remarkable aspect of this group of innovations is their long time lag. The most important technical ingredients for each of them were known as early as the 1920s. The development of invention into innovation was determined mainly by market considerations, with substitutability of the various products playing a key role, and the radio calling the tune for further introductions.

Electronic	1951 transistor	Bell Telephone Labs (USA)
Computers	1951 electronic computer	Remington Rand (USA)
	1954 silicon transistor	Texas Instruments (USA)
	1961 integrated circuit	Fairchild, Texas Instruments (USA)
	1971 micro-processor	Intel (USA)

Innovation of the electronic computer was preceded by the mechanical computer. The development of the first automatic mechanical computer, Aiken's Mark I in 1944, was supported by IBM. The electronic computer was innovated by outsiders, however, with considerable financial means being provided by the US army. IBM, which had not foreseen the potential of the computer, had to catch up from behind.

The innovation of the transistor, followed by many crucial improvement innovations (only a few of which are shown here), has had a far-reaching impact on many industries apart from the computer industry. This is an example of a basic innovation whose impact cannot yet be fully assessed. The semi-conductor industry is still going through important changes. In this long-wave downswing phase, however, labour-saving innovations dominate.

Motor Cars	1860 internal combustion engine	Société des Moteurs Lenoir (Fr)
	1876 four-stroke engine	Gasmotoren Fabrik Deutz (Germany)
	1888 motor car	Benz (Germany)
	1894 motor cycle	Hildebrand & Wolfmüller (Germany)
	1895 electric automobile	Acme & Immisch (GB)
	1913 assembly line	Ford Motor Co. (USA)
	1948 automatic transmission (passenger cars)	Buick (USA)
	1951 power steering (passenger cars)	Chrysler (USA)
	1967 Wankel motor	NSU (Germany)

A road vehicle was needed to replace steam-powered vehicles, and the modern bicycle (innovated in 1885) went some way towards meeting this need. The development of an electric car seemed logical, but the internal combustion engine (which replaced its predecessor, the gas motor) was cheaper and enabled motor cars to travel longer distances. The success of the four-stroke engine brought an end to research for a better electric car. While the motor car is a European innovation, the most important process innovation in the car industry, i.e. Ford's assembly line, was of American origin. It caused a drastic drop in production costs.

Innovations such as automatic transmission and power steering in passenger cars have been introduced with long time lags. Power steering was delayed by the Great Depression; moreover, after World War II the demand for cars was so strong that there was no incentive to equip them with power steering. This is a case of a sector which has produced very few radical innovations since its early beginnings. Demand has never been lacking, so that firms were not forced to introduce major innovations. Impulses to innovate another car engine (other than the internal combustion engine) have so far been weak.

Aircraft	1910 airplane	military airplanes (France)
	1938 helicopter	Focke-Wulf (Germany)
	1942 jet airplane	Messerschmitt (Germany)

Military demand has provided the major impulse for the innovation of the airplane, and also for the helicopter and the jet airplane. The helicopter could have been innovated much earlier, but the availability of the airplane made it unnecessary.

Photography	1888 portable camera	Eastman Kodak (USA)
	1924 Leica	Leitz (Germany)
	1935 colour photography	Eastman Kodak (USA)
	1948 Polaroid Land camera	Polaroid (USA)

Eastman Kodak (and celluloid film) helped to popularize photography. The photo industry left the invention of colour photography to outsiders, and Kodachrome was not developed until after the invention was introduced. A relationship between the life cycle of an innovation and the economic incentive for improvement innovations here seems very likely.

Our interpretation of the timing of innovations in the sectors discussed above can be briefly summarized as follows:

Sector	Nature of sector and timing of innovations
Printing	Cost-reducing innovations notably during recovery phases.
Oil refining	Derived demand (car industry, aircraft, petrochemicals); innovations as reaction to increasing demand from these sectors.
Resins, etc.	Technology push character dominates, but strongest growth is during prosperity phases.
Rayon, synthetic fibres	Technology push character dominates, but strongest growth is during prosperity phases.
Medicine	Innovations respond to dominant causes of death and illness; no relation with macroeconomic developments.
Rubber	Derived demand (car industry); innovations as reactions to demand increases in these sectors.
Steel	Derived demand (follows macroeconomic developments); innovations respond to increasing macroeconomic demand.
Illumination	Timing of innovation may have been determined by existing life cycle.
Telecommunications and related equipment	Timing of innovations determined by existing life cycles and scope for substitution.

Electronic com-puters	Cost-reducing innovations continue during depression phase.
Motor cars	Strong demand has evoked few major innovations.
Aircraft	Timing of innovations seems to be determined by existing life cycles and scope for substitution.
Photography	Timing of innovations seems to be determined by existing life cycles.

In only one sector, i.e. medicine, does there seem to be no relation between major innovations and macroeconomic development or industry life cycle. The timing of innovations in synthetic fibres and plastics seems to be determined by technology push rather than by demand pull. These sectors are dominated by large firms which are capable of financing large and long-lasting research programmes. In other sectors, either the long-wave phase or the life cycle phase offers clues as to when major innovations are to be expected.

The timing of innovations in the 13 sectors covered seems to conform reasonably well with the hypothesized timing of Table 8.3. While we acknowledge that discussion of particular cases can hardly serve as a proper test of an hypothesis, in retrospect Table 8.3 appears to be a useful framework for an understanding of why innovations are made at a particular time.

PART IV

THE FOURTH KONDRATIEFF DOWNSWING

XI

THE STAGNATION OF THE 1970s

WHAT CAUSED THE 1973-DOWNTURN?

In the spring of 1970, the OECD projected economic growth for the new decade for the major industrial nations. With 1970 output set equal to 100, Japan's national output was forecast to reach 265 by the end of the decade (implying an annual growth rate of 10.2 per cent). For other countries the projections were more modest: France 185 (6.3 per cent), Italy 177 (5.9 per cent), USA 164 (5.1 per cent), Germany 162 (5.0 per cent) and the United Kingdom 143 (3.6 per cent). None of these countries, however, achieved more than 50 per cent of the target set. Japan's increase in national output was only one-third of that expected by the OECD.

Why have the Western economies done so poorly in the 1970s? Was it the explosive rise in oil prices, as is often believed, or were more fundamental causes at work? The business cycle downturn of 1973 coincided roughly with the outbreak of war in the Middle East. Early in 1974 the export price of oil quadrupled compared to its level prior to October 1973. What followed was the most serious recession that the Western world had encountered since World War II, a recession which was followed only by a weak recovery which lasted from 1975 to 1979. The first oil price explosion was followed by a second: prices more than doubled in 1979/80. At the end of 1980 the price of oil was $34 per barrel; early in the 1970s it had been $2, in September 1973, $3.

The damage caused by the oil price explosion is impressive. In 1974 and 1975 all major industrial nations, with the exception of Germany, suffered double-digit inflation. The current accounts of OECD countries deteriorated sharply, turning negative in 1974 and staying so for the rest of the decade with the exception of 1978, which showed a small surplus. The increase in imports represented some one to three per cent of the GNP of individual countries. After the first oil crisis, the price rise was allowed to come through fairly rapidly, accelerating inflation and setting-up a new wage-price spiral. On the second occasion, government policies were more restrictive, aimed at lowering inflation. The tightening of monetary policy in the USA, however, led to record prime rates

Notes to this chapter may be found on p. 210.

which affected interest rates all over the world. In June 1977, an OECD team headed by Paul McCracken, chairman of the Council of Economic Advisers under President Nixon, concluded 'that the most important feature [of the severe problems of 1971-75] was an unusual bunching of unfortunate disturbances unlikely to be repeated on the same scale, the impact of which was compounded by some avoidable errors in economic policy' (OECD 1977: 14). And they continued: 'we see nothing on the supply side to prevent potential output in the OECD area from growing almost as fast in the next five to ten years as it did in the 1960s' (Ibidem: 16).

The view that supply-side shocks caused 'the Great Recession' of 1974-75 (not only did oil prices quadruple but crop failures also drove up food prices) is held by many economists. A major textbook as that by Lipsey & Steiner informs students: 'The years 1974 and 1975 saw major stagflation. The explanation is to be found in supply-side shocks and in the persistent inflationary expectations that held the inflation rate up in spite of a low level of aggregate demand' (Lipsey & Steiner 1981: 702). But the slow recovery following 1975 is more difficult to explain. The fear of accelerating inflation may have been a reason, but not a very satisfactory one, given the fact that some newly industrialized countries have managed to combine rapid growth with persistently high inflation.

Economic research on the impact of the oil crisis by Nordhaus (1980) suggests that the annual GNP growth rate of the OECD countries during the 1973-79 period was reduced only by 0.15 per cent because of the oil price increases. Furthermore, the annual inflation rate rose by an extra 0.6 per cent, the productivity growth rate dropped by 0.14 per cent, while the rate of growth in real income per worker showed a 0.41 per cent slowdown. These effects are comparatively minor. In Nordhaus's model, the oil price shock does not explain the retardation of growth that has occurred since 1973, nor the considerable drop in productivity growth. In another discussion of the macroeconomic consequences of OPEC and energy constraints, Tobin (1980) has argued that 'the 1974-75 recession and the low recovery path of 1975-78 cannot be attributed to the unavailability of oil.'

There is no doubt that the oil crisis, by driving up prices and by draining a huge flow of funds out of western economies, had a major impact on these economies. Nevertheless, it would be far too simple to blame the slow growth of the 1970s on the oil crises, just as it would be too simple to argue that the Great Depression of the 1930s was caused by the stock market crash of 1929. There were underlying weaknesses in the 1920s, most of which only became manifest after 1929. From about 1965 onwards, structural problems also developed, but most politicians and economists only came to realize their full impact after 1973. Consider for instance the following facts:

1. In the USA, a growth recession was under way well before the Arab oil em-

bargo. Even though the National Bureau of Economic Research dates the business cycle downturn at November 1973, the growth cycle chronology of the Center for International Business Cycle Research at Rutgers University marks March 1973 as the beginning of a growth recession. The oil crisis thus did not cause the 1973-75 recession; that would have come in any case, but would have been less severe.

2. Inflation was a major problem well before the quadrupling of oil prices. In the USA, the first significant increase in inflation occurred in 1965/66. By 1970 inflation in the major industrial countries, with the exception of Germany, had reached the five per cent mark. From 1970 through 1973, only the USA had nominal wage increases of less than 10 per cent. The first oil crisis thus did not cause high inflation; it merely accelerated it for a number of years.

3. The growth of industrial production had begun to slow down before 1973. In all four core countries (USA, UK, Germany and France) growth during the 1966-73 Juglar was lower than during the two preceding Juglars (1948-57 and 1957-66). If the role of manufacturing is seen as an engine of growth (see below), this is an important fact.

4. Profit rates had been declining since the mid-1960s. To the extent that profits provide an indication of the demand for a firm's products, the outlook has gradually deteriorated. This structural change also started well before the oil crisis (see Table 11.1). Sachs (1979) holds that the profit squeeze, intensified by the oil shock, is responsible for the prolonged stagnation in the European economies.

Table 11.1 *Rate of return on capital for private firms, before and after taxes*

| | United States | | United Kingdom | | The Netherlands | |
	before	after	before	after	before	after
1961-1965	14.1	8.3	10.9	7.9	7.9	4.7
1962-1966	15.0	9.0	10.7	7.9	7.6	4.4
1963-1967	15.1	9.2	10.4	7.8	7.3	4.25
1964-1968	15.1	9.2	10.1	7.7	7.2	4.2
1965-1969	14.4	8.6	9.3	7.0	7.2	4.1
1966-1970	12.9	7.7	8.4	6.1	6.9	3.95
1967-1971	11.7	6.9	7.7	5.6	6.7	3.85
1968-1972	10.9	6.2	7.0	5.1	6.3	3.6
1969-1973	10.1	5.7	6.5	4.6	n.a.	n.a.

Source: Van der Zwan (1975: 660).

5. Stock markets signalled a slowdown long before 1973. The Dow Jones industrial average showed a rising trend from 1948 until about 1965, when it reached a plateau on which it has stayed ever since. Breakthroughs of the 'magic' 1000-level have never been permanent. Occasional slumps, as in 1974,

dropped below the 600-level. If stock prices are expressed in real instead of nominal terms, the 1970s have shown a sharp decline of stock prices. Once again, the point is: the oil crisis merely accentuated a development which had been in progress since the end of the postwar long-wave prosperity phase.

6. Structural unemployment has been increasing since the mid-1960s. Although it was not realized at that time, later decompositions of total unemployment suggest that structural (as opposed to frictional and cyclical) unemployment started to increase at that time, an increase which has continued throughout the 1970s.

The 1966-1973 interval may be compared with that of 1920-1929. Both were typical long-wave recessions. Statistical comparisons may not bear this out completely, as the performances of individual countries during the 1920s were affected by their involvement in World War I and by the postwar transition. In Britain, for instance, some economic indicators (industrial production, capital formation) look better for the 1929-37 interval than for 1920-29. In other countries the 1920s brought record prosperity, and indeed, the feeling that prosperity would be permanent. Economic growth came to be taken for granted, as was also the case during 1966-73 even though structural problems were developing beneath the surface of carefree growth. On the positive side: both 1920-29 and 1966-73 saw the mass-produced availability of consumer durables – the spread of electric light, radio, the telephone, the refrigerator, and the automobile in the USA of the 1920s; the automobile (in Europe), colour television, hifi equipment in 1966-73. But structural problems were mounting, both in the 1920s and in the 1960s, reason why some long-wave authors (e.g. Mandel 1980) have interpreted the post-1913 and post-1967 years as part of a long-wave downswing. On the negative side we find over-expansion in a number of basic sectors: agriculture and the extractive industries, shipbuilding and (later on) the automobile industry in the 1920s; basic chemicals, oil refining, shipbuilding and (later on) steel and the automobile industry in the early 1970s. Both recession phases saw a downturn of the Kuznets or building cycle preceding the long-wave downturn: 1927 and 1972. In both periods significant merger waves took place, signalling attempts to acquire new product lines and accompanying profitability through diversification rather than through own research and technological innovation. These are all marks of an expansion which is coming to an end.

1973 was thus a watershed year, but it was not the oil crisis that brought an end to the great postwar expansion. In our opinion the following causes were pre-eminent.

A gradual saturation of many manufacturing sector growth markets,
coupled with a lack of major innovations to start up new growth sectors

Postwar growth in the manufacturing sector exceeded that of total output. Also
(a) the leading industries, whose growth far exceeded average growth, were
among the leaders in innovation; and (b) in international comparisons, the higher
the growth rate of manufacturing output, the higher the growth rate of total
output. Table 11.2 illustrates statement (a) for the United States. Strong growth
has gone together with high innovativeness (which of course does not mean that
above-average growth can only be realized with above-average innovativeness,

Table 11.2 *Top ten growers and top ten innovators, United States, 1956-73*

Top Ten Growers	annual rate 1956-1973	Top Ten Innovators	weighted inn. rate, 1953-1973
1. 30 Rubber & plastics	9.2	1. 38 Instruments	28.44
2. 28 Chemicals	7.9	2. 30 Rubber & plastics	14.73
3. 36 Electrical equipment	7.3	3. 36 Electrical equipment	12.05
4. 38 Instruments	6.3	4. 32 Stone, clay, glass	11.68
5. 26 Paper & allied products	5.0	5. 28 Chemicals	10.72
6. 35 Machinery	5.0	6. 35 Machinery	8.96
7. 22 Textiles	4.6	7. 37 Transportation equipment	7.77
8. 25 Furniture & fixtures	4.4	8. 33 Primary metal	6.54
9. 39 Miscellaneous	3.9	9. 21 Petroleum	5.18
10. 27 Printing & publishing	3.8	10. 34 Fabricated metal	3.04

Source: Van Duijn (1981a: 5).

witness paper and textiles). Table 11.3 suggests strongly that the manufacturing
sector has been the engine of postwar growth.[1] While the role of manufacturing
as the sector which propels the rest of the economy has been widely recognized
for less developed countries, it also performed that role in the postwar years for
the industrialized countries, which is yet another way of saying that technological innovations have been the key to growth.

One of the differences between the pre-1973 and post-1973 years, and in our
view an essential difference, is the slowdown of the manufacturing sector. As the
second part of Table 11.3 shows, post-1973 average manufacturing growth rates
dropped to the 1-3 per cent range (with even lower percentages in the case of
Norway and the UK). Aggregate output growth also fell, but relative positions
were reversed, with aggregate growth rates being somewhat higher than manufacturing growth rates. Only in the most mature economy of all, the USA, does
the manufacturing sector still lead.

This latter result is of considerable significance. Not only does it mean that
the U.S. economy showed some vigour in recovering from the 1975-trough, but

Table 11.3 *Average annual growth rates of aggregate output and manufacturing output*

	1951-1973		1973-1979	
	aggregate	manufacturing	aggregate	manufacturing
Austria	5.0	5.5	3.1	2.6
Belgium	3.9	4.9	1.7	1.5
Canada	4.6	4.9	3.2	2.8
Denmark	4.2	4.8	2.4	1.3
France	5.0	5.5	3.0	2.1
Germany	5.7	7.4	2.4	1.5
Italy	5.1	7.1	2.6	2.4
Japan	9.5	13.6	4.1	2.2
The Netherlands	5.0	6.1	2.4	1.9
Norway	4.2	4.3	4.2	0.2
United Kingdom	2.7	3.4	1.1	-0.6
United States	3.7	3.9	2.5	2.8

Table reprinted from Van Duijn (1981b: 4).

it also testifies to the role of innovation in economic development since manufacturing growth is based on the strength of a few innovation-packed sectors. The fact that innovation does not just displace jobs, as is often feared during depression periods, but is also responsible for their creation, is illustrated by Table 11.4. This table also provides a clue to the problem of slow economic growth: *countries with a strong (i.e. innovative) manufacturing sector will do better than others.* This conclusion holds for the older as well as for the younger industrial countries; it was true prior to 1973, and it is still true.

Table 11.4 *Top fifteen in employment growth, United States, 1974-1979*

SIC-code	annual growth rate
1. 3693 X-ray apparatus & tubes	16.3
2. 3832 Optical & analytical instruments	9.3
3. 382 Measuring & controlling instruments	7.9
4. 3573 Electronic computing equipment	7.6
5. 2331 Women's & misses' blouses and shirts	6.2
2452 Prefabricated wood buildings	6.2
2611 Pulpmills	6.2
8. 3713/6 Truck & bus bodies	6.1
9. 251 Household furniture	6.0
3911 Precious metal jewelry	6.0
11. 2328 Men's & boys' work clothing	5.9
2865 Cyclic crudes & intermediates	5.9
3555 Printing trade machinery	5.5
14. 3532 Mining machinery	5.3
15. 3623 Welding apparatus	5.2

Source: Table reprinted from Van Duijn (1981a: 9).

An over-expanded capital stock

In Chapter VII it has been argued that the leading sectors of a particular Kondratieff cycle require two kinds of infrastructural investment: industrial complexes for their own expansion, plus a general transportation and communication infrastructure. Both are likely to expand beyond a level necessary to meet demand. The results of over-expansion become most visible in the 'basic' sectors: steel, basic chemicals, oil refining, shipbuilding, construction. The subsequent lack of investment demand is the other side of the same coin.

A 'weakening of the hungriness motives'

This argument, given its name by Paul Samuelson, has recently come up in the re-industrialization and revitalization debates that are going on in almost all industrialized nations. The argument is that the belief in permanent affluence, fostered by 25 years of almost uninterrupted growth, has changed attitudes towards work and risk taking. In these terms, too, a long-wave expansion is self-destructive. The success of the welfare state has turned into the crisis of the welfare state.

This cause of the downturn is fairly fundamental. It is also universal in that changes of values and attitudes during prolonged periods of economic growth have not only occurred since the Industrial Revolution, but also appeared in the pre-industrial era.[2] Golden Ages have always been followed by Ages of Decline, partly because second generations have come to take economic affluence as a matter of course.

Uncontrolled growth of the government sector

Just as it proved too difficult a task for the private sector to expand its capital stock at a rate warranted by long-term growth potential, so have politicians been unable to check the expansion of the government sector, whose growth in the late 1960s and 1970s seemed to be determined by its own laws rather than by careful reflection on the desirable size of the government sector vis-à-vis the private sector.

This cause of decline is unique to this particular long wave. While the third Kondratieff upswing saw an increase in government intervention, the size of the government sector in the 1930s was so modest as to leave considerable scope for increased government activity as a means of combatting depression. In the present depression the opposite is the case. Government sectors have grown so large (see Table 11.5), mainly because of the excessive growth in welfare expenditure, that this depression is fought by curtailing the size of government to make room for the private sector. To what extent did increased government

Table 11.5 Structure and evolution of public expenditure

Country	Total[a]		Consumption		Investment		Transfers[b]	
	Average 1973-75	Change 1962-64 to 1973-75	Average 1973-75	Change 1962-64 to 1973-75[c]	Average 1973-75	Change 1962-64 to 1973-75	Average 1973-75	Change 1962-64 to 1973-75
Netherlands	49.8	13.5	16.9	1.7 (-4.7)	3.7	-1.0	24.9	11.4
Sweden	47.4	13.1	23.2	6.0 (1.6)	4.5	- .6	16.8	6.8
Norway	45.6	12.3	16.5	3.2 (1.3)	4.6	.6	21.9	7.9
United Kingdom	43.3	8.5	19.6	2.7 (- .6)	4.9	1.1	13.7	3.9
Denmark	42.2	13.3	22.0	7.4 (.4)	4.3	.5	14.0	4.9
Belgium	41.0	9.8	15.6	2.6 (- .9)	3.2	.6	18.0	5.7
Italy	40.9	8.2	13.7	.3 (-1.7)	3.1	- .5	19.8	7.0
Germany	40.5	6.2	19.1	3.4 (-1.0)	3.7	- .6	15.6	2.1
Canada	39.4	10.2	19.8	5.0 (1.6)	3.8	- .3	11.6	4.4
Austria	38.8	5.8	16.1	3.2 (-2.1)	6.2	.9	15.3	1.4
France	38.8	1.9	13.6	.0 (-2.7)	3.3	.2	20.0	2.8
United States	33.2	3.8	18.1	.3 (-3.0)	2.2	- .7	10.2	4.2
Australia	29.8	5.4	14.5	4.2 (- .2)	4.2	- .2	8.0	1.5
Japan	22.3	3.2	9.4	.6 (-4.3)	5.5	.2	6.5	2.1
OECD Total[d]	35.1	4.6	16.6	.6 (-3.1)	3.4	.1	12.2	3.8

a   Interest on public debt and other minor expenditure items, not shown separately, are included in the total.
b   Transfers to households and enterprises.
c   Bracketed figure is movement in constant 1970 prices; OECD total at 1970 exchange rates.
d   OECD total has been calculated in US dollars at the average exchange rates then prevailing.

Taken from OECD (1977: 309), with permission.

intervention play a role in causing the downturn? Surely, it would have occurred in any case, but the government sector has certainly encouraged it by growing at too rapid a pace during the long-wave recession phase. This expansion has had two negative effects: (a) it has gradually reduced manoeuvring room for the private sector – eventually giving rise to a large underground economy; (b) it has eliminated Keynesian expenditure policy during the ensuing depression.

Here we have a classic example of an economic agent, whose inertia gives rise to cyclical fluctuations. It took some time for government growth to get underway, but once it had gathered momentum it could not be stopped, despite the fact that the justification for continued growth had ceased to exist. Now, as economies struggle to get out of this depression, governments have finally begun to reduce their size.

The 1973 downturn had no single cause. Over-expansion of the capital goods sector and the maturation and finally saturation of growth markets may have been two prime factors; however, the length of the postwar growth era and the change in attitudes that growth brought about, eventually made expansion the victim of its own success, while politicians clearly proved themselves to be incapable of handling the distribution of growth. With a depression already in the making, the oil crisis of 1973 made it clear that the great postwar expansion had ended.

THE CURRENT DEPRESSION AND THE PREVIOUS ONE

Is this depression that we are suffering in the early 1980s as severe as that which struck the industrial world in the 1930s? So far not, neither in absolute nor in relative terms. Appendix F shows a number of commonly used economic indicators for the two depression phases, for the United States and the United Kingdom. The Great Depression was more severe in the USA than in most other nations; in the UK it followed a decade of slow growth and for some indicators even showed an improvement in comparison with the 1920s. In the USA the current depression is nothing like as bad as the previous one. GNP is well above the 1973 level; the unemployment rate, despite reaching a postwar high in 1982, is about one-third to one-half of that of the 1930s; personal consumption expenditures have continued to grow. Only gross capital formation has for most of the post-1973 years been below the level reached in the last of the upswing years. In the United Kingdom the main favourable difference with the Great Depression is that the unemployment rate, which averaged over 10 per cent during the 1920s and rose to over 20 per cent during 1931, 1932 and 1933, has remained in the range of five to seven per cent in the second half of the 1970s. GNP, personal consumption, and investment growth, however, have been less in the post-1973 years than after 1929! British output growth has therefore returned to its depression pace; only unemployment in the UK has not yet reached depression proportions.

To all this applies, of course: barring unforeseen developments. The present depression may run a different course. Built-in stabilizers (lacking in the 1930s) may have had a mitigating effect so far, but how long will they last? It may well be that at the present time (1982) the worst of this depression phase has yet to come. As we have seen, U.S. unemployment went to postwar record levels in 1982; the British rate reached double digits in 1981. There are no signs that the unemployment problem is likely to ease in the near future.

Even so, things are not as bad as they were in the 1930s. Why, then, do we call this a depression phase? The answer is: *because growth has slowed down considerably compared to its pre-1973 pace.* Britain is the only major exception. In many countries, growth rates have been cut in half. The growth rate of per capita income has dropped from the 3.5 per cent range to less than one per cent, and this is what counts for the present generation. It is easily forgotten that real per capita incomes are now much higher than they were in the 1930s (about two-and-a-half times as high in Western Europe; about twice as high in the USA and the UK).

Even if we have to make some sacrifices, therefore, we do so from a much higher income which is more equally distributed. This income distribution also results partly from an extensive social security system another form of defence against collapse which was lacking in the 1930s.

Other differences with the Great Depression, however, are less comfortable. That same social security system and the overall increase in the size of government, has left little or no room for stimulative policies of the Keynesian kind. Inflation, exacerbated by two oil price explosions but a serious problem in the Western world even before 1973, is another limiting factor and a possible source of future disturbance. Balance-of-payments deficits vis-à-vis OPEC-countries is a third. All this implies that some of the policy options that were available in the 1930s are now out of the question.

Finally, there is a difference between the 1930s and the present day whose significance we have only just begun to realize: *structural rigidities* which impair the adaptability to change. The oft-cited *Interfutures* Report sees two causes of these rigidities: 'They arise both from the conscious achievement of legitimate social objectives and from the involuntary accumulation of institutions, procedures and rules which are partly irreversible and are a source of ineffectiveness' (OECD 1979: 161). In our opinion, they result from 25 years of almost inter-rupted growth, a period which helped establish those institutions, procedures and rules, which could honour most claims for more, and which created feelings of risk aversion. In the 1920s, all this was unknown. If feelings of social security had existed during 'la belle époque' (1895-1913), they had been shattered by World War I. One symptom of rigidity is the slow response shown by some economic agents to stagnation. Some of the diverse reactions to the 1973 down-turn will be examined below.

THE SLOW RESPONSE OF SOME ECONOMIC AGENTS TO STAGNATION

Economic decision makers are known to react with a lag to structural, i.e. non-cyclical changes. If consumers grow accustomed to 4-5 per cent annual growth rates of real disposable income, as was the case in the 1960s, they need time to adjust their spending habits to 1-2 per cent growth rates, as many people have had to in the 1970s.

If government budget planning is based on trend rates of growth of three to four per cent, it is a painful business to have to adjust plans downward in order to make them compatible with a growth rate of only 1½ per cent. If labour unions have for many years been able to negotiate real wage increases of five per cent, they will need time to realize that this is no longer possible. If managers have come to take 10-20 per cent annual sales increases for granted, it is difficult for them to reorient selling strategies if the rates drop to 4-5 per cent.

No group in society can claim to be more alert than others in its response to changes, but some are forced to adjust more quickly, exposed as they are to the working of the market. Others can postpone the adjustment because they are protected from the market, i.e. because they can pass the buck. The ability to adjust also has a size dimension: typically, large institutions are slower in their reactions than smaller ones.

Differences in reaction to economic slowdown are illustrated in Table 11.6 in which we have traced developments of the major spending categories in four of the largest OECD economies: USA, UK, Germany and Japan. Taking GNP/GDP growth as a benchmark, it is possible to compare the three domestic spending categories: private consumption, government consumption and (private plus government) investment. In three countries (UK, Germany and Japan) government consumption was the fastest grower, outstripping both GNP/GDP and the other domestic expenditure components. Keynesians may consider this a posi-tive development – government spending as a cushion in times of stagnation. In this particular depression, the growth of government consumption may also denote the inability of governments to adjust to a slower growth trend. Further-more, if governments play an active role in combatting depression, should this not be with an eye towards the future, i.e. through government investment rather than government consumption? In the UK, however, investment by government has been cut in half since the onset of the depression. Table 11.6 does not show where government involvement has increased most, i.e. in the area of transfers to households and firms. In Table 11.5 we have seen that in 1973-75 transfer payments accounted for roughly 30 per cent of total govern-

Table 11.6 *The reaction to economic slowdown in the United States, the United Kingdom, Germany and Japan*

	1973	1974	1975	1976	1977	1978	1979	1980	1981
United States									
Gross national product	100	99	98	104	109	114	118	118	120
Private consumption	100	99	102	107	112	118	121	122	125
Government consumption	100	103	105	105	107	110	111	114	115
Gross private domestic investment	100	90	72	85	99	106	108	94	99
Exports	100	106	103	110	113	127	147	161	160
Imports	100	97	85	101	109	122	130	130	137
United Kingdom									
Gross domestic product	100	99	98	102	103	107	108	106	–
Private consumption	100	98	98	98	97	103	108	108	108
Government consumption	100	101	107	108	107	109	111	113	113
Gross private investment	100	92	78	92	98	101	106	87	84
Gross government investment	100	94	86	83	70	62	57	51	35
Exports	100	107	104	114	121	124	127	127	–
Imports	100	101	94	98	99	103	114	110	–
Germany									
Gross domestic product	100	100	99	104	107	111	115	118	117
Private consumption	100	100	103	107	111	115	119	121	120
Government consumption	100	104	109	111	112	116	120	123	126
Gross investment	100	90	83	93	96	99	112	113	104
Exports	100	112	105	117	122	127	135	143	155
Imports	100	104	108	120	125	132	146	155	158
Japan									
Gross domestic product	100	99	101	107	112	118	124	129	133
Private consumption	100	99	103	107	111	116	123	124	125
Government consumption	100	103	110	115	119	126	131	134	139
Gross private investment	100	96	86	89	92	97	107	108	107
Gross government investment	100	86	91	93	104	120	124	120	125
Exports	100	122	127	149	166	166	177	210	245
Imports	100	107	97	102	107	113	130	125	132

Sources: United States: US Dept. of Commerce: *Survey of Current Business* (various issues); other countries: OECD: *Quarterly National Accounts Bulletin* (various issues).

ment expenditure in Japan, the USA and the UK, and for almost 40 per cent in Germany. Since that time, however, these percentages have increased considerably, crowding out productive investment spending in the process.

The disappointing development of investment expenditures has been discussed earlier. Table 11.6 illustrates how poor investment performance has been compared with the 1973 level, and compared with overall economic growth. In the USA, the UK, and even in Japan, gross private investment hovered around the 1973 level during the remainder of the decade. In all four countries investment, as an expenditure category, has shown the slowest growth, a result which indicates the considerable excess capacity which was built up prior to 1973, and the lack of favourable prospects since that time. At any rate, once the present depression set in, private investors reacted very quickly. Fortunately, one typical reaction has so far been avoided: protectionism. Despite 'orderly marketing agreements' and the like, exports and imports have been growing rapidly since 1973. Japan and the USA, in particular, have greatly improved their trade balance, an improvement which was also partly due to the gradual transition towards less energy-intensive production.

All domestic expenditure components that have grown more rapidly than GDP are now under attack. Private consumption growth stagnated in 1980; government spending has to be cut back. Ways are sought by which to limit the growth of social security and welfare payments. The index of real disposable income could well fall below that of GDP. Everywhere in the Western world, and noticeably so in the USA, there is a trend towards reducing the role of government, as spender and as redistributor.

The problems of government have been compounded by two recent developments which, as such, can also be seen as lagged reactions to slowdown. One is the shake-out of labour during the 1980/81 recession. In the weak recovery that followed 1975, unemployment increased only moderately. When this upswing ended without any real improvement in the financial position of firms, jobs that had been kept through the recovery could no longer be maintained. A massive shake-out was the result.

A second problematic development is that of government debt servicing. The balance between receipts and government spending has deteriorated drastically since 1973 and government debts are now such that their servicing demands an ever-growing proportion of the budget.

Although private enterprise may have reacted quickly by reducing investment expenditure, in another respect it has been slow in responding to changing conditions, i.e. there has been a much publicized lack of innovation. In the course of the 1960s and 1970s the life cycle profile of manufacturing industry in many Western countries moved towards the maturity range. In other words, industries in their introduction or rapid growth phases were then less well represented than in the 1950s and 1960s. The industrialized countries now face the major task of rejuvenating their industrial package, i.e. to find new growth industries. This process of industrial re-orientation ought to have started in the second half of the 1960s, but the need for innovation was not recognized until the mid-1970s, after growth prospects had considerably deteriorated. Re-industrialization now has to take place under much more difficult conditions than would have been the case 10 to 15 years ago. As a result, there is much talk about the need for innovation, but little action. Technology is not the bottleneck: the technological foundations for new growth activities have already been laid. The hampering factor is the tardy recognition of changing demand structures, combined with the current lack of financial means with which to innovate. The Dutch chemical corporation AKZO, for instance, has had to postpone its plans for producing the new super-strong aramid fibre arenka (which competitor DuPont is producing under the trade mark kevlar) because of financial problems. In discussing innovation, the differences in adaptability between large and small firms again become significant. Innovation lags are likely to be longer for large than for small firms, as is testified to by the history of computer innovation. Developments in the field of bio-engineering may prove to be yet another case in point.

APPENDIX F

The current and the previous depression:
a comparison of the United States and the United Kingdom

Gross national product

United States				United Kingdom			
1920-29	4.3	1948-73	3.8	1920-29	1.9	1948-73	3.0
1929	100	1973	100	1929	100	1973	100
1930	90	1974	99	1930	100	1974	99
1931	83	1975	98	1931	95	1975	97
1932	71	1976	104	1932	94	1976	101
1933	69	1977	109	1933	96	1977	101
1934	76	1978	114	1934	103	1978	105
1935	83	1979	118	1935	107	1979	107
1936	95	1980	118	1936	110	1980	105
1937	100	1981	120	1937	114	1981	102

Unemployment rate

United States				United Kingdom			
1920-29	4.7	1948-73	4.8	1921-29	9.1	1948-73	2.0
1929	3.2	1973	4.9	1929	8.0	1973	2.6
1930	8.7	1974	5.6	1930	12.3	1974	2.6
1931	15.9	1975	8.5	1931	16.4	1975	3.9
1932	23.6	1976	7.7	1932	17.0	1976	5.3
1933	24.9	1977	7.1	1933	15.4	1977	5.7
1934	21.7	1978	6.0	1934	12.9	1978	5.7
1935	20.1	1979	5.8	1935	12.0	1979	5.4
1936	16.9	1980	7.1	1936	10.2	1980	6.8
1937	14.3	1981	7.6	1937	8.5	1981	10.6

Personal consumption expenditures

United States				United Kingdom			
1920-29		1948-73	3.7	1920-29	1.3	1948-73	2.7
1929	100	1973	100	1929	100	1973	100
1930	93	1974	99	1930	102	1974	98
1931	90	1975	102	1931	103	1975	98
1932	82	1976	107	1932	102	1976	98
1933	81	1977	112	1933	105	1977	97
1934	85	1978	118	1934	108	1978	103
1935	90	1979	121	1935	111	1979	108
1936	99	1980	122	1936	114	1980	108
1937	103	1981	125	1937	116	1981	108

Gross capital formation

United States				United Kingdom			
1920-29	6.2	1948-73	3.8	1920-29	5.5	1948-73	5.0
1929	100	1973	100	1929	100	1973	100
1930	76	1974	90	1930	100	1974	97
1931	51	1975	72	1931	98	1975	96
1932	28	1976	85	1932	86	1976	97
1933	25	1977	99	1933	89	1977	95
1934	31	1978	106	1934	108	1978	98
1935	43	1979	108	1935	112	1979	99
1936	59	1980	94	1936	123	1980	98
1937	66	1981	99	1937	127	1981	90

Note: Rates for 1920-29 and 1948-73 are annual averages (unemployment) and annual average growth rates respectively.

Sources: US Dept. of Commerce (1975); Feinstein (1976); OECD: *Main Economic Indicators* (various issues); OECD: *Quarterly National Accounts Bulletin* (various issues).

NOTES

1. The data in Table 11.3 obviously do not imply that other sectors of the economy could not have grown faster than the manufacturing sector. The fact is, however, that apart from mining and energy production, they have not done so if growth is measured in real output terms. We have not checked the data for all countries listed in Table 11.3, but for those that were checked, manufacturing output grew more rapidly than agriculture, services and the government sector. In macroeconomic terms the cause of this difference is, of course, productivity growth.
2. Interesting studies of value changes, correlating with the Kondratieff cycle, have been made by Namenwirth (1973) and Weber (1981).

XII

ECONOMIC POLICY DURING A DEPRESSION

WHAT WILL HAPPEN DURING A DEPRESSION PHASE?

In the previous chapter it has been shown that adjustment to structural change is a lengthy business. A long wave downturn as that which occurred in 1973 is such a structural change. People's adaptation to slowdown can be seen as a sequence of reactions, a typical example of which may consist of four stages.

Stage 1: There is nothing wrong

Despite the severity of the 1974/75 slump, few economists (or other observers of the world economy) anticipated the structural or long-cyclical nature of the downturn. The opinion was widely held that, apart from the impact of the quadruppling of oil prices, nothing had changed fundamentally and that, if anything, big slumps would breed big booms. Indeed, the immediate inventory-led recovery was beyond expectation; not until the second half of 1976, when fixed investment should have taken over, did a weaker than usual recovery pattern begin to develop (see Table 12.1). Consider, for instance, the following sequence of editorial comments in *The Economist*:

12 April 1975	Beware the coming boom. The great world boom is coming; that much seems certain.
12 July 1975	The promised world boom now seems likely to be postponed to 1977, despite recovery in America.
3 January 1976	That was a lousy year, but cheer up, boom is on the way.
28 February 1976	There is now a real prospect that the world may be returning to good economic growth with much lower inflation.
6 November 1976	The 1976-77 recovery has been fading.
1 January 1977	Investment-led stagnation?
27 August 1977	Hesiflation has continued long enough for some pessimistic businessmen and forecasters to begin the countdown to the next recession.

Notes to this chapter may be found on p. 225.

Table 12.1 *Forecast and actual growth of real GNP in the OECD area**

Forecast in for	1975 II	1976 I	1976 II	1977 I	1977 II	1978 I	1978 II
July 1975	3¼	4¼					
Dec. 1975	3¾	4	3¾				
July 1976		6½	4½	5¼			
Dec. 1976			3¼	4	3¾		
July 1977				4¼	4½	4	
Dec. 1977					3¼	4	3
July 1978						3¼	4
Actual rate	4.4	6.3	3.1	4.2	3.4	4.0	4.3

* Growth rates are percentage changes from previous half year, seasonally adjusted at annual rates.

Source: OECD *Economic Outlook* (various issues).

In Chapter XI we have referred to the well-known McCracken report (OECD 1977), which concluded that, despite some underlying changes in behavioural patterns and in power relationships, nothing had fundamentally changed in the years after the oil crisis. There was nothing on the supply side to prevent growth from resuming its pre-1973 pace. The views of the McCracken group were not shared by everyone, and dissenting economists began to raise their voices. Those who spoke of an upcoming period of slow growth, however, were in the minority.

Stage 2: Muddling through

Once it has become obvious that growth rates will not return to their former levels, a new phase sets in: muddling through. The goal of economic policy makers is then to maintain as much as possible, i.e. to protect acquired positions, hoping that the country will be able to weather the storm. This attitude is a defensive one. Consumers try to defend their spending patterns, despite sagging income growth; firms hope that government-backed loans and government subsidies will carry them through till better times; unions propose a shorter working week in order to avoid massive lay-offs; and governments make their initial attempts to curb the growth of spending and of welfare payments.

This phase may have lasted from mid-1977 until about the end of the 1970s. In Chapter XI and Appendix F we have seen that private consumption expenditure increased fairly rapidly until 1979, then slowed down slightly. The sharp rise in public spending began to taper off in 1977/78, when a number of governments introduced austerity measures, and taxpayers made it clear that they wanted no more tax increases.

Stage 3: Thinking of new growth strategies

If stagnation is long-lasting it will eventually become clear to everyone that the acquired positions can no longer be maintained. The defenders will be forced to withdraw. At the same time, awareness will grow that defensive strategies alone will not suffice. New solutions will need to be found. This third stage represents the transition from backward-looking, defensive views to forward-looking, offensive ones. On the one hand retrenchment is in full force, on the other hand new strategies are being formulated but not yet implemented.

From the technical point of view, this third stage begins when the business cycle expansion phase of the long wave depression phase comes to an end. In the United States and the United Kingdom this occurred in the second half of 1979; for the European Community as a whole the turning point can be located around December 1979. A business cycle contraction on top of a long wave depression really brings home the message of depression, most visibly in terms of rapidly increasing business failures and widespread layoffs.

These negative developments will dominate and strong pressure will be brought to bear for their mitigation with the aid of more defensive action, i.e. further cuts in government spending, wage freezes, postponement of the purchase of consumer durables and – to avert outside threats – protectionist measures.

The government's attitude is likely to be protective, but at the same time future-oriented strategies will be proposed. In 1980, for example, reindustrialization was the slogan in the USA and Western Europe. The election of a conservative president in the USA has brought supply-side economics to the fore, a new branch of political economy which also claims to offer a way out of present problems.

Now, in 1982, we are in the middle of this third stage, whose length will depend primarily on the length and severity of the recession which started in 1979. In 1981 the economy of the USA seemed to be on the upturn, but in the middle of the year it declined again, making the summer 1980 to summer 1981 business cycle upswing the shortest since 1919. By the end of the year the unemployment rate had set a new postwar record. In Europe, a recovery in 1982 has been hoped for, but as long as unemployment rates keep rising, government action will clearly continue to be defensive.

The length of stage three in the adaptation to slow growth process is not determined merely by business cycle conditions; the attitudes of policy makers become more crucial than ever. If they concentrate solely on defensive policies, these policies may well prolong the depression. If, on the other hand, they can instil a new spirit into society (as did the New Deal in the 1930s), they may be able to speed up recovery. The history of the interwar period illustrates the effect of government attitudes in recovering from the slump. The USA and a country such as the Netherlands provide contrasts. While the depression in the USA was much deeper than elsewhere, the mobilization of national energy invoked by Roosevelt's New Deal led to an earlier turnaround than was the case in the Netherlands, where the government clung to its defensive sound money policies until 1936. When these policies were abandoned, the economic situation improved immediately, but much later than necessary.

Stage 4: Offensive action

In this last part of the long-wave depression phase, attention is turned towards the future. New growth strategies are implemented. Concern with the past will continue, old structures will be abolished; but it is recognized that these measures are not sufficient to start new growth.

By this time too, the excess capacity of capital goods should have been worked off; the shake-out of labour of the previous business cycle recession should be completed. In other words, firms will have settled their accounts with the past and be prepared to embark on new ventures.

At the time of writing, no country seems to have entered this fourth stage. As has been argued above, the timing may differ from country to country, depending on the positive momentum that a government can generate. Moreover, the growth scenarios need not be the same for each country.

Some of the options now being investigated in the Western world will presently be discussed, but first we shall examine an extra complication of this depression phase, rigidity.

AN EXTRA COMPLICATION: RIGIDITY

Rigidity, which reduces adaptability to structural change, results from a quarter-century of almost uninterrupted growth. Prior to 1973 growth was taken for granted. It was thought that every demand could be met. Social objections became rights to which various groups felt they were entitled. Growth thus reduced flexibility and adaptability, and also reduced the willingness to take risks. Rigidity made its appearance in various areas, five of which will be discussed here.

Labour market

Now that unemployment has again become a major concern, it makes sense to look first at labour market rigidities. The several obstacles to a well-functioning labour market that have developed over the years include the following.

(i) *Lack of occupational mobility*
In a period of transition, when the source of growth has to be renewed, occupational mobility is essential. The increase of qualitative structural unemployment indicates that the adaptation of labour supply occurs only very slowly.

(ii) *Lack of geographical mobility*
Numerous examples can be cited of labour market mismatches caused by lack of geographical mobility. Low mobility may be a typically European problem, in the USA too there are signs of a reduction of labour mobility in recent years.

(iii) *The fixed nature of labour costs*
Whereas standard economic texts still treat labour as a variable input factor, economic growth has increasingly turned it into a fixed factor.

(iv) *Social security as a supply-limiting factor*
In some instances, social security regulations are known to have the perverse effect of providing an unemployed worker with a net income that is higher than, or equal to, that of his employed counterpart.

(v) *High marginal tax brackets may reduce incentives to work*

Most of these rigidities have been caused by government policies aimed at social protection of the work force. Now that adaptability is seriously hampered, however, governments will be forced to do away with them. This is not a question of abandoning social justice. In the long run, it would seem that social justice is better served by a labour market which functions well than by one which malfunctions.

Government invention

Government has recently come under attack as a principal contributor to rigidity, and this also has been due to growth.

(i) *The uncontrollable portion of the budget*
This is the part that is determined by earlier commitments and by existing laws. It is believed that 75 per cent of the United States budget is now uncontrollable, seriously limiting its effectiveness as an instrument of discretionary national economic policy. The largest single category of uncontrollable spending is that of welfare and social security payments.

(ii) *Regulatory policies*
The negative impact of regulatory policies is a main concern in the USA, even more than in Europe. The costs of complying with the huge number of federal regulations is mentioned as an important cause of the poor productivity performance of the United States economy.

(iii) *Unneeded government agencies*
Sometimes government agencies are maintained long after their work has been completed, representing memorials to old problems. 'Sunset laws' will be necessary to close such agencies.

(iv) *Bailing-out of companies threatened with bankruptcy*
By bailing-out companies government prevents their adjustment to new conditions, at a very high cost. Doing so, it also reinforces the popular notion that all major risks can be passed on to government.

(v) *Lack of cost-effectiveness measures for public expenditure*
Many government programmes are continued without any knowledge of their effects per unit of input. The implicit assumption seems to be that more money spent automatically means better results.

Institutional sclerosis

Postwar growth was only made possible by social consensus on the goals to be pursued, and by an institutional structure which permitted those goals to be realized. The institutions established to foster growth, however, may have developed their own objectives which no longer accord with the present need for economic revitalization. Having outlived their own usefulness, they now stand in the way of future growth. This phenomenon, known as 'institutional sclerosis', is widely recognized, and it is hardly surprising that calls for reindustrialization are invariably made together with calls for a 'new social contract' (*Business Week*, 30 June 1980) and a 'new sense of nationhood' (*Time*, 23 February 1981). In other words, a new social consensus will have to be developed, with the appropriate institutional structures. To illustrate how old structures can hamper change, we may take the experience of the Dutch Industrial Restructuring Company (NEHEM). NEHEM operates on the basis of tripartite agreements between the Crown, employers and unions. This method, which worked well for socioeconomic decision making in years of growth, has caused much frustration during these years of slowdown: firms with good prospects within an otherwise declining industry see little reason to share in that decline, while unions find themselves forced to cooperate with plans that foresee the loss of jobs. It has been partly due to such experiences that a widely acclaimed report on the place and future of Dutch industry (WRR 1980) has proposed that a new industrial policy should do away with the three-party format, and should instead rely more heavily on the knowledge of experts. Another example of an outdated institutional structure is the web of advisory bodies which covers almost all areas of public sector decision making – advisory bodies whose most conspicuous role now seems to be to cause delays in decision making.

Institutional sclerosis has also affected corporations. Entrepreneurs have been replaced by managers who emphasize high and rapid returns. When rapid growth is no longer certain in a company's own market, these managers look for diversification through horizontal mergers, thus reinforcing the emphasis on quick money making. In this respect the role of business schools is also important. By stressing short-run profit making rather than original thinking, they have created what has become known as the MBA syndrome.

In reaction to the shortsighted corporate culture, the entrepreneurial qualities of small and flexible firms have recently been emphasized, a rediscovery which in some ways implies a return to attitudes that were common thirty years ago.

Protectionism

This is one of the oldest forms of rigidity. By shielding industrial sectors from international competition, countries prevent their adaptation to new conditions. A first wave of protectionism, apparent around 1975/76, fortunately proved unsuccessful. A second wave seems likely to come in the wake of the present recession. Protectionism is not unique to this long-wave depression, but was a common reaction to slowdown both in the 1870s and the 1930s. Strictly speaking, therefore, it is not an extra complicating factor during this downturn, but it is a clear example of rigidity.

Inflation

A unique element of this depression is the continued high inflation. Although the problem has been very much aggravated by the two oil crises, inflation in the Western world was already high in the late 1960s and early 1970s. Economists are unable to reach agreement on the net welfare effects of inflation. In some countries inflation has been compatible with rapid economic growth and rising standards of living. Whether or not the redistributive effects of inflation are undesirable is by no means self-evident. It is clear, however, that inflation of the type experienced during the past decade, and the adjustments made for it, have increased rigidity.

1. In an inflationary environment with accompanying high interest rates, risky long-term investment projects are avoided; inflation hedges such as real estate steer capital away from more productive uses.
2. The prospect of paying back with devaluated money has extended government's borrowing limits, and removed checks on increased spending.
3. In all kinds of contracts indexation clauses reduce flexibility, for instance of real wages.

Many of these rigidities stem from, or have been influenced by, government action, but this does not mean that government should be held responsible for all the ills of society. On the contrary, the people elected the governments which created the laws, regulations and institutions that are now the cause of rigidity. The point is that only government can remove rigidity, to the extent that government caused it. If over-government is the result of growth during thirty years, then the balance can only be restored by reverse governmental action.

To put an end to rigidities will mean, above all, putting a premium on risk-taking behaviour. This applies to all five areas discussed above, whether it concerns increasing the own risk in social security, limiting subsidies to firms in danger, abandoning the tripartite formula, removing protectionist measures, or discouraging the use of capital for inflation-proof but unproductive investments.

The former development towards greater rigidity is not necessarily irreversible. Indeed, the consequences of slowdown are already making themselves felt. Once again, successful government action will be a matter of timely recognition of changing circumstances rather than of acting against time.

THE NEED TO OFFER A 'NEW DEAL'

At the beginning of this chapter it has been argued that the Western economies are now in the third stage of this depression phase: new growth strategies are needed, but the politicians' preoccupation is with the pressing problems of the present day, i.e. high unemployment and high inflation cause them to pursue defensive policies.

The length of this long wave depression phase could well depend on the determination and rapidity with which governments adopt more offensive strategies. The various policies now being conducted or proposed, whether offensive or defensive, will now be surveyed (see Table 12.2). It will be argued that defensive policies will only prolong the depression, and that offensive action, temporarily combined with paring down wherever necessary, will be the quickest way to achieve recovery.

Table 12.2 *Defensive and offensive depression policies*

Defensive policies	Offensive policies
(a) Retrenchment of government expenditure	(a) Expansion of the (semi-) government sector
(b) Protectionism	(b) Export promotion
(c) Reduction of labour costs	(c) Re-industrialization/Innovation
(d) Part-time jobs, reduction of the work week	(d) Supply-side economics
(e) Monetarism	(e) Industrial policy as an international issue

The following defensive policies might be adopted.

Retrenchment of government expenditure

Most Western countries are now attempting to cut down on government expenditure. Some are more drastic than others, but all realize very clearly that government expenditure cannot continue to grow in the style of the 1960s and 1970s. The growth of government spending was due mainly to the growth of transfer payments, an area which, together with the wages and salaries of civil servants, will need to undergo the most radical trimming.

This widespread response to depression illustrates one of the fundamental differences between this and the previous depression. If the 1920s were the years of *under-government* (leading to Keynesian government spending as a remedy), the 1960s and 1970s have been years of *over-government* (leading to retrenchment of government expenditure as a remedy, albeit not as a solution).[1] As a result of past government expansion, the major offensive policy option of the 1930s, i.e. Keynesian policy, has been put in reverse and in fact has become a defensive policy option.

Protectionism

Protectionism is a standard response to depression. Little needs to be said about it other than that previous Great Depressions were periods of increased protectionism. A protectionist mood is once again apparent, not as overt as in the 1930s but under the guise of 'orderly marketing agreements' and 'voluntary restriction'. With the possible exception of protectionism of infant industries, this is a strictly defensive and short-sighted policy.

Reduction of labour costs

The purpose of a reduction of labour costs is to give firms more breathing space. Exporting firms may become more competitive, if labour costs are in fact the cause of poor export performance, which for some industries is doubtful; it may also increase profits and investments.

In small countries such as the Netherlands, rising labour costs were the first to be blamed when depression struck, because the country is greatly dependent on its exports. Nowadays, of course, government expenditure is just as great a culprit. Yet a policy aimed at reducing the cost of export products can clearly only be successful if it is not also pursued by competing countries, enabling the relative position on the world market indeed to be improved. Such a policy has the same destructive potential for foreign trade as that mentioned previously: if pursued by all nations no one wins but all lose.

One argument that was used against labour-cost reducing policies in the 1930s does not now seem equally valid: the negative effect of a reduction of the purchasing power of wage income recipients. While it is obviously true that their purchasing power will be reduced, the allocation of the marginal dollar or pound sterling is quite different from what it was in the 1930s. Basic needs would still be fulfilled even if across the board real wages were reduced by 5-10 per cent. Moreover, new activities, the introduction of new products, etc., would apparently not be jeopardized by such a reduction.

Part-time jobs, reduction of the work week

There are two principal methods by which to combat the unemployment problem from the labour supply side. The first is to reduce labour supply by reducing the work week, by shortening the working age (both at the beginning and at the end), etc. The effect is that the number of jobs remains the same, but that the amount of time provided per job is reduced slightly. Proposals of this nature were common in the 1930s, and were rediscovered again after 1973. Their employment-creating potential is limited, the productivity of the marginal hour or year probably being much lower than the average. If slack time only is removed, there will be little need to hire new personnel. Such measures will usually have a chance to be effective only if they are accompanied by a reduction in wages and/ or pensions. Otherwise, labour costs will increase and firms will tend to replace labour by capital goods, thus nullifying the potential employment effect. True, unemployment would have been much higher were it not for the gradual reduction of the work week and the working age over the years, but the most appropriate time at which to implement such reductions is during long wave expansion phases, not during depressions.

A second way by which to combat unemployment is by dividing full-time jobs into part-time jobs so that, to put it simply, two people are needed for one job. The matter is not that simple, of course. Many jobs cannot be cut in half: overhead costs per man will increase; and people may prefer jobs for eight or nine-tenths of the time rather than only one-half. Nevertheless, the creation of part-time jobs may go some way towards alleviating a specific labour supply problem, viz. the increased number of women who may be specifically interested in less than full-time jobs. To that extent, the potential of this proposal may stretch beyond the current depression. Even so, this is also a defensive policy in that it does not create new sources of income.

Monetarism

Monetarists will disagree vehemently with the characterization of their policy recommendations as 'defensive'. They would argue that if their rules had been strictly adhered to, the depression would have been avoided. There is no agreement, however, on the role of monetary forces in causing or avoiding a depression, such as the Great Depression or the current one. The point is that strict control of the money supply by itself would not be sufficient, even regardless of questions about the amount of control that monetary authorities can exert in an open economy. Monetarism would be just as necessary as some of the other policies mentioned above, without in itself being sufficient to accomplish an economic renewal.

All five policy options have been or are being tried. The offensive strategies discussed below are mostly still in their conceptualization phase.

Expansion of the (semi-) government sector

Proponents of further expansion of the (semi-) government sector are now fairly rare, although they were quite common in the mid-1970s. Their proposals were truly Keynesian, and a whole generation of economists had learnt that Keynesian policies were the answer to an economic downturn. It is hardly surprising, therefore, that many economists called for an expansion of government expenditure (construction, urban renewal, quaternary sector activities) in order to combat depression.

This is a purely offensive strategy. G (government expenditure), like E (exports) and I (investment), is an expenditure component in the Keynesian demand model, which can be increased (G, E, and I are often assumed to be exogenous variables in the simple models) to raise national income through the operation of a multiplier effect. G is obviously the government's most direct grasp on the economy, so why not increase it?

The problem is that past cyclical and structural increases of G, have been subject to the familiar ratchet effect: they have been virtually irreversible. Scope for further expansion has thus been gradually eliminated in view of people's preference for an increase in own disposable income. For some time it seemed that an increase in the quaternary sector would provide a way out. Activities in this sector are (still) labour-intensive and create jobs with less investment per man than is possible in the industrial sector. It is felt, however, that further increase of this sector should be dependent upon a revitalization of industry. In other words, output increases from industry have to create the room for extra quaternary activities, many of which are subsidized by government.

Slow growth, and therefore lower tax receipts but higher social security payments, has thus left (semi-) government sector expansion as an offensive but impracticable strategy.

Export promotion

Export promotion is the counterpart of protectionism (just as expansion of the government sector is the counterpart of its reduction). It is ironic, therefore, that some governments which attempt to increase their exports (which must be another country's imports), simultaneously attempt to reduce imports (i.e. another's exports) through protectionism.

Export promotion is an old strategy, but one which is always important for small open economies such as that of the Netherlands. Recently, however, it has become a topic of debate in the USA. Export promotion can be approached from two angles: relative prices, and quality. The latter approach is by far the most important for the industrialized Western countries. Quality refers to product differentiation in existing markets, but also to the opening-up of new markets. In that respect it becomes part of the re-industrialization and innovation policy.

Export promotion is an offensive policy from an individual country's point of view. As indicated above, however, for a given amount of exports there is an equal amount of imports. From the international point of view, this means that such a strategy can only be successful if its defensive counterpart, protectionism, is abandoned.

Re-industrialization/innovation

Re-industrialization has so far been the slogan of the 1980s, succeeding to another popular and abused term: innovation. Both refer to the same kind of activity, however, i.e. the creation of new growth industries to replace those that had served us for 25 postwar years. This appears to be the most promising offensive strategy and, within the context of the long-wave theory presented in Chapter VIII, also the most recommendable. Re-industrialization attacks the problem of economic slowdown at its roots: insufficient sectors in their early life cycle phases. If such sectors could be developed, many if not most of the problems that have come with slowdown would be solved.

There are two schools of thought on how re-industrialization/innovation policy should be conducted: one favours a generic policy, the other a specific policy. The former aims at general measures that apply to the whole private sector and are intended to create a 'favourable business climate': tax measures, investment stimuli and de-regulation are the most important. The latter assumes some form of selection process on the part of government ('picking winners'). The selected growth sectors are then favoured at the expense of others, through subsidies, government procurement policies and possibly some form of infant industry protection. The danger of picking winners, of course, is that those winners may prove to be losers; focussing aid on the 'wrong' sectors entails that the 'right' ones are discriminated against. The argument against generic aid is that funds are too limited to be spread over all possible growth candidates. As a result none will really benefit.

The form or mix which will be chosen in practice may well depend on nation-specific, cultural factors. In Japan and France industrial policy will be more specific than in the USA or Germany. Most countries, including those that intend to conduct a specific policy, will try to improve the business climate through generic measures.

The selection of areas of future growth is obviously an important matter, but the crucial point of a re-industrialization policy is that *governments show their preparedness to pull the economy out of depression by offering some hope for the future*. They need not be very specific about which sectors will be the new growers as long as they show that they are backing industrial renewal through offensive action. In that respect, the early 1980s are comparable with the years immediately before and after World War II, when a number of Western governments were faced with a similar task of finding new sources of growth.[2]

Supply-side economics

It is with some hesitation that supply-side economics is labelled as an offensive answer to economic slowdown. A mix of defensive and offensive action might perhaps be more appropriate. Yet supply-side economics seems to be the closest approximation to a scientific revolution in economics since Keynesianism; as such, it could be instrumental in creating a more positive, even inspiring, opinion of the ability of policy makers to get their economies going again. That in itself would justify an 'offensive' label.

Is supply-side economics really a new paradigm? To the extent that it assumes causal relationships that are quite different from the prevailing Keynesian paradigm, the answer is in the affirmative. Many of the mechanisms that play a crucial role in supply-side models, are completely absent in Keynesian models.[3] The heart of supply-side economics is the notion that cuts in personal tax rates and business taxes provide incentives to produce new income, even as monetary policy fights inflation. In the Keynesian model higher growth comes from higher spending (leading to more inflation). In the supply-side model higher growth results from higher production (which lowers inflation). A cut in personal tax rates will take away disincentives to work; it will also increase savings, lowering interest rates, which in turn means higher investment. Thus, the supply of both production factors, capital and labour, is increased.

Supply-side economics is a specifically American reaction to the inadequacy of Keynesian policies. It claims to be able to solve two problems which, in the USA more than anywhere else, are seen as causes of the lackluster performance of the economy: low productivity and high inflation. Keynesian economics has little to say about them; Keynesian policies have not been able to solve them.

The quick rise to prominence of supply-side economics is reminiscent of the way in which Keynesian economics was embraced in the 1930s. Not a cure-all, but an approach to the economic problems of the day, indicating where and why conventional wisdom has failed. In that sense the emergence of supply-side economics is an exciting development. The intellectual stimulus it already has given to the economics profession, entirely justifies the 'offensive' label attached to it.

Industrial policy as an international issue

It has been indicated above that some, if not all, depression policies have international repercussions. Some are beneficial to other nations; in other cases, depression policies will have 'beggar-thy-neighbour' effects. Indeed, a not uncommon way by which nations deal with economic problems is to export them, but if many countries were to pursue this line, the world economy would spiral downwards.

This is the reason why many now advocate international cooperation in combatting the economic slump. The problem is that cooperative arrangements are more likely when the long-cyclical trough has been passed through than when countries are still in the third stage of the depression phase, as at present. It is hardly surprising, therefore, that even the beginning of a world-wide attack on depression still needs to make its appearance, and that partial attempts (as in the European steel industry) are continually thwarted.

This is an offensive strategy which has frequently been proposed, but which is still far from operationalization. At other levels, institutional structures may have power but have become ossified; at the international level, the little power that can be wielded is usually used to block offensive action rather than to stimulate it.

If anything is now becoming clear, it is this: defensive policies are not sufficient to get us out of the present depression. Offensive action, of which there are various forms, is needed. In our view the re-industrialization strategy is the most promising in that it would tackle our most basic problem: the lack of growth industries. It is understandable that economists in the USA stress supply-side factors. A lack of potential growth sectors may not be the key problem in that country (at the 3-digit SIC-level many innovative industries have shown considerable growth in the post-1973 years), and the true bottleneck might be formed by supply disincentives (because of inflation, regulation, etc.). Supply-side economics, however, is clearly compatible with a re-industrialization strategy. A lasting recovery will probably require a combination of the two.

NOTES

1. In 1980, President Carter was the first incumbent President of the USA to lose an election since Herbert Hoover in 1932. Hoover, a Republican, represented under-government, and lost; Carter, a Democrat, represented over-government, and also lost.

2. See for instance Wright (1939: 268) who argued that 'by careful study of the world market, pressure applied, not only on the right industries but at the right moment in the trade cycle, may transfer resources from stagnant to developing industries in such a way as to yield permanent real benefit and break down vested interests. It is with the aim of elucidating the possibilities of this type, designed to assist the transition to more profitable economic organization, rather than to buttress uneconomic and vulnerable interests, that the volume [i.e. Wright's book] has been written.'

3. For a comparison of Keynesian and supply-side models, see the interesting article by Keynesian econometric model-builder turned supply-sider Evans (1980).

REFERENCES

In addition to the titles referred to in this book, this list of references includes a selective bibliography of recent literature on the long wave.

Abramovitz, M. (1956): 'Resources and output trends in the United States since 1870', *Papers and Proceedings, American Economic Review*, 46, 5-23.
—— (1964): *Evidences of Long Swings in Aggregate Construction Since the Civil War* (NBER, Columbia University Press).
—— (1968): 'The passing of the Kuznets cycle', *Economica*, 35, 349-67.
Aftalion, A. (1913): *Les crisis périodiques de surproduction* (Marcel Rivière).
Andriessen, J.E. (1980): *Economie in theorie en praktijk* (6th revised printing, Elsevier).

Baker, R. (1976): *New and Improved*... (British Museum Publications).
Bernstein, E.M. (1940): 'War and the pattern of business cycles', *American Economic Review*, 30, 524-35.
Blair, J.M. (1972): *Economic Concentration* (Harcourt Brace Jovanovich).
de Bono, E. (ed.) (1974): *Eureka! How and When the Greatest Inventions Were Made* (Thames and Hudson).
Broersma, T.J. (1978): *De lange golf in het economisch leven* (Ph.D. Dissertation, University of Groningen).
Burns, A.F. (1934): *Production Trends in the United States Since 1870* (National Bureau of Economic Research).
Burns, A.F. & W.C. Mitchell (1946): *Measuring Business Cycles* (National Bureau of Economic Research, Studies in Business Cycles, No. 2).

Cassel, G. (1932): *Theoretische Sozialökonomie* (5th edition, A. Deichertsche Verlagsbuchhandlung).
Central Advisory Council for Science and Technology (1968): *Technological Innovation in Britain* (HMSO).
Chambers, J.C., S.K. Mullick & D.D. Smith (1974): *An Executive's Guide to Forecasting* (4th edition, South-Western).
Chapin, F.S. (1928): *Cultural Change* (Century).
Cherry, R.D. (1980): *Macroeconomics* (Addison-Wesley).
Cipolla, C.M. (ed.) (1973): *The Emergence of Industrial Societies* (The Fontana Economic History of Europe).
von Ciriacy-Wantrup, S. (1936): *Agrarkrisen und Stockungsspannen zur Frage der langen Welle in der wirtschaftlichen Entwicklung* (Paul Parey).
Clark, C. (1944): *The Economics of 1960* (Macmillan).
Clark, C., C. Freeman & L. Soete (1981a): 'Long waves, inventions, and innovations', *Futures*, 13, 308-22.
—— (1981b): 'Long waves and technological developments in the 20th century', in: D. Petzina & G. van Roon (eds): *Konjunktur, Krise, Gesellschaft* (Klett-Cotta), 132-69.
Clarke, H. (1847): 'Physical economy', *Railway Register*.
Claudon, M.P. (1917): *International Trade and Technology: Models of Dynamic Comparative Advantage* (University Press of America).
Cleveland, H. van B. & W.H.B. Brittain (1975): 'A world depression?', *Foreign Affairs*, 53, 223-41.
Club of Rome (1972): *The Limits to Growth* (Universe Books).

Cornwall, J. (1977): *Modern Capitalism* (St Martin's Press).
—— (1979): 'Macrodynamics', in: A.S. Eichner (ed.): *A Guide to Post-Keynesian Economics* (Macmillan), 19-33.
Croxton, F.E., D.J. Cowden & S. Klein (1967): *Applied General Statistics* (3rd edition, Prentice-Hall).

Dauten, C.A. & L.M. Valentine (1978): *Business Cycles and Forecasting* (5th edition, Southwestern).
Day, R. (1976): 'The theory of the long cycle: Kondratiev, Trotsky, Mandel', *New Left Review*, 99, 67-82.
Dean, J. (1950): 'Pricing policies for new products', *Harvard Business Review*, 28 (November), 45-53.
Deane, Ph. (1973): 'The industrial revolution in Great Britain', in: C.M. Cipolla (ed.) (1973), 161-277.
Delbeke, J. (1981): 'Recent long-wave theories: a critical survey', *Futures*, 13, 246-57.
Delfgaauw, G.Th.J. (1973): *Inleiding tot de economische wetenschap, Deel II: Macroeconomie* (Delwel).
van Duijn, J.J. (1977a): *Eb en vloed: de lange golf in het economisch leven* (Public lecture, Erasmus University, Rotterdam).
—— (1977b): 'The long wave in economic life', *De Economist*, 125, 544-76.
—— (1978): 'Dating postwar business cycles in the Netherlands, 1948-1976', *De Economist*, 126, 474-504.
—— (1979a): *De lange golf in de economie* (Van Gorcum).
—— (1979b): 'De betekenis van een innovatie-georiënteerd regionaal beleid voor Nederland', *Beleid en Maatschappij*, 6, 162-71.
—— (1980a): 'Another look at industry growth patterns' *(Faculty Working Papers 667*, College of Commerce and Business Administration, University of Illinois at Urbana Champaign).
—— (1980b): 'Comment on Van der Zwan's Paper', Chapter 20 in: S.K. Kuipers & G.J. Lanjouw (eds): *Prospects of Economic Growth* (North-Holland), 223-33.
—— (1981a): 'Innovation and economic growth in U.S. industries, 1956-1979' (Working Paper, Graduate School of Management, Delft).
—— (1981b): 'Economic policy during a depression' (Paper presented at the conference 'Managing the Unmanageable', Graduate School of Management, Delft, 22-23 April 1981).
—— (1981c): 'Fluctuations in innovations over time', *Futures*, 13, 264-75.
Dupriez, L.H. (1935): 'Einwirkungen der langen Wellen auf die Entwicklung der Wirtschaft seit 1800', *Weltwirtschaftliches Archiv*, 37, 1-12.
—— (1947): *Des mouvements économiques généraux* (Institut de Recherches Economiques et Sociales de l'Université de Louvain).
—— (1978): 'A downturn of the long wave?', *Banca Nazionale del Lavoro Quarterly Review*, 126, 199-210.

Easterlin, R.A. (1968): *Population, Labor Force, and Long Swings in Economic Growth: The American Experience* (NBER, Columbia University Press).
Eby Jr, F.H. & W.J. O'Neill (1977): *The Management of Sales Forecasting* (Lexington Books).
Economic Report of the President (1980) (US Government Printing Office).
Eelkman Rooda, F.E. (1978): 'De kapitaalgoederentheorie als verklaringsgrond voor de Kondratieff-cyclus', *Economisch-Statistische Berichten*, 63, 1216-20.
Eklund, K. (1980): 'Long waves in the development of capitalism?', *Kyklos*, 33, 383-419.
Enos, J.L. (1962): 'Invention and innovation in the petroleum refining industry', in: *The Rate and Direction of Inventive Activity* (National Bureau of Economic Research), 299-321.
Evans, M.K. (1969): *Macroeconomic Activity* (Harper & Row).

—— (1980): 'The bankruptcy of Keynesian econometric models', *Challenge* (Jan.-Febr.), 13-19.
van Ewijk, C. (1981a): 'A spectral analysis of the Kondratieff-cycle' (Research Memorandum 8111, Department of Economics, University of Amsterdam).
—— (1981b): 'The long wave – a real phenomenon?', *De Economist*, 129, 324-72.

Feinstein, C.H. (1976): *Statistical Tables of National Income, Expenditure and Output of the UK 1855-1965* (Cambridge University Press).
Forrester, J.W. (1975a): *Business Structure, Economic Cycles, and National Policy* (MIT System Dynamics Group, D-2245-2).
—— (1975b): *New Perspectives for Growth over the Next Thirty Years* (MIT System Dynamics Group, D-2251-1).
—— (1977): 'Growth cycles', *De Economist*, 125, 525-43.
—— (1979): 'Innovation and the economic long wave', *The McKinsey Quarterly* (Spring), 26-38.
Forrester, N.B. (1973): *The Life Cycle of Economic Development* (Wright-Allen Press).
Freeman, Chr. (1974): *The Economics of Industrial Innovations* (Penguin Modern Economics Texts).
—— (1979a): 'The Kondratiev long waves, technical change and unemployment', in: *Structural Determinants of Employment and Unemployment*, Vol. 2 (Reports prepared for OECD Experts Meeting in Paris, 7-11 March 1977), 181-96.
—— (1979b): 'The determinants of innovation', *Futures*, 11, 206-15.
Freeman, Chr., J. Clark & L. Soete (1982): *Unemployment and Technical Innovation* (Frances Pinter).
Frickey, E. (1942): *Economic Fluctuations in the United States* (Harvard University Press).
—— (1947): *Production in the United States, 1860-1914* (Harvard University Press).
Friedman, M. & A.J. Schwartz (1963): *A Monetary History of the United States, 1867-1960* (Princeton University Press).

Garvy, G. (1943): 'Kondratieff's theory of long cycles', *Review of Economic Statistics*, 25, 203-20
van Gelderen, J. (J. Fedder) (1913): 'Springvloed: beschouwingen over industrieele ontwikeling en prijsbeweging', *De Nieuwe Tijd*, 18, 253-77, 369-84 and 445-64.
Glismann, H.H., H. Rodemer & F. Wolter (1978): *Zur Natur der Wachstumsschwäche in der Bundesrepublik Deutschland* (Kiel Discussion Papers, 55, Institut für Weltwirtschaft Kiel).
—— (1980): *Lange Wellen wirtschaftlichen Wachstums* (Kiel Discussion Papers, 74, Institut für Weltwirtschaft Kiel).
Gold, B. (1964): 'Industry growth patterns: theory and empirical results', *Journal of Industrial Economics*, 13, 53-73.
Graham, A.K. & P.M. Senge (1980): 'A long-wave hypothesis of innovation', *Technological Forecasting and Social Change*, 17, 283-311.
Granger, C.W.J. & M. Hatanaka (1964): *Spectral Analysis of Economic Time Series* (Princeton University Press).

Haberler, G. (1937): *Prosperity and Depression* (Allen & Unwin).
Hamberg, D. (1966): *R&D: Essays on the Economies of Research and Development* (Random House).
Hanappe, P. (1975): 'Les "crises" contemporaines: vivons-nous un retournement du Kondratieff?', *Métra*, 14, 707-21.
Hansen, A.H. (1932): *Economic Stabilization in an Unbalanced World* (Harcourt, Brace & Company).
—— (1938): *Full Recovery or Stagnation?* (W.W. Norton).
—— (1941): *Fiscal Policy and Business Cycles* (W.W. Norton).
—— (1964): *Business Cycles and National Income* (expanded edition, W.W. Norton).

Harkness, J.P. (1968): 'A spectral-analytic test of the long-swing hypothesis in Canada', *Review of Economics and Statistics*, 50, 429-36.

Hartman, R.S. & D.R. Wheeler (1979): 'Schumpeterian waves of innovation and infrastructure development in Great Britain and the United States: the Kondratieff cycle revisited', in P. Uselding (ed.): *Research in Economic History*, Vol. 4 (JAI Press), 37-85.

Haustein, H.-D. & E. Neuwirth (1982): *Long Waves in World Industrial Production, Energy Consumption, Innovations, Inventions, and Patents and their Identification by Spectral Analysis* (International Institute for Applied Systems Analysis, WP-82-9).

Heertje, A. (1979): *Economics and Technical Change* (Halsted Press).

Hirsch, F. (1977): *Social Limits to Growth* (Routledge & Kegan Paul).

Hirsch, S. (1967): *Location of Industry and International Competitiveness* (Clarendon Press).

Hirsch, W.Z. (1969): 'Technological progress and micro-economic theory', *Papers and Proceedings, American Economic Review*, 59, 36-43.

Historical Statistics of the United States: Colonial Times to 1970 (1975) (US Department of Commerce).

Hoffmann, W.G. (1955): *British Industry 1700-1950* (Basil Blackwell).

—— (1965): *Das Wachstum der deutschen Wirtschaft seit der Mitte des 19.Jahrhunderts* (Springer-Verlag).

Imbert, G. (1959): *Des mouvements de longue durée Kondratieff* (La Pensée Universitaire).

Jantsch, E. (1967): *Technological Forecasting in Perspective* (OECD).

Jevons, W.S. (1884): *Investigations in Currency and Finance* (Macmillan).

Jewkes, J., D. Sawers & R. Stillerman (1969): *The Sources of Invention* (2nd edition, Macmillan).

Juglar, C. (1862): *Des crises commerciales et leur retour périodique en France, en Angleterre et aux Etats Unis* (Librairie Guillaumin et Cie).

Kahn, H. (1979): *World Economic Development: 1979 and Beyond* (Morrow Quill).

Kamien, M.I. & N.L. Schwartz (1975): 'Market structure and innovation: a survey', *Journal of Economic Literature*, 13, 1-37.

Kendrick, J.W. (1961): *Productivity Trends in the United States* (National Bureau of Economic Research).

Kitchin, J. (1923): 'Cycles and trends in economic factors', *Review of Economic Statistics*, 5, 10-16.

—— (1930): 'Production et consommation de l'or dans le passé et dans l'avenir', *Rapport provisoire de la délégation de l'or du comité financier* (Annexe 12, SDN), 57-64.

Kleinknecht, A. (1979): 'Basisinnovationen und Wachstumsschübe: das Beispiel der westdeutschen Industrie', *Konjunkturpolitik*, 25, 320-43.

—— (1981a): 'Überlegungen zur Renaissance der "langen Wellen" der Konjunktur ("Kondratieff-Zyklen")', in W.H. Schröder & R. Spree (eds): *Historische Konjunkturforschung* (Klett-Cotta), 316-38.

—— (1981b): 'Observations on the Schumpeterian swarming of innovations', *Futures*, 13, 293-307.

Klotz, B.P. (1973): 'Oscillatory growth in three nations', *Journal of the American Statistical Association*, 68, 562-67.

Klotz, B.P. & L. Neal (1973): 'Spectral and cross-spectral analysis of the long-swing hypothesis', *Review of Economics and Statistics*, 55, 291-98.

Kondratieff, N.D. (1926): 'Die langen Wellen der Konjunktur', *Archiv für Sozialwissenschaft und Sozialpolitik*, 56, 573-609.

—— (1928): 'Die Preisdynamik der industriellen und landwirtschaftlichen Waren', *Archiv für Sozialwissenschaft und Sozialpolitik*, 60, 1-85.

—— (1935): 'The long waves in economic life', *Review of Economic Statistics*, 17, 105-15.

van der Kooy, B.J.G. (1978): *Microcomputers* (Kluwer).

Korteweg, S., & F.A.G. Keesing (1978): *Het moderne geldwezen, Deel I – Macro-econo-mische uitgangspunten* (14th revised printing, Noord-Hollandsche Uitgeversmaatschap-pij).

Kotler, Ph. (1967): *Marketing Management: Analysis, Planning, and Control* (Prentice-Hall).

Kristensen, T. (1974): *Development in Rich and Poor Countries* (Praeger).

Krumme, G. & R. Hayter (1975): 'Implications of corporate strategies and product life cycle adjustments for regional employment changes', in: L. Collins & D.F. Walker: *Locational Dynamics of Manufacturing Activity* (John Wiley), 325-56.

Kuczynski, Th. (1978): 'Spectral analysis and cluster analysis as mathematical methods for the periodization of historical processes' (Paper for the 7th International Congress on Economic History, Edinburgh).

—— (1980): 'Have there been differences between the growth rates in different periods of the development of the capitalist world economy since 1850?', *Historisch-Sozialwissen-schaftliche Forschungen*, Bd. 6, 300-16.

Kuznets' S. (1929): 'Retardation of industrial growth', *Journal of Economic and Business History*, 1, 534-60 (reprinted in Kuznets 1953).

—— (1930): *Secular Movements in Production and Prices* (Houghton Mifflin).

—— (1940): 'Schumpeter's business cycles', *American Economic Review*, 30, 250-71 (re-printed in Kuznets 1953).

—— (1952): 'Long-term changes', *Income and Wealth of the United States* (Bowes & Bowes).

—— (1953): *Economic Change* (W.W. Norton).

—— (1972): 'Innovations and adjustments in economic growth', *Swedish Journal of Eco-nomics*, 74, 431-51.

—— (1978): 'Technological innovations and economic growth', in: P. Kelly & M. Kranzberg (eds): *Technological Innovation: A Critical Review of Current Knowledge* (San Fran-cisco Press), 335-56; reprinted in Kuznets (1979).

—— (1979): *Growth, Population, and Income Distribution* (W.W. Norton).

Lancaster, K. (1971): *Consumer Demand: A New Approach* (Columbia University Press).

Landes, D.S. (1969): *The Unbound Prometheus* (Cambridge University Press).

Lenoir, M. (1913): *Etudes sur le formation et le mouvement des prix* (Giard).

Leontief, W.W. (1953): 'Domestic production and foreign trade: the American capital posi-tion re-examined', *Proceedings of the American Philosophical Society*, 97, 332-49.

—— (1956): 'Factor proportions and the structure of American trade: further theoretical and empirical analysis', *Review of Economics and Statistics*, 38, 386-407.

Lescure, J. (1923): *Des crises générales et périodiques de surproduction* (3ième édition, Recueil Sirey).

—— (1933): *Hausses et baisses des prix de longue durée* (Domat-Montchrestien).

Levitt, Th. (1965): 'Exploit the product life cycle', *Harvard Business Review*, 43 (Nov.-Dec.), 81-94.

Levy-Pascal, E. (1976): *An Analysis of the Cyclical Dynamics of Industrialized Countries* (Central Intelligence Agency, Directorate of Intelligence, Office of Political Research).

Lewis, W.A. (1952): 'World production, prices and trade 1870-1960', *The Manchester School of Economic and Social Studies*, 20, 105-38.

—— (1978): *Growth and Fluctuations 1870-1913* (Allen & Unwin).

—— (1980): 'Rising prices: 1899-1913 and 1950-1979', *Scandinavian Journal of Eco-nomics*, 82, 425-36.

Lipsey, R.G. & P.O. Steiner (1978): *Economics* (5th edition, Harper & Row).

Long, C.D. (1940): *Building Cycles and the Theory of Investment* (Princeton University Press).

Lovell, M.C. (1975): *Macroeconomics: Measurement, Theory, and Policy* (John Wiley).

Maddison, A. (1977): 'Phases of capitalist development', *Banca Nazionale del Lavoro Quar-terly Review*, 121 (June), 103-37.

Mahdavi, K.B. (1972): *Technological Innovation* (Beckmans).

Mandel, E. (1978): *Late Capitalism* (Schocken).
——— (1980): *Long Waves of Capitalist Development* (Cambridge University Press).
Mass, N.J. & J.W. Forrester (1976): 'Understanding the changing basis for economic growth in the United States', in: *US Economic Growth from 1976-1986: Prospects, Problems, and Patterns*, Volume 6: *Forecasts of Long-Run Economic Growth* (Studies prepared for the use of the Joint Economic Committee, Congress of the U.S., December 15), 38-75.
Matthews, R.C.O. (1959): *The Trade Cycle* (Cambridge University Press).
Mensch, G. (1971): 'Zur Dynamik des technischen Fortschritts', *Zeitschrift für Betriebswirtschaft*, 41, 295-314.
——— (1972): 'Basisinnovationen und Verbesserungsinnovationen', *Zeitschrift für Betriebswirtschaft*, 42, 291-97.
——— (1975): *Das technologische Patt* (Umschau Verlag).
——— (1978): '1984: a new push of basic innovations?', *Research Policy*, 7, 108-22.
——— (1979): *Stalemate in Technology* (Ballinger).
Metzler, L.A. (1941): 'The nature and stability of inventory cycles', *Review of Economic Statistics*, 23, 113-29.
Mickwitz, G. (1967): *Marketing and Competition* (Centraltryckeriet, Helsingfors).
Mitchell, B.R. (1981): *European Historical Statistics 1750-1975* (Macmillan).
Moore, G.H. (1980): *Business Cycles, Inflation, and Forecasting* (National Bureau of Economic Research, Studies in Business Cycles, 24, Ballinger).
Mowery, D. & N. Rosenberg (1979): 'The influence of market demand upon innovation: a critical review of some recent empirical studies', *Research Policy*, 8, 102-53.
Mueller, W.F. (1962): 'The origins of the basic inventions underlying DuPont's major product and process innovations, 1920 to 1950), in: *The Rate and Direction of Inventive Activity* (National Bureau of Economic Research), 323-46.

Nabseth, L. & G.F. Ray (eds) (1974): *The Diffusion of New Industrial Processes* (Cambridge University Press).
Namenwirth, J.Z. (1973): 'The wheels of time and the interdependence of value change', *Journal of Interdisciplinary History*, 3, 649-83.
Nelson, R.R. & S.G. Winter (1974): 'Neoclassical vs. evolutionary theories of economic growth: critique and prospectus', *Economic Journal*, 84, 886-905.
Nordhaus, W.D. (1973): 'Some skeptical thoughts on the theory of induced innovation', *Quarterly Journal of Economics*, 87, 208-19.
——— (1980): 'Oil and economic performance in industrial countries', *Brookings Papers on Economic Activity, 1980-82*, 341-99.
Nordhaus, W.D. & J. Tobin (1972): 'Is growth obsolete?', in: R. Gordon (ed.): *Economic Research: Retrospect and Prospect — Economic Growth* (National Bureau of Economic Research).
Nota inzake de selectieve groei (Economische Structuurnota) (1976) (Tweede Kamer, 13 955, Staatsuitgeverij).
Nyström, H. (1979): *Creativity and Innovation* (Wiley-Interscience).

Ogburn, W.F. (1922): *Social Change* (B.W. Huebsch).
OECD (1979): *Facing the Future* (Interfutures Report).

Parvus (1901): *Die Handelskrisis und die Gewerkschaften* (Verlag M. Ernst).
——— (1908): *Die kapitalistische Produktion und das Proletariat*.
Patton, A. (1959): 'Stretch your product's earning years: top management's stake in the product life cycle', *The Management Review*, 48, 9-14, 67-79.
Pesek, B.P. (1961): 'Economic growth and its measurement', *Economic Development and Cultural Change*, 9, 295-315.
Pollard, S. (1962): *The Development of the British Economy 1914-1950* (Edward Arnold).
Prescott, R.B. (1922): 'Law of growth in forecasting demand', *Journal of the American Statistical Association*, 471-79.

Pruden, H.O. (1978): 'The Kondratieff wave', *Journal of Marketing*, 42, 63-70.

Ray, G. (1980): 'Innovation in the long cycle', *Lloyds Bank Review*, 135, 14-28.
Robertson, P. (1974): *The Shell Book of Firsts* (Ebury Press).
Rosenberg, N. (1974): 'Science, technology, and economic growth', *Economic Journal*, 84, 90-108.
—— (1975): 'Problems in the economist's conceptualization of technological innovation', *History of Political Economy*, 7, 456-81.
Rostow, W.W. (ed.) (1963): *The Economics of Take-Off into Sustained Growth* (St Martin's Press).
—— (1971a): *The Stages of Economic Growth* (2nd edition, Cambridge University Press).
—— (1971b): *Politics and the Stages of Growth* (Cambridge University Press).
—— (1975a): 'Kondratieff, Schumpeter, and Kuznets: trend periods revisited', *Journal of Economic History*, 35, 719-53.
—— (1975b): *How It All Began* (McGraw-Hill).
—— (1978a): *The World Economy: History and Prospect* (University of Texas Press, Macmillan).
—— (1978b): *Getting from Here to There* (McGraw-Hill).
—— (1980): *Why the Poor Get Richer and the Rich Slow Down* (Macmillan).
——, with the assistance of F.E. Fordyce (1978):' Growth rates at different levels of income and stage of growth: reflections on why the poor get richer and the rich slow down', in: P. Uselding (ed.): *Research in Economic History*, Vol. 3 (JAI Press), 47-86.
Rostow, W.W. & M. Kennedy (1979): 'A simple model of the Kondratieff cycle', in: P. Uselding (ed.): *Research in Economic History*, Vol. 4 (JAI Press), 1-36.

Sachs, J.D. (1979): 'Wages, profits, and macroeconomic adjustment: a comparative study', *Brookings Papers on Economic Activity*, 1979, 2, 269-319.
Samuelson, P.A. (1939): 'Interactions between the multiplier analysis and the principle of acceleration', *Review of Economic Statistics*, 21, 75-78.
—— (1980): *Economics* (11th edition, McGraw-Hill).
Scharlau, W.B. & Z.A. Zeman (1964): *Freibeuter der Revolution* (Verlag Wissenschaft und Politik).
Schmookler, J. (1965): 'Technological change and economic theory', *American Economic Review*, 55, 333-41.
—— (1966): *Invention and Economic Growth* (Harvard University Press).
—— (1972) in Z. Griliches & L. Hurwicz (eds): *Patents, Invention, and Economic Change* (Harvard University Press).
Schumpeter, J.A. (1927): 'The explanation of the business cycle', *Economica*, 7, 286-311.
—— (1928): 'The instability of capitalism', *Economic Journal*, 38, 361-86.
—— (1931): *Theorie der wirtschaftlichen Entwicklung* (3.Auflage, Duncker & Humblot).
—— (1939): *Business Cycles* (McGraw-Hill).
—— (1952): *Capitalism, Socialism and Democracy* (5th edition, George Allen & Unwin).
—— (1961): *The Theory of Economic Development* (paperback-edition, Oxford University Press; original English edition published in 1934 by Harvard University Press).
Shuman, J.B. & D. Rosenau (1972): *The Kondratieff Wave* (Delta).
Siegel, S. (1956): *Non-Parametric Statistics for the Behavioral Sciences* (McGraw-Hill).
Simiand, F. (1932): *Les fluctuations économiques à longue période et la crise mondiale* (Alcan).
Sirol, J. (1942): *Le rôle de l'agriculture dans les fluctuations économiques* (Sirey).
Solow, R. (1957): 'Technical change and the aggregate production function', *Review of Economics and Statistics*, 39, 312-20.
Soper, J.C. (1975): 'Myth and reality in economic time series: the long swing revisited', *Southern Economic Journal*, 45, 570-79
Stoken, D.A. (1978): *Cycles* (McGraw-Hill).

Tarde, G. (1903): *The Laws of Imitation* (Henry Holt).
Tinbergen, J. (1942): 'Zur Theorie der langfristigen Wirtschaftsentwicklung', *Weltwirtschaftliches Archiv*, 55, 511-49.
Tobin, J. (1980): 'Stabilization policy ten years after', *Brookings Papers on Economic Activity, 1980-81*, 19-71.
Trotsky, L. (1923): 'On the curve of the capitalistic evolution', *Vestrik Sotsialistischeskoi Akademii*, 4, 3-12.
von Tugan-Baranowsky, M. (1901): *Theorie und Geschichte der Handelskrisen in England* (Gustav Fischer).

US Department of Commerce (1973): *Long Term Economic Growth 1860-1970*.
—— (1975): *Historical Statistics of the United States: Colonial Times to 1970*.
—— (1979): *Statistical Abstract of the United States*, 100th edition.
—— (1980): *US Industrial Outlook 1980*.

Vernon, R. (1966): 'International investment and international trade in the product cycle', *Quarterly Journal of Economics*, 80, 190-207.

Wagemann, E. (1928): 'Probleme der Wirtschaftsentwicklung: die langen Wellen der Konjunktur', *Viertelsjahrshefte zur Konjunkturforschung*, 3, 1A.
—— (1931): *Struktur und Rhythmus der Weltwirtschaft*.
Wallerstein, I. (1979): 'Kondratieff up or Kondratieff down?', *Review*, 2, 663-73.
Warren, G.F. & F.A. Pearson (1935): *Gold and Prices* (John Wiley).
Weber, R.Ph. (1981): 'Society and economy in the Western world system', *Social Forces*, 59, 1130-48.
Weinstock, U. (1964): *Das Problem der Kondratieff-Zyklen* (Duncker & Humblot).
Wells, L.T. (1972): 'International trade: the product life cycle approach', in: L.T. Wells (ed.): *The Product Life Cycle and International Trade* (Division of Research, Harvard Business School), 3-33.
Wetenschappelijke Raad van het Regeringsbeleid (WRR) (1980): *Plaats en toekomst van de Nederlandse industrie* (Staatsuitgeverij).
Wilson, L.L. (1964): *Catalogue of Cycles*, Part I: *Economics* (Foundation for the Study of Cycles Inc.).
Wolf, J. (1912): *Die Volkswirtschaft der Gegenwart und Zukunft* (A. Deichertsche Verlagsbuchhandlung).
de Wolff, S. (1924): 'Prosperitäts- und Depressionsperioden', in: Otto Jensen (ed.): *Der lebendige Marxismus, Festgave zum 70.Geburtstage von Karl Kautsky*.
—— (1929): *Het economische getij* (J. Emmering).
Woytinski-Lorenz, W. (1931): 'Das Rätsel der langen Wellen', *Schmoller's Jahrbuch*, 55, II, 4.Heft, 1-42.
Wright, C.M. (1939): *Economic Adaptation to a Changing World Market* (Ejnar Munksgaard).

van der Zwan, A. (1976): 'Over de vergroting van de omvang in de produktie en de bekorting van de omlooptijd van het in bedrijven geïnvesteerde vermogen', *Economisch-Statistische Berichten*, 61, 60-65, 80-83, and 117-22.
—— (1980): 'On the assessment of the Kondratieff cycle and related issues', in: S.K. Kuipers & G.J. Lanjouw (eds): *Prospects of Economic Growth* (North-Holland), 183-222.

INDEX

Abramovitz, M., 15, 93
Aftalion, A., 62
Andriessen, J.E., 18
Australia
 long wave growth rates, 157
 public expenditure, 202
Austria
 output growth, 1951-79, 200
 public expenditure, 202

Baker, R., 174, 179
basic capital, *see* capital goods
basic goods, 83-92
basic sectors, 114-17, 136-38
Belgium
 long wave growth rates, 157
 output growth, 1951-79, 200
 public expenditure, 202
Bernstein, E.M., 70
Blair, J.M., 97
de Bono, E., 174, 179
Brittain, W.H.B., 69
Broersma, T.J., 63, 70
building cycle, *see* cycles, Kuznets
Burns, A.F., 15, 22, 27-30, 32, 150
business cycle, *see* cycles, Juglar
Business Week, 93, 216

Canada
 long wave growth rates, 157
 output growth, 1951-79, 200
 output growth in basic sectors, 1975-80,
 113
 public expenditure, 202
capital formation, fluctuations in, 158ff; *see
 also* infrastructural investment *and* investment
capital goods
 basic, 7, 66-67, 117, 136-38
 long waves, 112-28, 138-40
Carlson, Ch., 185
Carter, J.E., 225
Cassel, G., 70
Center for International Business Cycle Research, 197
Chambers, J.C., 25
Chapin, F.S., 43
Cherry, R.D., 19, 118

chronology
 business cycle, 19
 growth cycle, 10
 long wave, 79, 88, 102, 141, 143, 155,
 162-64
von Ciriacy-Wantrup, S., 69-70, 163-64
Clark, C., 68, 70, 117-18, 139, 163-64
Clark, J., 106, 108-10, 175
Clarke, H., 59
Claudon, M.P., 25
Cleveland, H. van B., 69
Club of Rome, 54, 119
Cornwall, J., 105
Cowden, D.J., 43
Croxton, F.E., 43
cycles
 growth, 9-10
 Juglar, 6-7, 11-15, 59, 80, 102, 104,
 122, 135, 141, 148-49, 158, 171
 Kitchin, 6-11, 80, 102, 158
 Kondratieff, 6-7, 18-19, *see also* long
 wave(s)
 Kuznets, 6-7, 15-18, 80, 102, 158, 169-
 70
 phases, 3, 5, 101, 135-36
cyclical fluctuations, *see* cycles *and* fluctua-
 tions

Dauten, C.A., 7, 16, 18, 77
Dean, J., 22
Deane, Ph., 46, 151
Delfgaauw, G.Th.J., 18
Denmark
 long wave growth rates, 157
 output growth, 1951-79, 200
 public expenditure, 202
depression
 current and previous, 203-04, 209-10
 economic policy during, 211-25
 stages, 211-14; *see also* cycles, phases
depression-trigger hypothesis, 124, 180-81
DeSimone, D.V., 97
van Duijn, J.J., 10, 26, 28, 132, 163, 172,
 199-200
Dupriez, L.H., 70, 163-64

Easterlin, R.A., 16
Eby, F.H., 25